The SS Officer's Armchair

Also by Daniel Lee

Pétain's Jewish Children

The SS Officer's Armchair

In Search of a Hidden Life

DANIEL LEE

JONATHAN CAPE
LONDON

1 3 5 7 9 10 8 6 4 2

Jonathan Cape, an imprint of Vintage,
20 Vauxhall Bridge Road,
London SW1V 2SA

Jonathan Cape is part of the Penguin Random House group of companies
whose addresses can be found at global.penguinrandomhouse.com

Maps by Darren Bennett (dkbcreative.com)

First published by Jonathan Cape in 2020
The author and publishers have made every effort to trace and contact
copyright holders. The publishers will be pleased to correct
any mistakes or omissions in future editions.

penguin.co.uk/vintage

A CIP catalogue record for this book is available from the British Library

ISBN 9781911214960 (hardback)
ISBN 9781911214984 (trade paperback)

Typeset in 12/14.5 pt Dante MT Std
by Integra Software Services Pvt. Ltd, Pondicherry

Printed and bound in Great Britain by Clays Ltd, Elcograf S.p.A.

Penguin Random House is committed to a sustainable future for
our business, our readers and our planet. This book is made from
Forest Stewardship Council® certified paper.

To the memory of Ryszard Seidenros, 1930–1942, who suffered the same fate as 1.5 million innocent Jewish children murdered during the Holocaust.

Contents

List of Illustrations and Maps

Illustrations

Maps

Dramatis Personae

Walter Bertsch – Minister of Economics and Labour in the Protectorate of Bohemia and Moravia; responsible for recruiting Griesinger to work for him in Prague

Rudolf Bilfinger – worked with Griesinger as a lawyer at the Stuttgart Gestapo before being posted to the Reich Main Security Office (RSHA)

Karl Hermann Frank – a leading Sudeten Nazi official, who in 1939 became Secretary of State for the Protectorate and was nominally in charge of Bohemia and Moravia after Wilhelm Frick assumed the role of Reich Protector in August 1943

Adolf Griesinger – father of Robert Griesinger, born in New Orleans, Louisiana in 1871

Albert Griesinger – Robert Griesinger's younger brother

Gisela Griesinger (née Nottebohm) – Robert Griesinger's wife, born in Hamburg in 1912

Irmela Griesinger – Jochen Griesinger's wife

Jochen Griesinger – son of Albert, and nephew of Robert Griesinger

Lina Griesinger (née Johns) – Robert Griesinger's grandmother, born in New Orleans in 1848

Robert Arnold Griesinger – Lawyer, SS Officer and an official at the Ministry of Economics and Labour in Nazi-occupied Prague

Robert Griesinger, Snr – Robert Griesinger's grandfather, born in Stuttgart in 1841

Wally Griesinger (née Passmann) – Robert Griesinger's mother, born in Duisburg in 1884

Joachim Grosser – Gisela's son from her first marriage; Robert Griesinger's stepson

Wilhelm Harster – deputy head of the Stuttgart Gestapo; later served in the Netherlands as head of the Security Police and the *Sicherheitsdienst* (SD)

Mrs Helmichova – Czech neighbour of Wally Griesinger, whom Wally sent to Prague after the war to discover Robert's fate

Alfred Hugenberg – newspaper magnate and leader of the nationalist party, the *Deutschnationale Volkspartei* (DNVP); served in Hitler's government in 1933

Jana* – the current owner of the armchair in which Griesinger's papers were discovered

Paul Emile Johns – Lina Griesinger's father, born in Kraków (Austrian Empire) in 1798 or 1800; later a composer and musician in New Orleans

Jutta Mangold (née Griesinger) – Robert Griesinger's daughter, born in January 1937

Konstantin von Neurath – Hitler's first Foreign Minister, and a Corps brother of Robert Griesinger from Suevia Tübingen; appointed by Hitler to be the first *Reichsprotektor* of Bohemia and Moravia in March 1939

Friedrich Nottebohm – Gisela's uncle; his experience of internment in the USA during the Second World War later resulted in his case being brought before the International Court of Justice in The Hague

Barbara Schlegel (née Griesinger) – Robert Griesinger's daughter, born in December 1939

Walter Stahlecker – chief of the Stuttgart Gestapo and later head of *Einsatzgruppe* A; killed in battle with Soviet partisans; funeral held at Prague Castle in March 1942

Ingeborg Venzmer (née Nottebohm) – Gisela's sister

Veronika* – Jana's daughter

Hans von Watter – a Corps brother of Robert Griesinger from Suevia Tübingen, who was later County Councillor of Prague

---

* Denotes that the name has been changed to protect the individual's privacy.

I do think that, as time went on, the children of people who had not been at the very top had a much more difficult time than we had: they were left surrounded by silence and lies. In our world, lies were impossible after the war – we knew where our fathers had stood. All we had to do was watch and read and listen, and accept the truth.

Testimony of Martin Bormann's son[1]

Introduction

Most residents of Stuttgart, capital of the German state of Württemberg, had ordinary plans for the weekend ahead as they set off for work on the morning of Friday 6 March 1936. There was a markedly different atmosphere in the city from the rush of energy and excitement of a few weeks earlier, during the Winter Olympics. The Games had been the Nazi leadership's first opportunity to showcase their spectacular economic achievements to the world. They had also hoped to put an end to rumours about the repression of political opponents and Jews inside Hitler's new Germany. After the closing ceremony, however, as visitors left, bunting was removed and anti-Jewish signs were swiftly restored to public spaces.[1]

The five lawyers working at section IIIc of the Württemberg Police Department had little to look forward to, over the approaching dull and cloudy March weekend. As Friday drew to a close and the sound of typewriters and ringing telephones died down, Walter, Wilhelm, Kurt, Rudolf and Robert left their first-floor office in the Hotel Silber, an imposing neo-Renaissance structure close to the tenth-century Old Castle in the centre of the historical Swabian city. But the weekend would prove to be far from quiet. Over the course of it, Hitler spectacularly – and illegally – remilitarised the Rhineland, marking a significant rupture with the terms of the Treaty of Versailles. As lawyers, the five men would have been concerned with future legal reprisals and the consequences of German reoccupation for multilateral diplomacy, so they would have had far more than usual to talk about when they returned to work on the Monday.

The five men formed a tight band, separate from the Hotel Silber's 200 other employees.[2] All in their late twenties or early thirties, three of them had studied law at the prestigious Tübingen University and, with the exception of Kurt Diebitsch, each had only joined section IIIc since the Nazis seized power a few years earlier. Outside the rigid confines of the Hotel Silber, the men and their families socialised together. The month before, they had celebrated the wedding of the tall, dark-haired and neatly dressed Robert Griesinger, the youngest and most junior of the five, who, after a drawn-out engagement, had finally married his sweetheart from Hamburg.

Since spring 1933 police section IIIc had played a distinctive role that allowed Nazism to take root and grow in Stuttgart. It was no ordinary police force. Rather, it was the headquarters of the Political Police for the state of Württemberg, known then and now by its more familiar name: the Gestapo. Under the Nazis, the Württemberg Political Police filled the Hotel Silber's 120 rooms, spread out over six floors. The basement contained the Gestapo's notorious torture cells. To this day, some of the elderly residents of Stuttgart continue to avoid Dorotheenstrasse because of the terrifying stories they heard as children about what took place in that basement. Walter Stahlecker was head of the Württemberg Political Police. A slender man with wire-rimmed glasses and shiny, thinning hair combed neatly back, he would go on to command *Einsatzgruppe* A, the mobile killing unit responsible for the murder of hundreds of thousands of Jews in the Baltic during the war. His stocky blond deputy, Wilhelm Harster, would serve in the Netherlands as head of the Security Police and the *Sicherheitsdienst* (SD) – the security and intelligence service of the *Schutzstaffel* (SS) – where he was instrumental in the deportation of more than 100,000 of the country's Jews. As Stahlecker made his way across the Baltic, and Harster tracked down Jews in the Netherlands, Rudolf Bilfinger, who had been a junior secretary in the Stuttgart bureau, remained in Germany, where he worked at the Reich Main Security Office (RSHA) as head of the Organisation and Law Group. An associate of Adolf Eichmann, Bilfinger was, in 1942, one of the legal masterminds of the Final Solution.[3] Later he was head of the Security Police and the SD in Toulouse.

Yet while the names of these three men can be found in studies of the Second World War, the same cannot be said of Kurt Diebitsch, the fourth lawyer, who was killed during the invasion of the USSR in 1941; or of the newly-wed Robert Griesinger, the fifth man, who finished the war working as a legal expert at a government ministry in occupied Prague.

Nazism had a devastating impact on the world and continues to fascinate, more than three-quarters of a century later. But most of us know the names of only a handful of Nazis who formed part of Hitler's inner circle. What about men like Diebitsch and Griesinger, who have so far escaped the attention of films, documentaries and history books? These low-ranking Nazis are doubly invisible: overlooked by historians, but also forgotten or deliberately suppressed in the memories of living relatives. The onerous task of first identifying and, later, understanding the experiences and feelings of some of the regime's nominal characters is important for what it communicates about consent and conformity under the swastika. Recovering lost voices from the past enables us to ask new questions about responsibility, blame and manipulation. They offer previously neglected insights into the rise of Nazism and the inner workings of Nazi rule.

This book tells two intertwined stories. One is the life of that young lawyer, Robert Griesinger. The other is the uncovering of that life, through a series of coincidences, research, cold calls, family lore, genuine or wilful forgetting and dead ends, and the ways in which the disturbing revelations reverberated in the lives of Griesinger's descendants. The first interests me for the insight it brings into the mundane workings of Nazi Germany. I am implicated personally in the second, for my pursuit of Griesinger led me to (among other people) his two surviving daughters, Jutta and Barbara, born in 1937 and 1939 respectively, who shared their memories and, in turn, came to regard me as a source of information about the father who died during their childhood, and whose absence overshadowed the rest of their lives. For Griesinger's daughters, the second generation of

Nazi perpetrators, their father was then – and remains today – anything but nominal. Spending so much time with Jutta and Barbara blurred the traditional boundaries between historian and subject. They were eager for any details I could provide, to help them build up a picture of a father they barely knew or remembered. As a Jewish historian of the Second World War, whose family was deeply marked by the disasters and atrocities of that conflict, I felt the keen ambivalence of the role.

For me, establishing facts was an act of justice. I wanted to know more about Griesinger, this seemingly peripheral figure, in order to find out if he was guilty of anything. Jutta and Barbara became, in my mind, representatives of the father they had lost; they should, or so I thought, make amends for his actions by bearing witness, by acknowledging the weight of the evidence that I placed before them. Faced with questions about his involvement in Nazi rule, they remembered little and had been told less. Their most vivid stories had the dreamlike quality of childhood recollections: a miniature porcelain toilet that sat on Griesinger's office desk; his light linen jacket soaked in blood as he carried the family's injured dog to the vet; the green cloaks the sisters wore as they and their mother fled from Prague at the end of the war. Throughout my interviews with Jutta and Barbara, questions hovered in my mind like accusations: How could you *not* know? Why are you shielding him? Yet when I approached them as a total stranger, decades after their father's death, they were kind, hospitable and willing to talk. As far as I could see them as people in their own right, I liked them. And one aspect of their experience strangely mirrored my own. For both our families, the traumas of the war were wrapped in an oppressive silence that became habitual over the course of generations. Secrets took on a palpable, looming presence, even if their existence was never acknowledged.[4]

We still know far too little about how low-ranking officials experienced the 1930s and 1940s, and Griesinger's life helps us understand why Nazi rule was possible.[5] The famous fanatics and murderers could not have existed without the countless enablers who kept the government running, filed the paperwork and lived side-by-side with potential victims of the regime in whom they instilled fear and the threat of violence. Griesinger also reveals the difficulty of trying to fit individuals into the categories usually applied to German people's experience under Nazism.[6] The young lawyer was neither a high-ranking Nazi nor one of the subordinates charged with overseeing the process of the Final Solution – those whose notoriety continues to ensure their remembrance. Nevertheless, his service at the Gestapo also excludes him from the category of 'ordinary Germans', which often lumps together everyone who, if not a political opponent, Jewish, Roma, disabled, black or homosexual, was therefore eligible to participate in the Thousand Year Reich. After all, to continue to go to work every day at the Hotel Silber as late as spring 1936 implies at the very least some support for the Nazi programme.

The narrative I trace will show how low-ranking officials might have existed in between two disconnected worlds; the first filled with the regime's well-known high functionaries, and the second that comprised the ordinary German population.[7] As many bureaucrats developed an intimate knowledge of the shape and scale of the new regime, even coming into contact with some of the Third Reich's key protagonists, they also shared the same spaces and interacted daily with the bulk of the population at whom the new legislation was aimed. Griesinger was not an ordinary German: he was an ordinary Nazi. As agents of the state, he and tens of thousands of lower-ranking men and women like him – Gestapo agents, SS and *Sturmabteiling* (SA) auxiliaries, party members, together with civil servants, judges, teachers and government officials – had the power to shape the lives of their neighbours and the wider community.

Griesinger's life allows us to understand what the rise of Nazism would have felt like at an individual level. Turning the gaze away from the German people as an indiscrete mass, and focusing instead on a single life, reveals how densely interconnected personal relationships and professional networks proved critical in allowing a new means of social organisation to take root and flourish in Württemberg, a German state previously renowned for its liberal parliamentary tradition and its aversion to political extremism.

*

Archival sources relating to Griesinger are limited, in part because of the destruction (deliberate or incidental) of records during the war. Through documents alone, he remains a colourless figure, defined by his professional trajectory and the broad outlines of his domestic arrangements. I wanted to know how he spent his evenings, the films he watched, the food he liked, what he read to his daughters. Knowing these things, I felt, would tell me something fundamental about those who perpetrated Nazi violence – a violence that devastated my own family and countless others. Where hard evidence ran out, I cast the net wider, watching him emerge in glimpses through the other characters with whom he shares these pages, and wondering what he might have done or seen at a given place and time.

'You look just like your father' were my first words to Jutta when I met her. Jutta's younger sister, Barbara, takes after their mother; and for decades the two have led separate lives, the final fragments of a family shattered by the traumas of war. Other links emerged along the way. Unexpected ancestors surfaced in New Orleans; and Griesinger's nephew, Jochen, with his wife Irmela, occupies the historical family home in Stuttgart, complete with the furniture of Griesinger's childhood. Both the daughter of the Czech woman who worked as Griesinger's maid in Prague and the granddaughter of his Jewish neighbours in Stuttgart, who were sent to Auschwitz, spoke to me. From this perspective, the 'ordinary Nazi' is defined by association as much as by absence – an empty space in a picture thronging with the people connected to him.

Why Griesinger? He entered my life unexpectedly. In 2011 I completed a PhD in history that examined the experiences of Jews in Vichy France. Within weeks of finishing, I moved to Florence to conduct research at a local university. Shortly after arriving, I hosted a dinner party for friends and colleagues. The amateur video showing the final moments of Colonel Gaddafi's life had just made the news and, as the evening was beginning to get under way, some guests huddled together on the sofa to stream the clip on a phone. It was here that I met Veronika.[8] She arrived with a mutual friend, who had called earlier in the day to ask if there might be room for an extra guest who wanted to meet me. Veronika, a tall Dutch woman in her late twenties, was in the city to begin a PhD in law. 'I'm so pleased to meet a historian of the Second World War,' she said to me. 'I would appreciate your advice on something that has *just* happened to my mother.'

When people find out I am a historian of the Second World War, they often share their family stories – about grandmothers in the French Resistance, uncles in hiding and relatives in concentration camps. I have heard hundreds of tales over the years, and no two are ever the same. My job gives people a chance to dig up like buried family heirlooms their stories, brush them down and show them off. On this occasion, however, something had only recently happened to Veronika's mother. And Veronika's opening gambit piqued my curiosity.

She began to recount the story of an armchair that her mother, Jana, in her early sixties, had recently taken for re-upholstering in Amsterdam.[9] When Jana returned to collect it a few days later, the chair restorer told her in no uncertain terms that he did not do work for Nazis or their families. To Jana's astonishment, the restorer presented her with a bundle of Nazi-era documents that he had found sewn inside the cushion of the chair. The man had assumed he was standing face-to-face with the daughter of a Nazi called Robert Griesinger – the name that appeared on every document. This Griesinger, as far as the restorer was concerned, had probably made the lives of the local Dutch population, including possibly his own relatives, a misery during the war. He did not believe Jana when she told him she did not recognise the name Griesinger or the documents and had no idea how his papers had ended up inside her chair.

From what Veronika told me, it was not obvious that Griesinger was a Nazi. After all, everyone at that time – even Jews – had swastikas stamped all over their official papers. Veronika explained that the armchair had been in her bedroom since she was a little girl and that, growing up, she had sat on it every day to do her homework. 'I just can't get out of my head that all that time I was literally sitting on Nazi papers, without even knowing it. I *need to know* who this man was, and how his documents ended up in my mother's chair.'

Veronika left me her mother's phone number and, the next day, I rang Jana in Amsterdam to find out more. Jana told me what little she could about the hidden papers and agreed to post the documents to Florence. It turned out that the chair was not an inherited family heirloom. 'The upholsterer who accused me of coming from a Nazi family didn't know what he was talking about,' she said. 'Neither my armchair nor the German man was in the Netherlands during the war. You see, I am not Dutch, and neither is my chair. I am Czech.'

Sitting in my office in Florence, with Jana on loudspeaker, I scribbled down notes. The chair, I discovered, had been on a long journey before ending up in Veronika's bedroom in Amsterdam. 'It first entered my life in 1968, when I was beginning my degree at the Charles University in Prague,' she said. Like generations of students before and since, Jana was on the lookout for cheap furniture for her student digs. One day she headed close to an area near the Old Town, full of artisan furniture shops. Jana recalled going into a number of such stores and not finding anything of interest. 'I had almost given up when a small shop on the corner of Celetná and Králodvorská caught my eye.' It was there that she found the armchair. 'It was exactly what I had in mind, so I purchased it immediately.' Jana did not recall the amount she paid, but was confident it could not have been terribly expensive. She told me the shop has since closed. She described the armchair as having a walnut veneer, a caned upper section and a cushioned seat. She said it was light and was suitable for the home, rather than for the office.

In the early 1980s Jana and her young family obtained permission to leave Communist Czechoslovakia to settle permanently in the Netherlands and were allowed to take with them on the train journey only a small number of objects. Even though they left so many things in Prague, Jana couldn't bring herself to part with the chair. 'It reminded me too much of my student days,

Photograph of the armchair

when I had barely any furniture, and my early years of being a mother.' She had kept the chair her whole adult life, owning it the longest of all her possessions, and it had relocated with her each time she moved house. In scores of family photos and home movies it's there in the background. Jana spoke movingly as our conversation drew to a close: 'Looking at these pictures with us smiling at the camera, it's chilling to think that, unknown to us, we were centimetres away from this Nazi's cache of swastika-covered papers.'

The discovery had unsettled Jana. It had never dawned on her that her cherished armchair had had a past life of its own, or that another person could have had an affinity with it in the same way she had. She almost felt betrayed. 'It may sound silly, but every time I go near it, I keep imagining that Nazi sitting in it.' Jana was desperate to know about Robert Griesinger, but the chair – her only witness – offered more questions than answers.

Jana's chair haunted me in the years that followed. I wanted to unlock the secrets of its past, so I began to follow its history. As I did so, I gained greater insight into aspects of Griesinger's personality, his life under Nazism and his ultimate fate. I was constantly amazed at how finding and pulling the right threads opened up new, unexpected avenues of research, which made me question what I thought I knew about our relationship with the past. The mystery of the hidden papers astounded archivists, experts and Griesinger's relatives, and granted me privileged access to private documentation, photographs and stories, which would otherwise be beyond reach. On numerous occasions, however, my obsession with the chair – gatekeeper to so many of Griesinger's secrets – gave way to feelings of annoyance. I was frustrated by the silences, the rabbit-holes and dead ends. What follows is not only the story of an ordinary Nazi. It is also a story of historical detection, with all the twists and turns, the frustrations and epiphanies that such an investigation entails.

A week after speaking to Jana on the phone, I received a package from the Netherlands. The assortment of documents inside came in different shapes, colours and sizes. Some were quite heavy, while others were mere scraps on yellowish paper that were crumbling at the edges. Several of the papers had the same-shaped hole, the size of a thumbprint, with similar, slightly jagged edges. Taking one of the documents, I circled the edge of the hole with my fingertip and thought about what might have caused it: perhaps these papers had been resting a bit too close to a metal spring in the chair, or perhaps a mouse had found its way into the bottom of the cushion and started to gnaw at the papers. One by one, I carefully arranged the fragile material chronologically across my desk. The first item was from 1933, while the last was from 1945. Dr Robert Arnold Griesinger's name was on each document. The papers revealed that he was a lawyer, who was born in Stuttgart in 1906 and was sent to work as a senior civil servant in Nazi-occupied Prague in March 1943. There was no reference to party membership or of participation in other Nazi organisations.

Unterschrift des Paßinhabers

M. Robert Griesinger

und seiner Ehefrau

Es wird hiermit bescheinigt, daß der Inhaber die durch
das obenstehende Lichtbild dargestellte Person ist und
die darunter befindliche Unterschrift eigenhändig voll-
zogen hat.

Stuttgart den 4. Dez. 1942
i.A.

Polizeisekretär

Nr. 30753 D/40

A page from one of Griesinger's passports

I studied Griesinger's photographs. In each one, he wore a light-coloured suit – civilian clothes. He was handsome, with slicked-back hair and a strong, distinctive face. I wondered how he had obtained the scar that ran across his left cheek. His hidden papers had obviously been chosen with care. There were wartime passports, certificates of war bonds, uncashed stocks and share receipts in cable companies, and a certificate showing that he passed the second stage of exams for the civil service in 1933, two years after completing his PhD in law. These were clearly his most valuable printed possessions: they were proof of an entire identity and existence, items that anyone would be lost without, especially in wartime. Yet what struck me was how little such papers actually reveal about anyone. I held Griesinger's documents in my hand and they told me everything, and nothing.

The German presence in the Czech lands lasted from 1939 to 1945, during which time the occupied territory was euphemistically called the Protectorate of Bohemia and Moravia. Searching through the assortment of papers, I tried to locate the particular ministry in which Griesinger worked, or a clue that revealed the nature of his work. The large number of central-European stamps inside his passport indicated that travel had been an integral part of his professional life, and I was particularly struck by one of the final stamps. In summer 1944, just weeks after the Normandy Landings and the Allied liberation of Rome, Griesinger went on holiday for three weeks to visit 'relatives' in Liechtenstein. Even at such an advanced stage of the war, Nazi officials like Griesinger continued to be granted holiday leave and would return from the tranquillity of a neutral country to their more dangerous postings. The trip was particularly perplexing because no relatives were mentioned in any of the other documents. In both of his wartime passports, someone had struck through in pen the section on 'wife and children', indicating that despite the Nazis' emphasis on pro-natalism and *Kinderreich* (child-rich) families, Griesinger was single and childless. I would learn that this was a lie.

I assumed Griesinger himself had stashed his personal papers in the armchair. Why would he choose to do this? If he felt the existence of the documents might compromise his future, then why did he not destroy them? What did he have to hide? Why didn't he ever return to retrieve his papers? I kept coming back to one of his passports, issued in Prague in June 1944 and valid for one year. Given what occurred in the city over the months that followed, it seemed likely that by the time the passport expired, it was already hidden inside the cushion. The documents were probably concealed during the Liberation of May 1945, a time when, after six years of gruelling Occupation, sections of the local population took part in sporadic killings against anyone who looked, or even sounded, German. Griesinger needed to mask his identity to get out of Prague alive. But would a senior civil servant with a doctorate in law have known what to do with a needle and thread? Perhaps he enlisted the services of a seamstress. Or perhaps he could rely on a trusted confidant, who could sew the papers in a way that was resilient enough to be left undisturbed for almost seventy years.

Griesinger's papers shed no light on what happened to him after the war. Had he been killed during the liberation of Prague, or captured by the Soviets and made a prisoner of war? He might even have been put on trial. Once the disorder of the liberation of western Czechoslovakia had subsided, People's Courts and local courts tried more than 150,000 Germans and their Czech collaborators. Did this composed, authoritative-looking figure end his days harried and haunted before a makeshift court, in which entire trials were known to last only a few minutes? From my desk in Florence, I could determine that Griesinger was not brought before the courts, nor was he formally executed, as his name did not appear on any of the post-war trial lists.[10] Perhaps, then, he spent the Liberation in hiding, or he might have escaped Czechoslovakia in disguise? If he managed to survive, it is likely that he swiftly adapted to post-war life and, given his date of birth, probably died in the 1970s or 1980s. However, learning anything about Griesinger after 1945 proved impossible. There was no trace of him: he was not mentioned in any books on occupied Prague or anywhere online. His significance during the Third Reich seemed negligible.

★

The very ordinariness of this man, who existed in only a handful of bureaucratic documents, made him all the more intriguing to me. I was determined to pursue him. I wanted to see whether following the trajectory of an anonymous man could reveal anything new about the complexities of living under Nazi rule. Would putting a human face on a shrouded past help to unravel the characteristically Manichaean terms of good versus evil so often associated with Nazism, or would it leave those awkward dichotomies unaltered?

My search for Griesinger was to last five years. It would lead me to Prague, Berlin, Stuttgart, Zurich, New Orleans and any number of German provincial towns where he had studied and worked. Along the way, I developed a new way of doing history. Academic history usually follows a standard path. After sustained engagement with secondary literature, the historian develops a hypothesis about a subject and will then look for primary sources against which to test their hypothesis. In a way, my pursuit of Robert Griesinger followed the reverse path: it began with the sources. I needed to reassemble the historical and social context in which Griesinger operated in order to discover how his personal documents came to be hidden.

After spending so long looking into Griesinger's case, what I eventually pieced together was the life of a good-natured boy from a wealthy family, a law student, later a bureaucrat within the Nazi regime, ambitious for promotion, fond of animals, aligned with racist ideology. I tracked the course of his army division across Europe during the war, looked at photo albums with his daughters and read his mother's diary. At times Griesinger's story also brought me startlingly close to my own family's past.

Chapter 1

A 'Real' Nazi

It all started with the armchair. The chair seemed to offer a way into Griesinger's subjective life, his taste, relationships and habits, in a way that his papers could not. From Florence, I had sent a photograph of the armchair to experts, hoping they might shed light on its provenance. Each agreed that it was inspired by the German-born cabinet-maker Michael Thonet, who had invented solid-wood bending in the 1840s. Models of Thonet's steam-bent laminated armchairs were popular among conservative buyers in the 1930s and 1940s, but by the 1960s they had become less fashionable.[1]

I visited Prague within a few months of first speaking with Jana, the armchair's current owner, hoping to establish where it had been manufactured and what I could of its intended buyer. Griesinger might have transported it from Germany to Prague, or he might have acquired it in the city, following his arrival. It was also possible that the armchair had been confiscated from the home of a Jewish family in Prague or even in Nazi-occupied western Europe, and later shipped east to make up for the furniture shortage affecting newly-arrived Reich employees and their families in recently conquered territories.[2]

At the library of the Museum of Decorative Arts in Prague I trawled through hundreds of architectural and home-design magazines from 1930s Czechoslovakia, each showcasing the latest conveniences of modern living, and in the scenes of living rooms and spaces I came across pictures of chairs that appeared identical to

Emil Gerstel Catalogue, Prague, p. 14

Jana's. The closest match appeared in collections of the Czech-Jewish designer Emil Gerstel, whose furniture company in Prague was taken over by the Germans in 1940. Gerstel's designs were expensive. The company specialised in historicist furniture, which corresponded to the tastes of its wealthy clients. To purchase a Gerstel design, clients had to visit the Gerstel shop on the bustling Senovážné Square, a historical site in the heart of Prague's New Town, peppered with tall symmetrical neo-Renaissance buildings with curving roofs. For those unable or without the time to buy an original, an easy solution was to hand. Gerstel's neo-rococo armchairs were easy to replicate, and imitation designs flooded the Prague market.[3]

On a rainy day in May, armed with multiple photographs of the armchair, I arrived in Prague's Old Town and began to make enquiries. Most of the Gerstel company's archives were destroyed during the war, and those that survived were lost when private enterprises were later nationalised.[4] I walked in and out of a dozen showrooms and ateliers.[5] Local chair-makers and furniture-sellers were divided on whether the armchair was an original Gerstel or an imitation. 'Every factory in Prague was churning out hundreds of chairs, just like this one,' the owner of one antique shop told me, as she stood in her doorway and examined the photo.

It is easier to purchase an original Gerstel today than it would have been when Griesinger arrived in Prague in 1943. The city's antique shops are now full of Gerstel pieces, which are neither rare nor particularly valuable. One restorer explained that the style is now considered simply too old-fashioned. In one antique dealer's shop I found two chairs identical to Griesinger's. The shop's owner was selling the pair for Kč 4,500, the equivalent of £150. It felt natural to prod the top of the cushion gently with my fingers to see whether I could detect anything inside. I handed Karel, the shop's owner, a photo of Griesinger's armchair and explained that documents from the Nazi era, covered in swastikas, were recently discovered inside the chair's cushion. I spoke slowly, pausing for effect as I uttered the word 'Nazi'. Karel glanced at the photograph and, after taking a puff on his cigarette, shrugged his shoulders and gave it back to me. His reaction turned out to be typical. Unlike the restorer in Amsterdam, none of the people I spoke to in Prague seemed especially surprised by the chair's use as a hiding place. 'This was Communist Czechoslovakia, for God's sake,' explained one, 'people had a reason to hide things; I find items concealed in furniture every day.' Other than banknotes, all the dealers and restorers I spoke to tend to throw out the items they find. One chair-maker said that he finds hidden letters and official documents from the Communist era in at least one in ten couches or armchairs that he restores. He told me he has never read any. It seemed as if a million paths for potential future historical investigations are being scrubbed from the face of the Earth. What thousands of people had hoped to hide from the regime temporarily, Karel and others like him were erasing for ever.

From 1948 right up until the fall of Communism, the people of Czechoslovakia lived under constant surveillance by the totalitarian state. The Czechoslovak secret police, the StB (*Státní bezpečnost*), monitored the population with vigour. By 1989, in addition to its regular staff of 15,000–17,000 employees, the organisation had an extra 30,000 informants on file, tasked with denouncing anyone suspected of acting against the regime. In an era marked by tapping devices and fear-mongering, it is hardly surprising that many ordinary citizens chose to conceal anything that could potentially incriminate them and their families.[6]

While I was in Prague, I also began looking in local archives for evidence of Griesinger's existence in that city. After a day of endlessly streaming through reels of microfilms at the Czech National Archives, I eventually found a document on Griesinger in a police file. Every newcomer to Prague was requested to register their address and personal information with the authorities. Griesinger's form disclosed that he first arrived in Prague from Stuttgart in early March 1943, that he was Protestant and that his parents were Adolf and Wally. But Griesinger's police file also revealed something else: in the documents that he had hidden inside the chair he had concealed an important fact. His wartime passports up to as late as 1944 stated that he was a childless bachelor. But he *had* married. In his police file in Prague, he confirmed in his own messy handwriting that he had married a woman named Gisela Nottebohm.[7] Who was he trying to deceive by withholding this information? Whatever his reasoning, Griesinger's efforts to mislead his own contemporaries remained effective seventy years later: he had pulled the wool over my eyes all too easily.

Not content to have uncovered only a single document, I headed the next day to the Archive of the Security Services, which I had heard also contained files of Germans who lived in Prague during the Nazi occupation of the Czech lands. I hoped to uncover Griesinger's name mentioned in something such as a testimony from a former Reich employee, to help me piece together how he spent his days. When I arrived at the archive, located inside a dated Art Deco building with a dark, grubby façade, I handed the cover page of Griesinger's police file from the National Archives to the archivist on duty. She took off her glasses to read the document, placing them on top of a stack of old books that she had on her wooden desk. She asked me to wait in a room full of filing cabinets which had a subtle, musky smell while she went in search of a file.

The large walls of open shelves contained thousands of files with different-coloured jackets. When the archivist returned, she handed me a document in which Griesinger's name appeared on a list of 'German Public Employees in Prague'. Only a few details were typed alongside his name: his date and place of birth, his address in Prague and his role as an employee of the German state government ministry in Prague – most of which I already knew from the National Archives and from the documents in the chair. The final detail, however, contained new information. Alongside his vague employment details, I read that Griesinger was in the SS. He was listed as an *SS Obersturmführer* (senior storm leader).[8]

The trail of this everyday piece of household furniture had led me to a member of one of the last century's most sinister organisations: the *Schutzstaffel*, or SS. Just seeing those two letters next to his name automatically transformed my preconception of Griesinger. The image that I had built up of him was beginning to crack. Until that moment I had thought I was on the hunt for an unremarkable civil servant. I had even momentarily entertained the idea that Griesinger was apolitical. Now it seemed I was on the trail of someone more significant. SS members – recruited only after meeting strict racial, height and health criteria, and after swearing an oath of allegiance to Hitler – remain associated with the most perverse aspects of the Third Reich. If Griesinger had chosen to join the SS, it was likely that he agreed with the main tenets of Nazi ideology, including, of course, its racism and anti-semitism. Griesinger was no longer just the polite, well-educated bureaucrat, dressed smartly in a light-coloured suit. Another image, admittedly speculative, began to form in my mind: Griesinger wearing his intimidating SS uniform, beating up terrified Jews on the streets of Stuttgart and Prague. I felt the sheer irony of this SS officer's most precious documents ending up in the possession of a British Jew.

I had begun this journey to help Jana and her daughter Veronika uncover how Griesinger's papers ended up inside their family's armchair. However, the more material I collected on Griesinger from Czech sources, the more my interest in the armchair dwindled.

While I still hoped to solve the mystery of Griesinger's hidden documents, I also wanted to explore more about the SS officer – not only his time in Prague, but who he was at his core, what he had done and why he had done it.

Before Veronika first approached me with Griesinger's story, I had never studied the SS in any depth. I had always thought that involvement in the organisation was a full-time position, one that defined the existence of its members. SS officers, I had believed, wore the black uniform of the organisation every day and spent each waking moment terrorising the local population. Griesinger's example shows this must not always have been the case. As a lawyer at a government ministry, Griesinger already had a full-time job that had nothing to do with his SS membership. As I delved deeper, I discovered that so too did tens of thousands of doctors, lawyers and civil servants.

Shortly after learning that Griesinger was in the SS, I travelled to Berlin to see whether I could find his SS dossier. I wasn't optimistic: two-thirds of the one million SS members' files were destroyed by Allied bombing during the war. The surviving SS dossiers are held at the Bundesarchiv in the sleepy Berlin suburb of Lichterfelde. As I went into the building I seriously wondered whether my interest in this unknown Nazi was taking up too much of my attention, sending me as it had to another city, one with a less than fifty–fifty chance of having any information. But the possibility of handling Griesinger's SS dossier was too tantalising to ignore. In the unlikely event of finding anything, I might have the chance to read his own words, the closest I could come to 'meeting' this man, whom I had only known from a passport photo and official documents.

Upon arriving, I discovered to my relief that not only had Griesinger's SS file survived, but it was available for consultation. The archivists didn't seem to be in a hurry to fetch the documents from the holdings, but eventually someone handed me the files, on top of which was written: 'Dr Robert Griesinger, SS number: 161,860'. His SS number was etched onto the page in old Gothic handwriting. Griesinger's immense file contained dozens of letters that he had sent to Berlin, and as I began to read his correspondence from the mid-1930s, I was hearing for the first time his voice in each line. It was a calm and detached voice, devoid of all emotion. After the censor and the SS staff in Berlin, I was probably only the third person to read Griesinger's words. The letters and reports in the file did not uncover the nature of his role in the SS, as I had hoped they might. It did not expose him as an SS desk killer or a concentration-camp guard. Rather, they were concerned solely with family affairs and his work as a civil servant.

It was not until seeing Griesinger's SS file that I learned he was a father. A 1941 document contained details of his children. In addition to a stepson, Joachim, the product of his wife Gisela's first marriage, it mentioned two daughters: Jutta, born in January 1937, and then another daughter, born in December 1939. There was no additional information about Jutta or her younger sister, whose name I later discovered was Barbara.⁹ If his daughters had managed to survive the war and were still alive, they would be in their seventies. Perhaps they still lived in Stuttgart. The file revealed that in order for their marriage to be approved by the SS, both Gisela and Griesinger needed to produce a family tree to demonstrate Aryan ancestry.

Griesinger's tree showed that neither of his parents was born in Stuttgart. Wally, his mother, was born in 1884 in Duisburg, a German town twenty-five miles from the Dutch border, where her family had lived for centuries. Griesinger's father, Adolf, originated from even further afield. Adolf was not born in Germany. He was not even born in Europe. Rather, he was born in 1871 in New Orleans, Louisiana. As I ran my finger up the family tree, I saw that Griesinger's family, many bearing the names of French noble families, had lived in the American South for generations. His family was not as historically German as I had presumed. Griesinger struggled to complete all the parts of his American family tree. He did not know details of a large number of his American ancestors. He was also without several crucial documents, including his father's birth certificate and a marriage certificate for his paternal grandparents. His entry into the SS, in the absence of such crucial

documents, casts doubt on the reputation of the SS as an organisation for the German elite, one that was equipped with a rigorous
application process. The authorities apparently took Griesinger at
his word when he stated that his ancestors in New Orleans were
of desirable racial stock.[10]

According to Hitler, all good Germans could connect to their
country's glorious past through their ancestors, who once worked
the German land. The Nazis went to great lengths to foster a
philosophy of Blood and Soil (*Blut und Boden*), which promoted
Germanic ties to the land, at the expense of the 'inferior races'
such as Jews, Slavs or Roma, who it was argued had no historical
connection. Griesinger's American background challenges
commonly held conceptions of German identity during the Third
Reich. Only one strand of his ancestry could speak to this idyllic
portrayal of rural life. It was a little odd that I found out all of
these intimate details from information obtained for Griesinger's
membership to a violent paramilitary organisation. But the Nazi
obsession with bloodlines and progeny made the gathering of all
types of emotional, sexual and family details an imperative of SS
membership. Despite its repugnant purpose, documentation assembled for the enforcement of racial purity paradoxically resembles
other modes of genealogical research. Using it, we can trace the
paths of kinship across generations.

Discovering that Griesinger had ancestors born in the United
States, and that he was a father, meant that the Berlin archives
produced more questions than they answered. They told me
nothing about Griesinger's war, nor could they shed much light on
his day-to-day life as an ordinary Nazi in Stuttgart during the Third
Reich. For that, I had to go elsewhere.

The Stuttgart that I encountered seventy-five years after the end
of the war bore only a partial resemblance to the city in which
Griesinger spent his early life. Like so many German cities, Stuttgart
was the victim of intense Allied bombing. Fifty-three Allied air
raids destroyed almost 60 per cent of buildings in Stuttgart, killing
4,562 people. This included a raid on 12 September 1944 by the 101

Squadron of the RAF, in which 957 were killed and 1,600 injured.[11] That night, eighteen-year-old Sergeant David Bernett, my grandfather, was a Special Duties Operator on board a Lancaster bomber. My research assistant in Stuttgart paused as we strolled through the city centre and looked suddenly uncertain when I divulged this information. 'So, you too have relatives who inflicted pain on others,' she said sharply. While, for me, my grandfather's raid over Stuttgart was only a minor, if necessary detail of his war record, this was not the case for the people of that city who, decades after the end of the war, are still affected by his seven-and-a-half-hour bombing spree. Until then, as a British Jew, I had never expected that somebody might associate me with a wartime tragedy.

When the French liberators arrived in April 1945, the city was covered in 4.9 million cubic metres of rubble.[12] Responsibility for rebuilding the city centre fell to the city's mayor, Arnulf Klett. His priority, during his thirty years as mayor, was to rebuild the city's devastated economy, industry, housing and transport system as quickly as possible. He paid little attention to architectural detail and ignored calls to restore Stuttgart to its pre-war historical Gothic splendour. Instead, over the ruins of the city, a mishmash of raw concrete eyesores and pedestrian zones sprang up.[13]

I spent my first few days in Stuttgart combing through various archival repositories scattered across the region, trying to piece Griesinger's life back together. Fading papers filed away for more than seventy years shed light on his various transfers and promotions at the Württemberg Ministry of the Interior. I found details of Griesinger's student days, his salary and the positions he occupied within the ministry until the outbreak of war. Above all, the papers presented the image of an earnest and rather unspectacular civil servant, committed to forging a career under the auspices of the new and untested Third Reich. More so than anything else, the local archives revealed Griesinger's legal training to have been his greatest asset, propelling him into social arenas that might otherwise have been out of reach.

Uncovering details of his Nazi past proved more of a challenge. Hoping to come across bulkier files, I tried to find out whether the

authorities investigated Griesinger after the war as part of denazification process – an ultimately failed campaign set up by the victorious
Allies to purge Germany of all traces of Nazism. When I went to
the Staatsarchiv Ludwigsburg, where the denazification files are held,
I ran my finger down the list of names of people beginning with
'G' who were subject to post-war sanctions, but rather than Robert,
it was Wally Griesinger, his mother, whose name leapt off the page.
In April 1946 Wally was accused of having been a Nazi because of
her involvement with the *NS-Frauenschaft*, the Nazi party women's
league. Robert's name was nowhere to be found. Robert, a card-
carrying party member and an *SS Obersturmführer*, did not have a
file, whereas his mother, who was not a party member, faced investigation. Another example of how family histories sometimes read
strangely when placed next to official narratives from the archives.[14]

Gleaning details of Griesinger's role in the SS in Stuttgart was
also testing. There was no local SS archive to speak of that contained
files either on individual SS members in Stuttgart or on the nature
of the organisation's local branches. In April 1945, when it was
thought that the American army was only days away from liberating
Stuttgart, local SS leaders destroyed the organisation's archives.
They had privileged access to the fuel and oil needed to burn more
than fifteen years' worth of paperwork. As Wilhelm Murr, the
fanatical Nazi Gauleiter of Württemberg was ordering the people
of Stuttgart to fight until the bitter end, flames devoured the SS
files of Robert Griesinger and those of his closest comrades, oblit-
erating their secrets for ever. The destruction of the SS papers was
not confined to Württemberg and the south-west. As Allied victory
approached, SS personnel set fire to their papers in towns and
villages across Germany and the occupied lands.[15]

But written sources can only ever tell part of a person's story.
Other clues survived the war and did not go up in smoke. While
I was in his home town, I hoped to find and meet someone who
had known Griesinger personally.

On a whim, I picked up the local phonebook and began cold-
calling all the Griesingers listed. Some of the people kindly racked
their brains, trying to think of a Robert in the family, although

most thought I was a telesales rep and promptly hung up. Then I reached 'J'. I called the first name, Jochen Griesinger.

'I had an Uncle Robert,' responded the hoarse voice down the line. 'He was my father's brother. May I ask why you're interested?'

What could I say? 'Hello, I found your Nazi uncle's papers hidden away inside the cushion of an armchair in Amsterdam – are you free for a coffee?' It was preposterous. 'I'm doing research on German lawyers in the 1930s,' I said, stretching the truth. 'I am in Stuttgart for research and would really like to meet you.' I felt the sweat in my palms as I waited for him to respond.

'Very well,' said Jochen, sounding mildly intrigued. 'Come over to my place tomorrow at midday.'

I noted the details and hung up. It was the same address Griesinger had lived at when he was a bachelor. I was going there to meet his nephew.

The Griesinger house is perched on a hill in the south of Stuttgart. Shortly before midday I began to make my way along the street, passing a succession of large 1920s houses and villas. The buildings, each with their own front lawn, were a fair distance away from one another. At three storeys high, the Griesinger residence was among the larger houses in this affluent neighbourhood. The house was painted a soft peach, its many windows decorated by white wooden shutters. The German flag fluttered next to the front door. Unlike the other houses in the area, four rather out-of-place grey classical columns surrounded the building's main entrance. To access the house, I needed to pass through a large gate that bore the letter G in solid black metal. I rang the bell. I was anxious, still unsure how Jochen would react to my interest in his family. Perhaps Griesinger's daughters were present. Jochen could have alerted his cousins to my phone call. The gate opened and gave way to a paved staircase that went uphill, cutting across the front lawn. I climbed up, realising as I did so that it was the first time I was following in Griesinger's actual footsteps.

Jochen stood upright, waiting for me in front of one of the columns at the entrance to the impressive house. He had short silver hair and a trimmed white moustache. A strong, solidly built man, he wore his light-blue shirt with jeans in a way that imparted confidence. He was an impressive septuagenarian. After we shook hands, Jochen ushered me round the side of the house towards the back garden, where a slender blonde woman was laying a table. Noticing our arrival, she turned to welcome me, introducing herself as Irmela. She wore skinny jeans with a fitted black top. She looked in her fifties. I was unsure whether she was Jochen's wife or his daughter.

We sat around a wooden garden table at the back of the house, protected from the sun by a floral parasol. I had hardly taken out my notepad and pen before Jochen and Irmela told me they found my interest in Robert bewildering. 'The man was a real Nazi,' said Irmela, without hesitating.

She had brought it up, not me. 'What makes you say that?' I asked, relieved the subject was out in the open.

'Albert, my husband's father, told me,' she said, gesturing towards Jochen.

'I just don't understand why you want to know about Robert,' interrupted Jochen. 'He wasn't important.'

'I'm not sure you'll believe me, if I tell you,' I said, reaching back into my bag to remove a photocopy of Griesinger's hidden papers. I handed them the documents and told them the story of their recovery, placing in front of them an enlarged colour photograph of the chair. Wanting to be sure of my words, I spoke slowly. I had dropped all pretence of conducting research about 1930s German lawyers.

'It's amazing. I can't believe it,' repeated Irmela as she and Jochen slowly turned the pages of Griesinger's documents.

Jochen stayed quiet. 'I haven't seen this chair before,' he finally said, bringing the image closer to inspect it properly, 'but it certainly looks familiar.'

'We inherited similar chairs that have been in the house since the time Robert lived here,' said Irmela, sounding excited. She stood up and beckoned me inside.

As I stepped into the house, I felt as if I had gone back in time. Elaborately gold-framed family portraits, some of military figures,

hung around the walls of the room. Almost all the furniture was
wooden and appeared hand-crafted: an ornate cabinet replete with
gold handles, a collection of copper ornaments sitting on top of a
baroque-style wooden chest. Nothing seemed to have changed since
the interwar years. I was surely experiencing the living room in the
same way Robert had.

Gisela and Robert in his parents' house, *c. 1937*

Still holding the photograph in her hand, Irmela pointed out
three bentwood chairs with woven cane backs that bore a striking
resemblance to the one in the photograph. Most of the furniture
in the Griesingers' enormous living room was sizeable. A large
wooden armchair that looked almost like a throne dominated
another of the corner spaces. Irmela caught me admiring it. 'That
was Lina's chair,' she said as she lifted some magazines off the seat
to reveal the quilted cushion. 'Lina was Robert and Albert's
American grandmother. She died at the end of the First World
War.' I was impressed that she seemed to know every detail of her

husband's family history. 'Grandmother Wally lived into her
nineties. Towards the end of her life, I spent a lot of time with her
alone in this house. I heard a lot of stories.'

We returned outside to the veranda and resumed our places
around the table. 'What happened to Robert?' I asked. 'I haven't
managed to find any trace of him after 1945.'

'You mean you don't know?' said Irmela as she sat up in her
seat. She looked at Jochen, who remained still. 'He died in Prague
at the end of the war,' she continued. 'He was in hospital in Prague
when soldiers – I'm not sure if they were Czech or Russian – came
in and shot him. They threw his body on a mass grave.' As she
said this, Irmela brought her hands close to her chest and pulled
an invisible trigger with her finger.

Jochen continued where his wife had left off. 'After the war,
Grandmother Wally paid a Czech person she knew, called Mrs
Helmichova, to go to Prague to find out what happened to Robert.'
Jochen told me that even though Helmichova returned to Stuttgart
in 1946 with a death certificate on which was listed 'infectious
disease' as the cause of his uncle's death, the family dismissed the
official version of events as a whitewash. Helmichova claimed to
have learned about what really happened to Robert from people
she met in Prague. She even brought back to Stuttgart a jar that
she said contained earth from Robert's grave. 'My grandmother
never got over Robert's death,' said Jochen, shaking his head.

I asked Jochen whether Gisela and his cousins, Jutta and Barbara,
managed to make it out of Prague.

'They survived.'

I waited for him to elaborate, but he and Irmela remained silent.

'Are they still alive?' I asked. 'I presumed Gisela must have died,
as she would be more than one hundred, but what about the girls?'
I wondered if they still lived close by.

'I think they're alive, but it has been many years since we had
news from them,' said Jochen firmly.

Irmela explained that, in the aftermath of Wally's death in 1976,
an inheritance battle had divided the family. They had not heard
from Jutta or Barbara since then.

'Did they both marry?' I asked, hoping for the women's married names.

They had. Both women gave up the name Griesinger. Irmela explained they were now known as Jutta Mangold and Barbara Schlegel. 'Jutta was living in Switzerland in the 1970s. Perhaps she is still there,' said Irmela.

I asked Jochen, born on the eve of the Second World War, whether he remembered his uncle. Everything he knew about Robert, he said, were stories and anecdotes he had heard from other people while growing up. I told Jochen I was interested to learn how Robert first became involved with the Nazis, and asked whether it was something he might have inherited from his parents. Jochen shook his head vigorously. Neither Albert, his own father, nor his grandparents – Robert's parents – were at all interested in Nazism. From the archives, I knew that neither Adolf nor Albert Griesinger had had a denazification case brought against them. But Wally's denazification dossier continued to linger in my mind. Even though she was not a member of the party, she did join the NS-Frauenschaft, the Nazi party's women's league. She clearly found some elements of the Nazi project appealing.

'Robert's father hated the Nazis,' chipped in Irmela from across the table. 'He was an old-fashioned military royalist; a confidant of the King of Württemberg,' she said, proudly. After arriving in Stuttgart from New Orleans, Adolf Griesinger embarked on a distinguished military career. 'Grandfather Adolf had sworn his allegiance to the king for life,' she continued. 'When the Nazis came to power, they asked him to work with the army in some capacity, but he refused.' Irmela recounted other examples of the family's aversion to Nazism, which included Adolf and Wally's friendship with the Stauffenberg family, prominent residents of Stuttgart. Adolf knew Count Alfred von Stauffenberg from the royal court of Württemberg. Count Alfred and Countess Caroline were the parents of Claus von Stauffenberg, who attempted to kill Hitler in the 1944 July Plot and was executed when the plan failed.

As Irmela spoke, Jochen listened and nodded, jumping in intermittently to clarify an occasional detail. 'Grandfather had no time for the Nazis,' he said at one point. He explained that Adolf saw in Nazism nothing more than a vulgar populist movement, led by a brutish Austrian corporal.

'All of the house's employees were against the Nazis, because of Adolf,' said Irmela. I wondered if this heroic image of Adolf might not be a bit exaggerated. Possibly sensing my scepticism, Irmela went away and returned a few minutes later with a photo album to prove her point. 'This is Albert and Gertraut's wedding album from 1938. Look for yourself.' She handed it to me. 'No one would have dared show up at the ceremony in a Nazi uniform, because of Adolf.' I began to look at the images. Nazi uniforms were nowhere to be seen. Only a few military uniforms were visible. One of the photographs captured the formal arrival of Adolf, then in his mid-sixties, at the church, dressed in his old imperial uniform. He wore a classic piece of headgear, his *Pickelhaube*, a helmet with a spike, synonymous with imperial Germany. He displayed his medals proudly on his chest, with his Iron Cross 1st Class taking prime position. Adolf's sword hung from a buckle on his left side. I couldn't help but think that he resembled Bismarck.

Adolf and Wally Griesinger outside the church on the occasion of
Albert and Gertraut's wedding in 1938

As I looked at the photographs, I spotted Robert among the crowd, standing with Wilhelmine, his eighty-eight-year-old maternal grandmother. He looked very smart. He was dressed in top hat and tails and wore a white waistcoat and white bow tie. According to Jochen and Irmela, Adolf forbade Robert ever to wear his SS uniform in his presence. 'He was certainly not allowed to wear the thing in the house,' said Irmela, assertively. 'His SS uniform suited his arrogance,' she let slip.

'What makes you say that?' I broke in. 'Did Wally ever speak of her son in that way?' I asked.

'Of course not. In his mother's eyes, he could do no wrong. Bobby, as she called him, was perfect.' Irmela explained that when she first lived in the house in the 1960s, a lot of the staff had worked for the Griesingers for decades. 'They kept vivid memories of Robert,' said Irmela. 'I remember the gardener and the driver telling me that none of the staff ever liked Bobby.'

'They thought he was a snob,' exclaimed Jochen.

'And that he was ice-cold,' added Irmela. 'Apparently, you couldn't look into his eyes.'

Irmela recalled a post-war conversation with Wally's niece, who had nothing good to say about her cousin. Irmela made sure to tell me that this relative was married to a prominent member of the Resistance.

Robert was beginning to sound like a perfect monster. It was a side to him hidden from the administrative documents that I had seen so far, which gave few hints of the nature and temperament of this seemingly insignificant Nazi. To me, Griesinger was an abstract figure from the past, who appeared only in obscure historical sources. This contrasted with the assessment of his relatives, who, having grown up with stories of Robert, could give voice to someone who had long since ceased to exist.

I looked at one of the photographs of Robert, from Albert and Gertraut's wedding album. Underneath the image of his brother, Albert had written, 'And here comes Mr Regierungsrat' – a sarcastic jibe at Robert's supposed self-importance. I asked Jochen whether his father and Robert had been close.

'Not at all,' said Jochen firmly. 'They were completely different.' He explained that Albert was always at the stables. He loved horses and went on to make a career out of it, moving to Düsseldorf in the late 1920s to become a horse trainer. Robert rode horses, but had little affinity for them.

According to Jochen and Irmela, Robert's greatest passion was women. Irmela told me that the family even had to 'pay off' one woman when she discovered that she was pregnant with Robert's child. 'Because the baby was illegitimate,' said Irmela, 'Grandmother did not recognise the child as a Griesinger.' She did not know any further details about this undocumented episode in Robert's life. What she seemed to know a lot about, however, was Wally's intense dislike of Gisela. Wally considered her daughter-in-law an evil temptress, who had corrupted Robert and prised him away from his beloved parents. On the back of another photograph of her were the words 'the evil one' in Wally's handwriting. According to Irmela, Robert fell for Gisela's party-girl approach to life. Wally was convinced that Gisela had led her son down a dangerous path.

The truth was more complicated. Jochen and Irmela's open disdain carried some of the perpetual relish of gossip in a family that had seen its share of feuds, but it might also have served a deeper, less conscious purpose. After the war, German families needed strategies to help heal the emotional wounds brought about by Nazi rule. One of these was the identification of a particular relative as the 'real Nazi', a family member with a 'brown past', upon whom a collective sense of blame for acquiescence in the regime could be focused and contained.[16] Perhaps it was useful to paint Robert as the black sheep: after all, the Griesinger most implicated with the Nazis had died in Prague, rendering him – then and now – the ideal scapegoat.

Towards the end of my visit, I told Jochen I was intrigued by the way the house did not seem to resemble any of the others on the street. Jochen told me he had recently discovered the building's blueprints from the mid-1920s, which he had framed and arranged in a neat display in the lobby. He explained that Adolf had wanted his new house to remind him of his childhood in post-Civil War

Louisiana. Adolf insisted on having four towering Corinthian columns on the porch, on top of which sat a large balcony. The result was like something out of *Gone with the Wind*.

The Griesinger house on Auf dem Haigst (photo taken *c.* 1953)

Even though he later became a patriotic German, Adolf Griesinger's southern roots remained a key part of his identity, thanks in part to the influence of his mother, Lina. Adolf, an only child, enjoyed a close relationship with his mother, who spent her final years living under her son's roof. Even though separated by an ocean, the Griesinger family in Stuttgart knew all about their American relatives, thanks to Lina, who maintained a regular correspondence with them in English. I wanted to discover more about the ideas and character traits unique to Louisiana that the future SS officer inherited from his ancestors. It was obvious that a visit to New Orleans was the next step.

I had spent the whole afternoon in Jochen and Irmela's home and it was starting to get late. Just before taking my leave, I asked them whether they had any documents about Robert. 'I'm afraid not,' said Irmela after a slight pause. 'We did have some things – letters and that sort of thing – but we threw them all out.' She said that it had not crossed her mind to send the documents to Jutta and Barbara, as they were no longer in touch.

I wasn't sure whether to believe her. It didn't seem that anything had ever been thrown out of this house. Throughout the afternoon, on each occasion Irmela went in search of a different photograph collection, I saw cupboards and drawers full to the brim with old letters, postcards and newspaper clippings. Tempted though I was to push the matter further, I realised it would be unwise to do so. It was already decent enough of the couple to receive me and answer my questions. They were under no obligation.

'I really don't think we have anything,' said a seemingly disheartened Irmela, 'but I'll let you know if anything should turn up.'

I scribbled down my address as I left, suspecting I would never hear from them again. Later that evening in my hotel room I typed 'Jutta Mangold' into the online Swiss phonebook. There was only one hit in the whole country. Her address and phone number were listed.

Chapter II

Inheriting Ideas from the New World

'You have ten minutes to finish up, and then we really have to ask you to leave,' said a nervous-looking archivist at the New Orleans Notarial Archives, still managing to maintain a southern charm as heavy rain pounded the building's windows. 'The archives will remain closed until further notice,' she continued.

I had until then been seated alone in the reading room, surrounded by piles of notarial acts belonging to Griesinger's ancestors, which I had intended to read that day. It was March 2016 and my last day in New Orleans. As I hurriedly made digital copies of the material, the archivists were preparing for the worst. Rainfall had reached three inches an hour in some parts of the state, and New Orleans was bracing itself for a deluge. After Hurricane Katrina, which had devastated the city in 2005, destroying a significant proportion of its collections, staff at the Notarial Archives were leaving nothing to chance. From then on, the archivists had a plan in place to avoid the loss of thousands of documents to flooding. The facility went into lockdown. Staff suddenly appeared out of nowhere. On hands and knees, they pulled open cupboards and drawers, removed the contents and moved them to safety, high above ground.

I had left Europe knowing that Griesinger's father was born in New Orleans and that he always remained proud of his American ancestry. Other than their names, Robert Snr and Lina, I knew nothing about Griesinger's grandparents. Wanting to understand the family's core values and the environment in which Robert Snr and Lina raised their son, I arrived in Louisiana looking to find out more about the circles in which they mixed and the impact of the American Civil War on their lives. I also intended to uncover whether they came from families that enslaved people. By asking these questions, I hoped to discover what attitudes and ideas Lina and her husband might have passed down to their children and grandchildren from the nineteenth-century American South and whether Griesinger's American ancestry might somehow have influenced his worldview during the Third Reich.

I was not disappointed. Even after Katrina, papers shedding light on Griesinger's ancestors remained largely intact. Griesinger's father, Adolf, was born in New Orleans in 1871, at a time of immense change following the Civil War (1861–5) and the Reconstruction era. It was a period of shortages and severe racism. Adolf's father, Robert Griesinger (Snr), was German-American. He had arrived in New Orleans from Stuttgart in his mid-twenties in 1867, without speaking English or French.[1] He was able to settle down quickly, thanks to the city's enormous ethnic German population. In the years that followed the Civil War, demand for labour was strong and immigrants from Germany were welcomed to New Orleans with open arms. The thousands of Germans who had sought political refuge in the United States after the botched revolutions in 1848 were joined by hundreds of thousands of economic migrants, who left in search of work. In the years between 1830 and 1860 more than 1.5 million Germans left their homeland for the United States.

Robert Griesinger was one of 2,594 Germans who settled in New Orleans in 1866–7. When he arrived, he found a vibrant German Quarter. In 1860 the German-American population of 19,752 accounted for almost 12 per cent of the city's population. New Orleans was then home to four German newspapers, fifteen German Protestant churches, eleven German schools and various other German societies and organisations. German plays were constantly performed in the city's theatres, attracting some of the most recognised actors of the era.[2]

Thousands of the new arrivals from Germany found work in cotton, which at the time was the driving force of the city's economy. By the 1820s New Orleans was the financial capital of the American South and lay at the heart of the world's cotton trade. The city was a corner of the 'cotton triangle', linking the ports of New Orleans, New York and Liverpool. Robert Griesinger (Snr) began life in the American South as a cotton agent at the firm Clason and Co.[3]

Griesinger's future wife, Lina, was not German-American. At the time of their meeting, Lina lived in New Orleans with her sister and brother-in-law. She had been orphaned in 1860, aged only twelve. Slavery and its after-effects would have made an impact on Lina's early years. In 1860, 14,484 black or mixed-race people were enslaved in New Orleans – 8 per cent of the population – distributed among 4,169 owners. It was unusual at the time for a white person to own more than one enslaved person. In this urban setting, most enslaved people were domestic workers, or sometimes labourers. Outside the city, things were very different. In 1860, 331,726 people lived in slavery in Louisiana alone, and while the average Louisianan planter owned forty-nine enslaved people, some families owned up to 200.[4]

On the eve of the Civil War, New Orleans was home to the country's largest domestic slave market. Unlike other southern cities, where the buying and selling of enslaved people was confined to a single building or street, New Orleans offered more than fifty sites where auctions of enslaved people took place, including the courtyards and luxury hotels of the French Quarter.[5]

Lina was sixteen when the Union victory in the American Civil War ended the practice of slavery in Louisiana. Even though neither she nor her husband ever owned another person, I wondered whether Lina's ideas about the world were formed while growing up with an enslaved worker in her house. If Lina's father was one of New Orleans's 4,169 enslavers, she would probably have inherited racist ways of thinking about whiteness, blackness and the differences between people. She might later have passed attitudes on white supremacy down to her children and grandchildren. On the other hand, Lina might have held racist views even if her father was not an enslaver. Plenty of people who grew up in the United States in the 1850s and 1860s without an enslaver as a relative believed in the supremacy of the white race, and this was not confined to the South. We are apt to forget that racial prejudice was endemic among Northern whites, thousands of whom championed rigid racial separation. Even before the Civil War, Jim Crow laws and regulations that required racial segregation were born and enacted in states including New York, Massachusetts and Pennsylvania, far north of the Mason–Dixon Line.[6]

Paul Emile Johns, Lina's father, was the city's most celebrated composer and musician in the nineteenth century. He is credited, among other things, with the first US performance of a Beethoven piano concerto in New Orleans in 1819. Johns performed in all the city's music halls and later developed an international name, thanks in part to his friendship with Frédéric Chopin, whom he met on a trip to Paris. Chopin was so impressed with Johns that he even dedicated his five mazurkas of Opus 7 to 'Monsieur Johns de la Nouvelle-Orléans'.[7]

Lina grew up in a house full of musical instruments, sheet music and song recitals. She also grew up surrounded by slavery. It was due to Johns's role in the city's musical scene that Lina's father was able to acquire his first enslaved worker. The city's notarial records document the transaction of a fourteen-year-old light-skinned boy named Reuben, between Johns and the composer George Manouvrier.[8] The grandmother of SS member Robert Griesinger, who I discovered later enjoyed a special bond with her grandson, had grown up with an enslaver father at a time when the slave trade was booming.

I also discovered that Lina's maternal grandparents, Nicolas and Manuela Favre D'Aunoy, were active in buying and selling enslaved people. In 1826 Lina's grandmother sold a thirty-one-year-old woman called Susanne. Manuela had been given Susanne as a gift from her uncle when he was in Charleston, looking to buy enslaved workers for his own daughters. 'Please accept this négresse,' wrote Manuela's uncle, 'as a token of my love and attachment to you.'[9] By examining the notarial acts, it was possible to trace Griesinger's family in New Orleans almost all the way back to the founding of the city in 1718. I discovered a world of ambitious relatives: plantation owners and cotton merchants, each one of whom, men and women alike, owned enslaved people.

Lina's great-great-grandfather, Jean Baptiste Honoré Destrehan de Beaupré (1700–65), had 166 enslaved workers on his plantation. Alongside his seven legitimate children he had a daughter, Catalina, with an enslaved woman called Geneviève. Catalina remained an enslaved worker for thirty-five years before finally buying her freedom.[10]

Two hundred years later, preventing sexual relations between Aryans and non-Aryans was a central component of Nazi ideology. According to the Nazis, the 24,000 black people living in the Third Reich represented such a grave threat to the racial hierarchy that legislation was brought in to exclude them from Germany's future national community. The famous Nuremberg Laws that removed citizenship from Jews, and prevented marriage and sexual relations between Jews and Aryans, were extended to blacks and Roma in November 1935. The children of white German mothers and French colonial soldiers born during the French occupation of the Rhineland after the First World War were singled out for special discrimination. A special commission was set up in 1937 to locate these 500–800 Afro-German children, derogatorily called 'Rhineland Bastards', then in their early to mid-teens. Once found, about half of them were forcibly sterilised by the regime. Many had even been taken from school without their parents' permission. Speaking about his experience sixty years later, one Hans Hauck recalled being sterilised along with five other teenagers without full anaesthetic. Immediately after the vasectomy, Hauck was taken to the Gestapo headquarters in Saarbrücken, where he was made to sign an agreement stating that he would never have sexual relations with a German citizen.[11]

Given the Nazis' insistence that black people were among the lowest elements in the new racial hierarchy, Griesinger would have been appalled to discover the existence of Marshall Honoré Jr, a living black relative. Honoré, whom I tracked down living in Baton

Rouge in his mid-nineties, was a direct descendant of Catalina, the mixed-race daughter of Griesinger's ancestor, Jean Baptiste. Marshall Honoré Jr grew up in racially segregated Louisiana at the same time his distant cousin worked at the Gestapo. While neither had any knowledge of the other, their paths almost crossed when, in 1943, Honoré was sent to the European theatre as part of a segregated unit, where he fought in Normandy and at the Battle of the Bulge. By spring 1945 Honoré had crossed the Rhine River. As he advanced deeper into Germany, he was, unbeknownst to him, hot on his cousin's trail.[12]

The four-year Civil War coincided with Lina's coming of age. In April 1862 Union forces captured New Orleans. Albert Johns, Lina's older brother, was taken prisoner. In the weeks that followed the capture of New Orleans, the local population resisted attempts to submit to Federal authority. The women and girls of New Orleans proved particularly hostile to Federal troops. Many turned their backs on Union soldiers, exited streetcars or even burst into Confederate song when the men appeared. In mid-May 1862 Union general Benjamin Franklin Butler issued his infamous 'Woman Order' in New Orleans. According to the Order, any woman who insulted a Union soldier 'by word, gesture or movement' would be regarded as, and held liable as, a prostitute. The city's residents were alarmed, inferring from the Order the threat of rape by Union soldiers against southern women.[13]

With post-Civil War Reconstruction came an upturn in Lina's fortunes. In the June of 1870 twenty-one-year-old Lina married twenty-eight-year-old cotton agent Robert Griesinger Senior. Later that month Lina and Robert travelled to New York and then on to Europe for their honeymoon. As I tried to uncover more information about this, I discovered that Kate Chopin, the great feminist writer, was also celebrating her recent marriage to her husband, Oscar, on board the same ship. Moreover, it turned out that the two couples were already friends – from New Orleans.[14] Even at the time the young Kate, whose later novel *The Awakening* remains a key text in the American literary canon, was an avid writer, inscribing in a commonplace book her essays, poems and sketches. Her diary from the summer of 1870 reveals that the Griesingers and Chopins travelled extensively together during their honeymoons across Germany, taking in the scenic views by train and boat and visiting churches, gardens and museums. The days were long and hot, while the evenings were lively and at times even raucous. In Bonn the couples attended a garden concert where they became animated after drinking too much wine, and Kate wrote in her diary later that the phlegmatic Germans seemed unimpressed with the group's 'American sociability'. The outbreak of the Franco-Prussian War in mid-July interrupted the Chopins' travel plans. They accompanied Lina and Robert to Stuttgart, where Kate spent a morning with Lina and the mother-in-law she had only just met, shopping for the lace and linen for the housework that she knew she would be expected to carry out as a newly married woman.[15]

Lina became pregnant a short while after returning from the honeymoon. On 17 November 1871 she gave birth to Adolf. Things continued to go well for the Griesingers. Professionally, Robert was in a good position, and even became one of the founding members of the New Orleans Cotton Exchange. A few months after Adolf's birth, Clason and Co. took out an advert in the *New Orleans Times* to announce that Robert Griesinger had been made resident partner. During the next year the family moved from the French Quarter to the desirable Garden District, where they settled into a house on Louisiana Avenue.[16]

Just as Robert and Lina began to start their family, New Orleans entered a period marked by heated racial tension. As young Adolf Griesinger grew up in 1870s Louisiana, membership of white supremacist organisations took off, sometimes reaching 50 per cent of the white male population. SS member Robert Griesinger's grandparents mixed in circles in which it was perfectly acceptable to hound, beat up and, sometimes, murder local black people. Their friend Oscar Chopin, Kate's husband, joined the notorious White League and took part in the bloody Battle of Liberty Place in September 1874. The League and other paramilitary groups terrorised New Orleans, openly intimidating free blacks and Republican candidates. When the Nazis took to the streets five decades later, openly espousing similar views on race and miscegenation, did Adolf draw a connection to words and actions already familiar from his youth and the world of his parents? If he did, he was not alone. During the mid-1930s scores of leading German lawyers looked enthusiastically to the United States for inspiration on how best to implement their new racist order. As it turned out, most found the American system too racist to attempt to replicate in Nazi Germany. This is best seen in the case of American anti-miscegenation laws. To develop their racial classifications, the Nazis looked closely at laws in thirty US states that criminalised interracial marriages. Some legislators, such as Senator Theodore Bilbo from Mississippi, considered any person with even 'one-drop' of black blood to belong to an inferior race. This one-drop rule, which consigned Marshall Honoré Jr to a segregated military unit during the Second World War, was deemed too extreme by the Nazis, who defined Jews as anyone with three or four Jewish grandparents.[17]

The Long Depression (known as the Great Depression, until the Wall Street Crash of 1929 usurped the name) struck during 1873 and lasted six years. It marked the end of the Griesinger family's good fortune in New Orleans. Cotton was one of the Depression's biggest victims: its price fell by almost 50 per cent. The fabric, once the source of the Griesingers' wealth and social standing, now threatened its ruin.[18] Amid the downturn in fortunes, a return to Germany seemed the only option. Lured by its economic prosperity and the creation of a middle class that was taking place in imperial Germany under Bismarck, the Griesinger family moved to Stuttgart in the early 1880s. Robert Snr had lasted in America less than twenty years. As a German-American, fluent in the German language and steeped in German culture, ten-year-old Adolf adapted swiftly to life in the *Kaiserreich*. His parents sent him to the Royal Central Cadet School in the Lichterfelde area of Berlin. It was there that the young American cadet began a lasting friendship with Walther Reinhardt, who went on to become one of Germany's most important military figures.

Adolf Griesinger while a cadet at Lichterfelde *c.* 1885

Adolf's father was one of fifty to sixty million migrants who moved from Europe to the Americas in the Age of Mass Migration that began with worsening socio-economic conditions and failed revolutions in 1848 in the Habsburg Empire, France and the German and Italian States, and ended with the outbreak of the First World War. The stories of the men and women like Robert Snr who set sail, hoping to live out the American Dream, have been endlessly recounted. But for some, the dream quickly became a nightmare, and one in three immigrants returned to their home country. Yet historians have spilled little ink exploring this reverse migration and its effects.[19]

While I was in New Orleans I realised that the portico of the Stuttgart house in which Robert Griesinger grew up was emblematic of surprising continuities. Those crossing eastwards over the

Lina and Robert Griesinger Snr *c.* 1905

Atlantic, such as the Griesingers, brought with them American ideas, cultures, codes of behaviour and even a taste in furniture that proved influential in building a home in Germany. SS member Robert Griesinger inherited all of these traits from his father and grandmother, from whom he also inherited an ease with brutally racist attitudes and practices. Even though Griesinger's enslaver ancestors contributed only one piece to the total mosaic of his racist character during the Third Reich, the influence of southern racial hatred proved significant. These enduring concepts, which came from beyond the boundaries of the German nation state, coalesced with the antisemitism of Germany from the 1880s onwards – including Nazi racial thought – to shape Griesinger's worldview.[20] The armchair that protected his documents, so similar to the living-room furniture he had grown up with, connected his two worlds of the Deep South and the Third Reich. It was no coincidence that the Czech-made rococo-style armchair so closely resembled the sizeable antebellum furniture of his youth. A smaller or less distinct piece would have been out of place in Griesinger's domestic imagination.

Chapter III

'Zero Hour'

Shortly after arriving in her home, I handed Jutta Mangold an enlarged photograph of the armchair. She scrutinised it for several seconds. 'I have thought so much about this picture ever since receiving it in the post with my father's documents.' She handed back the photograph. 'I'm sorry, but I don't remember ever seeing it before.' I had travelled to meet Jutta in a suburb of Zurich, where she had lived since the end of the Second World War. Jutta was tall, with short white hair, and was warmly charismatic. As she took my coat, she told me that she had been looking forward to my visit. I was pleased; Jutta was the first child of a perpetrator that I had ever met. In turn, I was the only person who had ever enquired about her father's Nazi past. As I walked through her front door I noticed a faint trace of cigarette smoke. I think we were both nervous.

Jutta has lived alone on the ground floor of a small post-war residential block since her husband died in 1997. Her flat was small and open-plan. When I visited in November 2014 there were no photographs on display, no keepsakes – no memories. Instead, in a room filled with lots of miniature colourful china objects and 1970s furniture, pictures of scenic landscapes hung on the walls. In the centre of the room a white tablecloth covered the dining-room table, on which Jutta had neatly arranged a selection of teas and pastries on gold-rimmed porcelain plates. At a safe distance from the food and drink was a large padded envelope, on top of which were laid Griesinger's two wartime passports, which Jana and Veronika had sent Jutta a few weeks earlier from Amsterdam.

As she poured the tea into two porcelain cups that she had inherited from her grandmother Wally, Jutta painted a picture to me of an idyllic upbringing in occupied Prague. She told me about her school friends – the sons and daughters of other Germans stationed in the Protectorate – and the games they played, including details she had not thought of for more than seventy years. At the same time that Jutta was trying to ply me with pastries, she described the large family home in an affluent suburb where she lived with her parents, half-brother and sister, and two German-speaking Czech servants.

When I asked about her father, who had died when she was eight, Jutta placed her teacup back on its saucer and began to stir her tea with her spoon. Still maintaining eye contact as she gently clinked the spoon in her cup, she told me quite firmly that she had little information to share. 'Until I received your letter, I thought my father was an ordinary lawyer. I know very little about his career during the time the Nazis were in power,' she said. Jutta did not know where her father had studied, the sort of law he practised or who had employed him. While she knew he had worked south of Stuttgart before the family moved to Prague in spring 1943, she did not know what he did there, nor did she have any knowledge concerning the nature of his work in the Protectorate. Jutta referred to her father as an 'ordinary office type', perhaps because she retained a vivid memory of being taken by her mother to her father's place of work. She recalled entering his office in a historical building and seeing him seated behind a large wooden desk. What she remembered most of all was a miniature porcelain toilet perched on his desk. Why a German lawyer in occupied Prague would have this model on open display was something Jutta still wondered about. 'I later thought he might have used it as a model for something professional. I never asked at the time. I can still see it,' she said.

Just as Jutta knew nothing of her father's professional life, she also knew nothing of her father's relationship to the Nazi party.

'Politics,' said Jutta, 'was kept out of the home.' She was adamant that she could not recall any Nazi iconography from her childhood. She didn't remember her parents making any supportive comments of Hitler, nor did she recall either the Führer's portrait or a swastika flag being in the family home. Yet even if she did not recall it, Jutta probably heard her parents use the compulsory 'Heil Hitler!' greeting when shopping or in the street. At school she would, like all German children, have saluted the flag each day and sung, 'Adolf Hitler is our saviour, our hero'. Jutta would not have thought anything of it then, as a child: such actions would have seemed completely normal. She could not have grasped their significance.

Jutta's memories were more vivid when discussing the end of the war. In 1945 she saw her father for the last time. 'After we escaped Prague, my father was supposed to join us a short time later, but he never came.' She remembered their final goodbye. On the morning of their departure, just as the Germans began evacuating thousands of women and children from the Protectorate, the thirty-eight-year-old lawyer escorted his wife and children along the short path of their house, to where a small truck waited for them. Jutta recalled kissing her father before he lifted her onto the back of the vehicle. As the truck pulled away, her father stood waving his family goodbye from the end of the garden path. A few months later she and Barbara were two of Germany's 1,250,000 fatherless children. By the time she was old enough to ask questions about her father's Nazi past, it was too late: Jutta's mother had remarried in Switzerland. With a new stepfather and, later, half-brothers, any discussion of Jutta's father was avoided. There were no photographs or other reminders of him in her new family home. Jutta remembered trying to ask the difficult questions as a child, but was shut down by her mother. 'The past was taboo. We knew not to speak about it.'

Such secrecy was not uncommon. Just as most Germans after the war built a 'memory wall' against the recent past, so they also sought to create fresh identities and make a clean break with the past, a process they called *Stunde Null*, or 'Zero Hour'. For most families, other things took precedence in the immediate post-war years. Desperate shortages of food, coal, medicine, clothing and other essentials, coupled with the threat of sexual violence from the Occupation forces, ensured that life in Germany during the first year of peace was even more difficult than during the final year of the war. By 1947 juvenile crime and infant mortality had increased, and people were having to survive on rations of 1,000 calories a day. Thousands of displaced German children were depressed, mistrustful and suffered from nightmares, regularly wetting their beds.[1] By the 1950s West Germans remembered the war years selectively, positioning themselves as a nation of victims. Instead of reflecting on the suffering Germans had caused to others, including Jews, political opponents and victims of the euthanasia programme, most West Germans focused instead on their own injustice: displacement, the lives of the men who continued to languish in Soviet POW camps and the loss of the 'German east'.[2]

For much of the post-war period a collective silence shielded most Nazi perpetrators, collaborators and bystanders from having to recount incriminating details from their pasts. By the early 1950s, when German children were old enough to ask their parents about their actions under the Third Reich, most were met with silence. Only the sons and daughters of those who had been at the very top of the regime, whose crimes were already public knowledge, knew about their family's Nazi pasts. For everyone else, the extent of their parents' complicity remained a mystery that hung over and moulded intergenerational communication. Recalling the period many years later, one German woman wrote that she experienced her family's constraint as conspiratorial: 'it lay like a heavy, thick blanket over most post-war children and teenagers'.[3] The majority of West Germans 'forgot' or 'cut out' their earlier acceptance, support and complicity for the regime.[4] The struggle to rebuild in the first post war decade was a testing period for familial relations that had broken down with the end of the war. Suspicious children learned not to bring up the subject, for fear of being disloyal to their parents' version of events or, worse, being labelled a *Nestbeschmutzer* – a family member who soils the nest.[5] In lieu of asking questions, many children preferred to maintain an idealised version of their parents' wartime records. Similarly, people with a past they wanted to hide employed strategies intended to gloss over their lives in the 1930s and 1940s, at the very least by responding vaguely to any question. To prevent unwelcome probing, the oft-used expression 'Well, it was war' served to normalise the ghosts of the Third Reich and play down Nazi atrocities.[6]

Such evasion tactics played out in many families. Dieter Hahn, born before the end of the war in Karlsruhe, a city close to Stuttgart, recalled his father refused outright to discuss the Nazi period. His mother responded with half-answers, which included the worn-out line that 'there were many awful things done by that regime which we only slightly perceived, but didn't really understand'. Hahn eventually gave up asking questions.[7] Silence also reigned in the house of Wilhelm Ströbel, one of Griesinger's associates from the SS in Stuttgart. After the war Ströbel went on to enjoy a glittering career as a lawyer. When I tracked down his son, Peter, also a successful lawyer in Stuttgart, he said his father never spoke about the years 1933–45 and that he had never seen any documentation relating to his father from the Nazi period.[8]

In the late 1950s the timespan between the present and the concentration camps seemed as long as the one between the present and the medieval witch trials, observed one commentator. To be cut off from the recent past was not without consequence. Some young Germans were angry at the way in which recent history had been hidden away and forgotten. As one twenty-three-year-old observed in 1959, 'we don't have any past – because under your guidance as adults, we've forgotten it, or regard it almost like some sort of exotic monstrosity that doesn't directly concern us'.[9]

The post-war silence within families persisted for decades, some-times for ever. Those of the second generation in perpetrator families who did discover their parents' Nazi pasts sometimes did so by accident, while at other times it was relayed to them by a relative or someone else in their community. How these children of Nazis dealt with their complicated and sometimes shameful ancestry varied, with some skirting around or even defending their parents' actions, and others cutting off ties with their parents completely or changing their relationship with their own children. Without necessarily realising it, their parents' actions shaped the lives and relationships of Jutta's generation, giving them an uncertain sense of security and identity.[10]

Secrecy in the family mirrored events at the national level, allowing silence to prosper. When post-war trials against Nazis occurred, they generally ignored low-level functionaries and killers and aimed to convict only prominent members of the regime. The first and best-known trial of leading Nazis occurred between 1945 and 1946, at the International Military Tribunal in Nuremberg. Amid a frenzy of international attention, twenty-four surviving senior Nazis – including Hermann Göring, Joachim von Ribbentrop and Hans Frank – were tried for crimes against peace, war crimes and crimes against humanity. Twelve further trials took place at Nuremberg in the three years that followed, in which the paltry figure of 183 former Nazi officials and military leaders, senior party members, industrialists, lawyers and doctors were indicted. These were known as the Subsequent Nuremberg Trials, and twelve of the defendants were sentenced to death, while eight were given life sentences and seventy-seven were sent to prison for various amounts of time. Despite thousands of investigations being launched in the first post-war decade, fewer than half resulted in a conviction. Between 1945 and 1958 only 6,093 former Nazis were convicted of having committed a crime – a drop in the ocean when we remember that in 1945 the Nazi party had eight million members.[11] The sentencing of Nazi criminals was further hindered by the anonymity afforded to them by the new West German chancellor, Konrad Adenauer, who amnestied former Nazis in 1949, allowing them to reintegrate into the fold. By January 1951 the new legislation had amnestied 792,176 Germans, including functionaries of the SA, the SS and the Nazi party.[12]

Things began to change a bit in the late 1950s thanks, in part, to the publication of Anne Frank's diary in paperback in 1955 and a series of trials of former Nazis that continued up to the mid-1960s, which drew public attention to Nazi atrocities. The first took place

in 1958 in Ulm, south-east of Stuttgart, where Griesinger worked
prior to joining the Gestapo. The conviction of former Nazis gained
considerable publicity locally and nationally and prompted the estab-
lishment of West Germany's chief investigative bureau of Nazi-era
crimes. Nevertheless the government's priority for amnesty ensured
that the bureau failed to get off the ground, allowing former Nazis
to hide in plain sight. Trials of the 1960s and 1970s were famous
for doling out acquittals or light sentences to those indicted.

Even though the trials drew international interest, Jutta claimed
she never gave a thought to the precise nature of her father's job
in occupied Prague, or the extent of his support for the Nazi party.
This included the 1967 trial of Wilhelm Harster, who had spent the
years 1929–37 as a lawyer in Stuttgart, the same city in which Jutta's
father practised the same profession at the same time. Excerpts of
Anne Frank's diary were read out in court during Harster's trial,
an event at which Anne's father, Otto, testified in person. The trial
was a major affair and received ample coverage in the Swiss press.
As newspapers reported at the time, the trial marked the first time
in the history of West Germany that Nazi war-crimes charges were
levelled at such a prominent 'desk murderer', a mass killer and
predator who, in the words of the judge at the Eichmann trial,
exercised his 'bloody craft behind a desk'.[13] By the late 1980s, more
and more Germans of Jutta's age, spurred on by the uncomfortable
questions that the students had asked in 1968, found ways to question their parents and speak frankly about their family's past.[14] That
the children of Nazis had discovered a voice did not mean their
parents were willing to respond, however. Hundreds of thousands
of Germans who had lived as adults through the Third Reich refused
ever to discuss their past with their children.

But it is even harder to ask these questions of the dead. As an
adult, Jutta had never contemplated delving into her father's past.
Despite knowing the horrors of the Third Reich from school, books
and cinema, she never suspected that Griesinger might have been
complicit in the regime's atrocities. It was the most common
response shared by hundreds of thousands of Germans of the
post-war generation.[15] It is possible to infer from this that Jutta

ignored her father's history for fear of what she might uncover. But this might not be the reality. After all, how much do any of us know about our parents' lives before us? Why should children of Nazis who can't chart their parents' wartime records be held to a different standard? Few had the financial means, or even the know-how, to learn anything more than the half-told stories from home. Jutta had never heard any passing comment at family gatherings about support that Griesinger might have shown for Nazism, nor had any evidence ever surfaced in the press, in a book or online that connected him to the regime. In Prague she had seen for herself that he worked behind a large desk in an office, dressed in a smart suit and tie. In Jutta's mind, abstract legal subjects, and perhaps porcelain toilets, preoccupied her father's working life. It was other children's fathers who wore a sinister uniform to patrol the streets or work in a concentration camp.

And, of course, there were no family documents to contend with. Jutta told me she had never seen a document with Robert's name on it and did not even know what his handwriting looked like. She believed everything had been lost or destroyed during the war. Until, that is, a Dutch furniture restorer pulled her father's swastika-covered documents out of the armchair.

'It's just all so amazing. I really can't believe it,' she said, as she looked down at the table to make sure everything was in its correct place. 'My father died when I was just a little girl. It's incredible that after so many years he should unexpectedly re-enter my life. I can't tell you how happy I am.' That Griesinger's message in a bottle to his daughter took the form of papers covered in swastikas did not seem to deter her enthusiasm. 'Holding these papers and learning about their incredible journey is a way of giving me back a piece of my past.' She told me she was eager to learn more from my research.

Other historians have shown how hard it is to find children of Nazis who are willing to speak to a stranger about their family's pasts.[16] I was more fortunate. The allure of Jutta's father's papers, and my research into his actions during the Third Reich, meant that I had information Jutta wanted to hear. On one level, our encounter was dependent on a simple exchange of information: I was keen to flesh out my image of a handsome, low-ranking Nazi. Jutta hoped to learn about her father from me. But on another level, Jutta and I were at cross-purposes. I was collecting evidence against a perpetrator whose culpability I saw increasing with every discovery. She was looking for information about a father she loved, and whose absence had shaped her life from an early age. The facts that I could share might not be in question, but their meanings and psychological impact, as I told them and as she heard them, were worlds apart.

Most German parents in the post-war era covered up their earlier consent for Nazi rule and passed these mental habits on to their children. Despite the curiosity that Jutta expressed to me about her father's Nazi past, I thought I could see this culture of emotional evasion playing out in her response. At no point, over the course of our first day together, did Jutta jot down a single note to herself. While it was no doubt easier this way for her to listen and process the information, I wondered how she planned to retain it all. The only time she became animated, and suggested she would person-ally seek out additional knowledge, came during our discussion of Frédéric Chopin and his friendship with her great-great-grandfather, Paul Emile Johns, star of New Orleans's music halls in the mid-nineteenth century, whose name meant nothing to her.

When I met Jutta's younger sister, Barbara, at her home in northern Bavaria, her response was similar. Barbara, who was five when their father died, could not recall a single memory of him that was her own. Like Jutta, she had tried to ask her mother for information about their father, but to no avail. Robert Griesinger represented one of millions of Nazis who became an unspoken memory within his family after the war. But, like his hidden iden-tity papers inside the armchair, the secrets of the past were never far from the surface as his daughters were growing up. Whether Gisela's silence stemmed from a continued sense of grief or a desire to forge a new post-war life, it worked, and eventually Barbara stopped asking questions too. After Griesinger's death, it was his mother, Wally, who took on the role of chief mourner, and her house, unchanged, became a shrine to her son. Wally's increasing animosity towards Gisela, however, damaged Jutta's and Barbara's relationship with their grandmother. In the end it was Irmela, Jochen's wife, who looked after the matriarch in her old age and, even while making her distaste for Robert clear, became the keeper of family knowledge about him.

After meeting Jutta and Barbara and travelling to New Orleans, I decided to return to Stuttgart to visit Jochen and Irmela again. I tell my students never to expect to learn anything on a first interview; it is in the second one that people truly begin to open up.

Irmela greeted me warmly and ushered me inside. Almost three years had passed since my last visit. Easter was approaching and the house was covered in festive decorations. Jochen was seated reading a newspaper by the window. He smiled as I approached and apologised for not getting up to meet me – he had recently been unwell, but was recovering. I sat down on the couch next to a coffee table, on top of which was a large plate piled high with fresh pretzels smothered with butter and chives.

As we ate our pretzels on a sofa beneath Wally's portrait, I asked Jochen and Irmela for more information on how the appearance of Gisela in Robert's life altered his relationship with his mother. 'You probably don't remember,' began Irmela, as she stood up and guided me towards a window overlooking the back garden, 'but on your last visit there was a large oak tree just there,' she said, pointing at the slope. 'It was a tree that Robert sent his mother in 1938 to apologise for being unable to make it home for Christmas.' Christmas was a big deal in the Griesinger household. Wally wanted 1938 to be particularly special, as it was the first Christmas both of her sons were married. 'Wally was incredibly angry that Robert wasn't coming home. She felt Gisela was stealing Robert away from her,' said Irmela. The problems only escalated. Before long, Robert had had enough of his mother's meddling. 'During the war they had a big fight,' said Irmela, shaking her head. 'It was one they never got over.'

'How do you know so much?' I asked.

Irmela recounted a couple of short anecdotes she had told me on my previous visit, such as her close relationship with Wally during the 1960s and her discussions with staff members who had known Griesinger. She then injected a striking new detail. 'Ahead of your visit, I had a look round the house to see whether I could find anything that you might find interesting,' she said, as she moved into an adjacent room. She returned a few moments later, clutching what looked like a wooden drawer. She knelt down and gently placed it on the carpet and began rifling through and moving papers around, until she found what she was looking for. 'Here it is.' She handed me an envelope. Two stamps of Hitler in the top right corner, one bright red and one blue, caught my eye. The letter was addressed to Robert in Prague. Its postmark read 'Stuttgart, 31st March 1945', but the envelope clearly never made it out of Germany. The Allied advance temporarily suspended the regular mail's activity. A short time after the arrival of French troops in Stuttgart on 21 April 1945, the letter was returned to Adolf and Wally Griesinger, after first being opened and vetted by the censor.

In this four-page letter Adolf wrote to his son in blue ink on the main body of the page, while Wally wrote her message in pencil, taking up every inch of space that her husband had not used along the margins of the sheet. In her note, Wally attempted desperately to patch things up with Robert, telling him of her hopes that one day he would recognise how much he meant to her. It was a touchingly affectionate final message from a mother to a son, conveying her regret that they would never again have a real conversation. Wally bade Robert farewell, convinced that within days she and her husband would be killed either by an aerial bomb or by the advancing Allied troops.[17]

'Could I have a look at some of the other papers inside?' I asked. Jochen and Irmela seemed to trust me more this time. As Jochen sat watching us from the sofa, I joined Irmela on the pale-green carpet and together we went through the drawer's contents. Alongside a mass of black-and-white photographs dating back to the mid-nineteenth century were some old letters and postcards from New Orleans. It seemed that even after Lina emigrated to

Stuttgart, she maintained contact with her nieces and nephews for the rest of her life. They sent her family news from New Orleans and, in return, she wrote of her life in the *Kaiserreich*.

A photograph sent in 1910 by Emil Christ to his aunt, Lina Griesinger, of his father's new house in New Orleans

As we approached the bottom of the drawer, I caught sight of two soft-bound leather books. I opened one and saw straight away that it was Wally's diary. Her first entry in March 1917 read, 'I am writing this book that I hope to destroy when we win.'[18] As I flicked through, I saw that Wally wrote an entry almost every day for two years, in which she chiefly reported on the news and German prospects in the war. She also included press clippings about the war's progress from the *Süddeutsche Zeitung*, which she attached to the top of some of the pages with now-rusty paperclips. One of the printed articles caught my eye because it still had the bright-red pencil markings at one side that Wally had drawn, to signal its need for preservation. The clipping was from late 1918. Its title was 'hope' and it suggested that things might get worse for the German nation before they got better. The author wrote that even if German society spiralled into 'avarice; the rule of the Jews (*Judenherrschaft*); immorality and a slump in the birth-rate', such suffering should only be taken as a sign of how far God 'bends his people, for whom he has greater things in store'.[19] Reinhard Mumm, the author, was a Protestant pastor and a renowned antisemite, whose father-in-law, Adolf Stöcker, was one of the most prominent antisemites in imperial Germany.[20]

Wally's wartime diary called into question some of Jochen and Irmela's theories about Adolf and Wally's position during the Third Reich. Her diary revealed that Wally would have been attracted to certain elements of the Nazi project, especially its *völkisch* nationalism and rejection of democracy. While it is supposed that the Griesingers, like thousands in conservative military circles, were at first wary of the Nazis' revolutionary appearance, their disdain probably subsided over time. Wally's diary not only disclosed her opinions on the progress of the First World War and the home front, but also revealed the conservative, Protestant and antisemitic daily, the *Süddeutsche Zeitung*, as her newspaper of choice. The newspaper's intended readership was the patriotic Protestant middle class. Wally's selection of antisemitic, xenophobic and homophobic clippings from the staunchly conservative newspaper to which she adhered shed light on her character and political leanings. It also revealed the nature of the sort of discussions Robert would have encountered while growing up.[21]

The second leather book I discovered at the bottom of the drawer was Robert's 'Child Book', an account Wally kept of Robert's development, which she began the week he was born in November 1906. In most of the early entries Wally noted baby Robert's weight (3.75 kilograms at birth), his height and commented on his general appearance. She included details of hospital visits and his baptism, and later marked all his significant milestones, recording the arrival of his first tooth (10 July 1907) and the date he took his first steps (31 January 1908). Above all, she put into writing her reaction to becoming a mother and the changes this brought to her everyday life. As Robert got older, Wally's entries became longer. She was more thoughtful and took greater care recording aspects of her son's personality.

Still sitting cross-legged on the carpet in front of Jochen and Irmela, I began to flick through the first pages of the book. 'The children are leading a god's life, in which they have never shed a single tear,' wrote Wally on 6 March 1911, when Robert was only four.[22] Unusually, she kept up her baby book until 22 April 1925, the day Robert left home to go to university. I asked Jochen and Irmela if I might take both soft-bound books away with me for a few hours in order to make copies. They agreed.

Chapter IV

The 'War-Youth' Generation

The year Robert was born, 1906, was a key moment in the history of Stuttgart. In the years immediately preceding Griesinger's birth, the town experienced great political and economic change. As the capital of the Kingdom of Württemberg, the city had been incorporated into the German Empire following unification in 1871. Unlike other parts of Germany, the people of Stuttgart at the turn of the century were largely unaffected by political extremism on the left or the right. The popularity of the Social Democrats in Stuttgart increased steadily during the first decade of the century. In 1898 the city held the German Empire's initial First of May parade. And in 1907 Griesinger might have passed Lenin, Jean Jaurès or Ramsay MacDonald as he was pushed in his crib through the English-style Rosenstein Park. In that year Socialists from across the globe converged on Stuttgart to attend the International Socialist Congress and the first International Conference of Socialist Women. At a time when no country had ever formed a Socialist government, organisers singled out Württemberg as the only state in Germany where they could guarantee freedom of speech to their delegates.[1]

Under the new German Empire, industrialisation and urbanisation on a large scale took rapid hold of Stuttgart. In 1906 the city's automobile and electrical industries thrived, with Daimler and Bosch employing thousands of workers at their plants. Stuttgart's 1875 population of 107,000 inhabitants more than doubled, to reach a quarter of a million people by 1907. Tramlines were built and roads paved. The development of urban gas, water, electricity and sewage systems changed Stuttgart for ever.[2] Workers completed the late-Gothic-style new town hall in 1905. A bronze statue of *Stuttgardia*, a goddess to protect the people of Stuttgart, was installed above the main entrance to the building. The statue was modelled on Else Weil, a seventeen-year-old Jewish girl who as an adult later fled to America, escaping Nazi persecution.

Still, the city's transformation occurred within limits. Württemberg did not enjoy the kind of raw materials that had catapulted the Ruhr into becoming a major industrial region. Even though Stuttgart's population had doubled, that of other German cities had quadrupled. Change occurred at a slower pace there. At the time Griesinger was born, a strong semblance of traditional rural living went hand-in-hand with the benefits of modernity. In 1906 the city in which Hegel was born and where Schiller wrote his first play remained one of the most beautiful in Germany. It was a captivating municipality, adorned with historical narrow lanes, buildings and monuments. The early fourteenth-century Marktplatz, surrounded by tall timber-framed houses, lay at the centre of the old town and dominated city life. In summer the smell of jasmine and lilac lingered in the air.[3]

After leaving Jochen and Irmela's house with a bag bursting with Wally's journals and hundreds of scraps of paper, I headed to a small café in the centre of Stuttgart to sift through the documents and arrange them into some sort of order. I began to read some of the documents Wally had chronicled about starting a family in the same city a hundred years earlier. Her papers had not been touched in decades. Wally's long entries in her diary and Robert's Child Book described the events of her son's early years with great attention to detail. They revealed Robert's idyllic childhood, during which his doting parents had the financial means to ensure the future SS officer grew up without want of anything. Every few pages in the Child Book, Wally included a new photograph of her son. In some images Robert was alone, but in others he was with his parents, smiles beaming across their proud faces. He was a healthy-looking boy, without a trace of the scar on his cheek that

I had first noticed in the photos of him that were discovered inside the armchair. In these pictures Robert was dressed in first-rate, quality clothing, sometimes in a muslin dress and at other times in a pleated skirt. As he became a toddler his outfits took on a more nautical theme, typical for the *Kaiserreich*, and in some photos he sported a white beret.[4]

Even though the Griesingers employed a full-time governess, Wally maintained an active role in her son's development, playing games and reading to him. 'He only wants stories,' wrote Wally when Robert was five. He had a particular liking for Hans Christian Andersen's classic folk stories and fairy tales. At around the same time Robert's other main interest was a little girl named Erika Tobel, his 'first love', wrote Wally humorously. Nevertheless, neither Wally nor Erika could compete with Grandmother Lina, when it came to being the prime object of Robert's affection. Robert was besotted

Adolf and Robert Griesinger *c.* 1908

A page from Wally Griesinger's Child Book that includes a
photograph of Wally, Robert and Albert Griesinger, 1910

with his American grandmother, the most important person in his
life, whom he worshipped. They were inseparable. She was 'his
entire life', wrote Wally in one diary entry.[5] Even though Lina learned
German, her pronunciation was infused with the distinctive melody
of a Creole accent. It's likely she would even have used some Creole
words to speak to Robert as a toddler. It was, after all, the 'language
of childhood' for generations of children born in nineteenth-century
New Orleans, who learned it from their nannies and nurses.[6] If

Robert was hungry for stories, then Lina's own childhood would have given her plenty to pass on, revelling in the exploits of the Lafitte Brothers – French pirates who plundered Spanish ships in the Gulf of Mexico – or Marie Laveau, New Orleans's most celebrated Voodoo Queen. Lina was also a link to Robert's American cousins who remained behind in New Orleans. Lillian, Dunbar and Anna Christ were born close to the same time as Robert.[7]

When Robert came to visit Lina at her home on Kronenstrasse, she entertained her grandson while seated in an ebonised, barley-twist-style armchair. Lina probably bought it in Stuttgart in the 1880s or 1890s when ebonising furniture was in vogue.[8] After Lina's death when Robert was eleven, Adolf moved the chair into the family home. As Robert grew up, the iconic piece of furniture dominated a corner of the Griesingers' living room, where it remains to this day. Thanks to the chair, Robert had a permanent reminder of his beloved grandmother and the stories she had told him. He saw, from an early age, that furniture served a function that went beyond mere practical usage. Heirlooms had a sentimental value. They were not readily disposable.

Lina Griesinger (née Johns) in her armchair c. 1915

Robert's parents were able to enjoy a comfortable life in imperial Germany, thanks to the money they received from Wally's father, Arnold Passmann, a wealthy timber merchant and industrialist from Duisburg. While the family's money came largely from the maternal line, Robert's father's position as a confidant of the King of Württemberg ensured that the family enjoyed important status in Stuttgart. Before the First World War, Adolf Griesinger was a major of the king's cavalry in the Royal Württemberg Army. The Griesingers lived on the second floor of an apartment on the Alexanderstrasse in the centre of the city. The street's proximity to the Württemberg War Ministry on the Olgastrasse ensured the area was made up almost entirely of military personnel and their families.[9] Such a conservative environment meant that Robert's upbringing took on a traditional military rhythm, attending concerts by military bands and taking part in events, such as the annual Sedan Day celebrations, that commemorated Württemberg's glorious military past.

His privileged childhood was brutally interrupted by the Great War. When war broke out in 1914, seven-year-old Robert had only 'an inkling' about the significance of contemporary events. He spent the summer playing 'Germans against French' with his friends. Her diary reveals that, like most of the population, thirty-year-old Wally was confident about the outcome of the war. Even though Russia, France and Britain surrounded her 'wonderful German lands', it was only a matter of time before the nation triumphed. There were new challenges closer to home to contend with, as well. Not only was Adolf called away to serve on 9 September, but it was also Robert's first day at school. Thanks to their favoured position, the Griesingers were able to send their son to the Eberhard-Ludwigs-Gymnasium, where Hegel had once been a pupil. Ebelu, as it was known, was a school for the children of the city's elite.[10]

School did not come easily to young Robert. In autumn 1915 Wally wrote almost daily of her disappointment with her son, then aged nine, for falling behind in his studies. 'He's healthy and sweet, but everyone who gets to know him realises he is terribly lazy.' The future SS officer struggled at the Gymnasium, which prided itself in teaching knowledge of the Classics and classical languages. His school work did not improve, and his behaviour suffered as a result. An abysmal grade in Latin proved the final straw for Wally early in 1916. She pulled Robert out of the school and sent him instead to a school in which he would receive more classroom attention, to help him catch up. Within weeks at the new school Robert's grades had improved. The move brought about a love of reading, and Robert spent the Easter holidays that year immersed in books.[11]

During even the early years of the war, most people in Germany were suffering from periods of illness and severe shortages. The Allied naval blockade of Germany, which lasted from 1914 until 1919, prevented foreign food, fertiliser and other imports coming into the country by sea. Its consequences were disastrous. 'To win this war [...] we starved the children of Germany,' wrote George Bernard Shaw in 1919.[12] Over time, the droning of traders, the smells of fruits and meats and the assortment of stalls brimming with fresh products, which for centuries had characterised Stuttgart's Marktplatz, disappeared. They were replaced by long queues of tired women waiting for hours, often sitting on old chairs they had brought from home, holding empty baskets and ration cards.[13]

Fortunately for them, the Griesingers' wealthy background ensured that their experience of the home front differed strongly from that of the majority of the German population. For large parts of the war, life went on almost as normal for Wally, who continued to clothe and feed her children and send them to school. The family even spent peaceful summers at a late-medieval castle owned by Wally's father in Slangenburg in the Netherlands, which had remained neutral, close to the German border. When she left the house to do her bit for the war effort, Wally did not enter a factory, like so many working-class German women. Rather, like other society ladies in Stuttgart, she worked with Queen Charlotte at the Württemberg Red Cross, where she helped to produce cotton, one of the many raw materials in high demand. Unlike most German families, the Griesingers managed to spend every Christmas of the war together.[14]

It was only in early 1917 that Wally indicated in her diary that the tide was beginning to turn. Griesinger's tenth birthday in November 1916 marked the start of the 'Turnip Winter' when, owing to the failure of the potato crop, poor-quality turnips suddenly replaced the potato as the main staple of the German diet. During these months rations slumped to 1,150 calories a day, far below the recommended minimum daily requirement.[15] As Robert joined his new school, the Reformrealgymnasium in 1917, the Griesingers were slowly being drawn into the problems faced by the rest of the population.[16] From this point on, Wally wrote almost every day about limits on burning gas and the lack of bread and other shortages.[17]

Malnutrition took its toll on the children of Stuttgart. Conditions were so bad that thousands of children in the city stopped growing between 1917 and 1918.[18] Sickness was endemic, due to an absence of soaps and disinfectants, which affected domestic hygiene. Wally worried about Robert's health and appearance. He was too pale, and his body was not in shape. He fidgeted and lacked focus. The hardships of war affected Robert at a pivotal moment in his childhood, the consequences of which cannot be underestimated. He was frequently absent from school and his grades suffered. During his first school year at the Reformrealgymnasium, Robert's behaviour was poor, which upset his mother. In 1917–18 Wally had few kind things to write about her son. It was the first low point of their relationship, which until then had been so warm and loving. She wrote stinging remarks about Robert's performance at school, commenting that even the 'less talented kids' could redeem themselves by drawing. Wally employed the services of a private tutor to get Robert through the end-of-year exams.[19]

In the absence of foreign armies on German soil, and having secured so many territorial gains over four years, Germany's capitulation in November 1918 came as a shock to Wally and most of the population. Only from the middle of October 1918 did Wally realise the game was up: it was like 'living on a volcano'. The steadiness and stability that had marked the Griesingers' world became undone in November 1918. Not only were the Allies about to shame and disgrace Germany internationally, but closer to home change on an epic level was imminent. 'Revolution in Stuttgart' was the opening of Wally's diary entry on 9 November, the day the war ended, and the day Robert turned twelve. The young man was probably crushed. Family friend Claus von Stauffenberg, who turned eleven a few days later, refused all celebration on the 'saddest birthday of his life'.[20]

November 1918 marked the end of the German Empire. Across the country all twenty-two German monarchs abdicated, as the Kaiser fled to the Netherlands and a new republic was declared. Stuttgart served immediately as the capital of the newly created Free People's State of Württemberg. The new government of Württemberg was led by Wilhelm Blos, a Social Democrat. The abdication of the King of Württemberg, whom Adolf had served for twenty years and who had become a lynchpin in the rhythm of family life, was an enormous blow to the Griesingers, who feared Blos's new government would succumb to a Spartacist (German Communist) coup. Overnight the prospect of anarchy and civil war became a real threat for residents of the newly created state. During this tense time Wally's fear of Bolshevism shone through on every page. She wrote of the storming of the royal palace and of crowds gathering on squares and main streets, waving red flags. Wally feared the 'dark and heavy' future that lay ahead, as a Spartacist coup seemed imminent during the early months of the Weimar Republic.[21] In January 1919 the Spartacists managed for a time to take control of Stuttgart's town hall and train station, and in early April they erected barricades across Stuttgart. The insurrection did not last long. The new government of Württemberg violently attacked the Communists, with the help of the right-wing Free Corps, volunteer paramilitary units.[22] Living in the centre of the city, Robert could have witnessed the upheaval from his doorstep.

Conditions for many German children only got worse with the end of the war. The onset of the influenza epidemic that began in early 1918 and lasted until late 1919 killed more than 200,000 Germans.[23] But this was not all. At a time when the vanquished nations struggled to produce enough food and coal, the Allies kept

the blockade in place after the armistice was signed. Its enforcement ensured the persistence of famine and poverty for millions
of German and Austrian children. While in 1917–18 there was only
enough milk in Stuttgart for children under two, pregnant women
and nursing mothers, by 1919 the milk supply was worse than at
any stage of the war, with the city receiving only one-fifth of its
pre-war levels of milk. Hundreds of babies died within days of
birth.[24] In August 1920 Ramsay MacDonald, Noel Buxton and Joseph
King, three influential Labour politicians, published a letter in *The
Nation* that referred to German children as 'a whole generation on
the verge of breakdown'.[25] They were referring directly to Robert
Griesinger's generation.

Even if Robert did not suffer much in comparison to the rest of
the population, he saw with his own eyes the scale of the difficulties facing the new republic. The legacy of war engulfed the public
spaces of the city. As Griesinger came of age, he encountered a
nation in mourning. More than two million German men were
killed in the Great War. In addition there were 2.7 million disabled
veterans, 1.2 million war orphans and 533,000 war widows. Most
of these were, like most of the dead, aged under thirty.[26] At school
and in the streets the young Robert could not have failed to notice
the large numbers of orphaned children and widows dressed in
black. He witnessed how disfigured veterans such as Dr Pfeiffer,
his geography teacher at the Reformrealgymnasium, learned to
adapt to post-war life using prosthetic limbs.[27]

For the first two months of 1919 the military requisitioned
Robert's school building on Neckarstrasse in central Stuttgart. Amid
the upheaval, the Reformrealgymnasium boys sought distraction.
They had temporarily decamped to a local girls' school, the Königin-
Katharina-Stift, where they shared the building, but otherwise led
entirely separate lives from the girls. So desperate were some boys
to make contact with the girls that they used the ink-bottle holes,
located in the corner of their oak-wood benches, as a postbox to
exchange letters. The system flourished and was never discovered
by the teachers. Pupils who were at the Reformrealgymnasium at
the same time as Griesinger also recalled cheating during exams

and playing tricks on teachers. Even though they had just lost a war and were living in uncertain times, German schoolboys displayed a similar attitude to children in all industrialised Western countries.[28]

Griesinger formed part of a so-called 'war-youth' or 'Weimar-youth' generation, along with Himmler, Heydrich and many thousands of others who, born between 1900 and 1910, had been too young to fight in the war. This generation witnessed the absolute collapse of the values and certainties of their parents' world. It was a generation shaped by the devastating experience of war, national humiliation and the disorder that plagued the early years of the new post-war republic. While Griesinger could not have realised it at the time, he was permanently scarred by the events of 1918–19.

Growing up, the future SS officer enjoyed a close bond with his mother, sharing with her his thoughts, feelings and hopes for the future, much of which Wally recorded in her diary. She paid close attention to her teenage son's physical and mental development, and to his emerging extreme nationalist political views. Her entries between 1920 and 1925 portray Robert as a friendly, popular and healthy boy, with numerous hobbies. While many of the traits often associated with potential Nazi perpetrators – such as a broken or impoverished family background, or youthful involvement in Nazi circles – are absent from Wally's descriptions of these years, some common traits are present, such as a highly educated Protestant background that manifested itself in a form of extreme nationalism.[29]

Although Robert got off to a difficult start at his new school, Wally's decision to remove him from the Eberhard-Ludwigs-Gymnasium was vindicated by his progress after his second year at the Reformrealgymnasium. Gone were the days of bad behaviour and finishing near the bottom of his class. Instead, Robert adapted to his new environment during his second year of school, making friends easily. While he was no genius, he managed to perform to a level that did not concern his teachers. During his spare time in his early teenage years Robert was passionate about reading and collecting stamps. He was also good at helping around the house. Even though, like the other fifty-two boys in his school cohort, he was unfit and uninterested in sports, he liked to go ice-skating in winter, one of the few physical activities he enjoyed.[30] Throughout the family summers in Slangenburg in the Netherlands he spent most of the time helping to arrange the castle's archive. Wally consistently described her son as a happy, friendly and humble boy, who did not cause trouble. In an entry from May 1921, one month after his confirmation, she wrote, 'When I was recently talking to him, I realised there was nothing terrible or bad in him.' Friends and relatives who received the photograph sent by Wally to mark the occasion could easily have mistaken fourteen-year-old Robert for an altar boy.[31]

Robert Griesinger's confirmation photograph, 1921

Unlike Albert, his younger brother who suffered from various ailments, Robert did not have any serious illnesses in his teenage years. In February 1922, aged fifteen, he was among the tallest boys in his class, and by Easter 1923 he towered over his mother. I was struck by Robert's impressive height of 183 cm (six feet), something that was not obvious from the pictures inside the armchair. As he grew older, Robert developed new interests that superseded his liking for ice-skating and stamp-collecting. The history of art became one of his three main passions, and he would spend hours each weekend visiting Stuttgart's galleries and exhibitions. He was so committed to the subject that, for a time, he intended to study it at university.[32]

Then there were young women: aged seventeen, Robert originally complained when Wally sent him to dance lessons against his will, but soon withdrew his protests, for ballroom dancing was his first opportunity to spend time in the company of young women of his own age. Not only that, but he actually got to hold and touch them. He attended lessons at every opportunity. The young society women noticed the tall, slim and elegant Robert Griesinger, who had begun to take greater care of his appearance, making sure he always looked smart in his new suits. Wally was thrilled that Robert confided in her his innermost feelings about the women he met at dances, such as Ilsi, one of his dancing partners, on whom he had his first proper crush.[33]

Politics was Robert's third passion. His visits to galleries and dance halls in the early 1920s coincided with one of the most violent and unstable moments in German history. The immediate post-war years were critical in the formation of the 'war-youth' generation. United by a longing for a renewed sense of identity and collective action, and inspired by romantic interpretations of the camaraderie of the trenches, they were suspicious of liberal democracy and instead aimed to create a new community based on a revival of nineteenth-century *völkisch* (folkish) ideas that centred on the mystical blood bonds unifying the German people. These young men believed that only a return to traditional structures of social and political authority could offer a solution to Germany's political and economic turmoil. Many of this war-youth generation shared traits of coldness, hardness, determination and an exaggerated sense of importance.[34] According to the family lore passed down to Irmela, Robert had indeed embodied all of these characteristics. While it was not inevitable that Griesinger would later turn to Nazism, and many Germans born in the first decade of the twentieth century did not, his upbringing ensured that he was more susceptible than most. His parents were ardent supporters of the overtly monarchist *Württembergische Bürgerpartei*, a subsidiary of the nationalist and anti-Weimar German National People's Party (DNVP). His school life also pushed him strongly to the nationalist right – pupils at the Reformrealgymnasium later wrote that the nationalism of their teachers, who longed for the rebirth of a militarist Germany, rubbed off on them.[35]

A series of events in the early 1920s transformed Griesinger from a gentle schoolboy, interested in stamps and Renaissance art, into a political agitator. Just as he reached adulthood, the resurrection of the fatherland seemed possible when, to the delight of the schoolboys of the Reformrealgymnasium, barricades returned to the streets of Stuttgart. In March 1920 extreme-right elements of the officer corps, discontent with the republic, attempted to seize power in Germany by staging a coup. Wolfgang Kapp, a Prussian civil servant who had been born in the United States, led a group of *Freikorps* paramilitaries to Berlin and, after forcing the national government to flee to Stuttgart, proclaimed himself chancellor. Kapp had the backing of thousands of DNVP supporters, such as the Griesingers.[36] Yet the putsch failed to materialise. A nationwide general strike ensured that, after four anxious days, the right-wing coup was aborted. The government and the press swiftly returned to Berlin, leaving in their wake the schoolboys of the Reformrealgymnasium despondent that the excitement was over.

At the time of the Kapp Putsch in 1920, thirteen-year-old Griesinger was too young to comprehend fully the implication of the events that unfolded on his doorstep. Three and a half years later, when Germany was on the brink of political and economic collapse, the situation was different. In summer 1923 the government declared a state of emergency. Problems had begun to escalate in January of that year when, in the aftermath of Germany's failure to pay reparation instalments, French and Belgian troops marched into the country and occupied the Ruhr, the industrial heartland of Germany. German workers reacted with passive resistance and went on strike, ensuring that output ground to a halt. When the government began printing money to compensate the striking workers, a monetary crisis ensued. The creeping inflation that began in 1914 and continued throughout the war years suddenly turned into hyperinflation, causing the mark to spiral out of control; 1923 was the year of soaring prices and farcical anecdotes about the buying power of the Reichsmark with which Weimar Germany is synonymous. While at the beginning of the year Wally Griesinger could buy a postage stamp for twenty Reichsmark, by November 1923 she wrote anxiously that its price had risen to twenty million Reichsmark. Like millions of Germans, she struggled with the quantity of the near-worthless banknotes she needed to carry with her each time she left the house.[37] The whole of Germany, it seems, knew a person who momentarily left a wheelbarrow full of paper money unattended outside a shop, only to return a short time later to discover that a thief had first tipped out the money, before making off with the wheelbarrow. It remains among the worst experiences of inflation in world history.

Wally's diary revealed that before Griesinger had finished secondary school, a reactionary brand of nationalism was already a defining feature of her son's personality. At sixteen, Griesinger relished the deluge of jingoistic reaction that swept the nation during the Ruhr crisis.[38] In 1923 Griesinger was no longer the child who in 1914–18 was entirely dependent on his parents to grasp what was going on in the world around him. Rather, in this new context of French belligerence and economic disaster, he looked for ways outside the family home to explore and embrace his nationalist beliefs. He got his first taste of life within a paramilitary organisation, joining the Bismarck Youth, the youth wing of the conservative DNVP, which recruited young men and women from predominantly upper-middle-class and noble backgrounds. Curiously,

Wally's diary contains the only surviving reference to Griesinger's membership of the Bismarck Youth.[39] In archives that I discovered in Berlin, I saw that even when asked directly by Nazi-party officials whether he had previously been a member of any political organisations, Griesinger always stated that he had not.[40]

As part of the Bismarck Youth's *völkisch* and conservative world-view, members were instructed to 'keep their blood clean' to preserve the purity of the German nation.[41] By the time of his seventeenth birthday in November 1923, Griesinger was entirely dedicated to the nationalist cause. Wally depicted him for the first time as a grown man, capable of holding lucid and intelligent ideas. She was 'astonished' by his knowledge of the political situation. Thanks to his parents' close friendship with General Walther Reinhardt, the former chief of the German army, Griesinger was politically better informed than almost any other young man of his age. Nevertheless, his respect for Reinhardt was limited. Reinhardt, a staunch German nationalist who remained a monarchist at heart, was, in Griesinger's eyes, too eager to defend democracy and, in the seventeen-year-old's words, 'not right-wing enough'.[42]

Griesinger's racist nationalism did not begin with his entry into the Bismarck Youth. It surrounded him from a young age. Conservative military families blamed Jews for starting the Great War and, throughout its duration, accused them of undermining the fatherland. A resurgence of antisemitism, starting with the infamous 'Jew Count' in 1916, increased following the war, especially within the reactionary circles frequented by Griesinger's parents, who loathed Weimar's 'Jewish Republic', which they thought responsible for the twin evils of Communism and Social Democracy. After the First World War, antisemitic references to 'Jewish world dominance' filled the pages of the *Süddeutsche Zeitung*, which piled racial abuse on Jewish figures in Württemberg.[43] In the early 1920s the Griesingers' political party, the DNVP, held a position on Jews that appealed to its electorate, who sought *völkisch* policies to preserve the purity of German blood. At this time the DNVP openly demanded the introduction of measures to protect the German people from Jewish control. In April 1924 the party barred Jews, and Germans married to a Jew, from becoming members.[44]

When Griesinger was growing up, Stuttgart had a small Jewish population that numbered 4,500. Even though several Jews lived within 200 metres of the Griesingers on Alexanderstrasse – including the Dessauer and Engelberg families – Adolf and Wally would not, given their politics, have mixed in the same social circles as these or other Jews.[45] School marked the first occasion that Griesinger came into regular contact with Jews. In 1925, the year he completed his schooling, nineteen Jewish boys were enrolled at the Reformrealgymnasium, out of a total number of 552 pupils (3.5 per cent of the total student body).[46] It took until 2008, and the remarkable efforts of a history teacher, Judit Vamosi, for the school to investigate properly the fate of its Jewish pupils under Nazism. Vamosi and her students managed to uncover seventeen Jewish pupils whose lives, and in many cases deaths, they charted in an exhibition.[47] On class registers that I discovered in local archives, pupils' names appeared alongside their address, their father's profession and their religion. Jewish children were immediately identifiable when they didn't go to religious Christian classes run by local priests or pastors. It would have been impossible for a Jewish boy to hide the fact that he was Jewish.

There were four Jewish boys in Griesinger's cohort at the Reformrealgymnasium. Even though three of them were not in his class, it's likely he knew them. While one of the boys, Edgar Fleischer, lived in a different part of the city, two of them, Walther Stern and Walther Hummel, lived in the same part of Stuttgart as Griesinger. They might even have taken the same tram to and from school. Whereas the archives left no indication of what became of Walther Stern after the Nazis came to power, Edgar Fleischer managed to leave Germany in 1934 and emigrated to Peru, where he was killed in a plane crash in 1937. Walther Hummel remained in Germany until 1942, when he was deported with his mother to Izbica, a transit ghetto in central Poland that fed the extermination camps of Belzec and Sobibor.[48]

Hugo Stern was the only Jewish boy in Griesinger's class of twenty-four pupils. Stern went on to study medicine at university. He later worked in Stuttgart for two years, before he lost his job because of the Nazis' racial laws. Records showed that in 1937 Stern emigrated to the United States, where he set up a medical practice in Syracuse.[49] Within a few days of writing to representatives of the Jewish community in Syracuse, I found myself speaking on the phone to Judy Kaplan, Stern's daughter. Surprised that anyone should take an interest in her father so long after his death in 1970, she told me the little she knew of his life as a Jew in Stuttgart. 'My father never spoke to my brother and me about antisemitism at school, I only recall him telling us about being targeted at university,' she said. 'He didn't really tell us anything about his schooling. Until now, I did not know he was the only Jewish boy in his class.'[50]

In the year before his final exams for the *Abitur*, Robert remained undecided over his chosen subject of study at university. By late 1924 he had gone off the idea of art history and was leaning instead towards economics. He was sure, however, that he would join a Corps, a traditional student fraternity, which for Wally would involve 'stupid old fashioned customs like fencing and [ritual] drinking'. It was around this time that Wally noticed a change in her son's attitude to his school work. Realising that his entire future depended on his exam results, scheduled for February 1925, he began to take his studies seriously, declining invitations to attend dances and turning down the chance to go on holiday over Christmas. To his mother's delight, Robert passed his *Abitur*, finishing in fourteenth place in his class. It was all that was required to be accepted onto a course at a good university. Robert had performed reasonably well in religious studies, German literature, history and philosophy. He passed most other subjects with satisfactory or sufficient grades, but fared worse in Latin and drawing, finishing bottom of his class. To celebrate his admission to university, he went hiking for a few days in the Black Forest with three school friends.[51]

When he moved out of his parents' house, eighteen-year-old Griesinger was an extreme nationalist who was at ease mixing in antisemitic and anti-Communist circles. Despite this, neither he nor most of his peers had joined the Nazi Party that had formed in 1920. Griesinger left home in spring 1925 to begin his degree in law at the University of Tübingen, a small picturesque university town, with cobblestoned streets and timber-framed houses. Wally was inconsolable the day her son set off for university. She took to her Child Book within minutes of him leaving the house. Having kept it since Robert was less than a week old, this was her final entry, in which she wrote of the pain she was feeling at losing her 'good good boy', an expression she repeated throughout the entry. 'I have lost everything,' she wrote solemnly. She could not face looking at his desk and bed because they invoked such painful feelings. The knowledge that she would never again tuck him into bed at night weighed heavily on her heart.

Robert did not seem to feel the same way towards his over-protective mother when he left Alexanderstrasse. His parting words, when he asked his mother not to visit him too often, brought her almost to tears.[52]

Chapter v

Hollow Talk

Griesinger's time at university coincided with the end of hyperinflation and the beginning of the 'Golden Years' of Weimar. Compared to the years that preceded it and those that followed, the years 1924–9 were a period of relative stability and prosperity. Four days after leaving Stuttgart, Griesinger would have celebrated the election of Field Marshal Paul von Hindenburg as German president on 26 April 1925, which led the nationalist right to swell up in patriotic fervour. It felt like the dawn of a new era.

Tübingen was amongst Germany's most distinguished universities, as well as its most nationalist and reactionary. In his first year Griesinger lived in an apartment above a bakery on the cobblestoned Neckargasse, one of the oldest and liveliest shopping streets in the heart of the medieval town.[1] When he began his studies, the faculty and student body was overwhelmingly hostile towards the new republic.[2] The First World War and its consequences formed a powerful backdrop to Griesinger's life at Tübingen. At campus ceremonies, nationalist speeches designed to stir up students' emotions glorified imperial Germany. They also venerated the fallen soldiers and denounced the shame of Versailles.[3] Only those prepared to reconquer the lost territories by force, said the university's rector in one speech from this time, had the right to sing 'Deutschland über alles'.[4] In this pan-Germanic *völkisch* setting, antisemitism flourished long before the Nazi seizure of power.

As a student at Tübingen in the early 1920s Walter Stahlecker, later Griesinger's associate from the Stuttgart Gestapo, led the staunchly antisemitic German Nationalist League for Protection and Defence (DVSTB), which was founded in 1919 as an umbrella organisation for smaller antisemitic associations.[5] Antisemitism was also prevalent among the university's faculty, especially in theology, where Adolf Schlatter and Gerhard Kittel – renowned teachers who inspired generations of pastors in the church of Württemberg – described Jews publicly as opponents of Christians and Germans, who should not be allowed to marry Aryans.[6] It is unlikely Griesinger ever came into contact with a Jewish student or professor while at Tübingen. Even before Hitler's antisemitic decrees were enacted nationally, the university had an unwritten policy of not accepting Jewish students or faculty staff.[7] He might, however, have encountered ideas on eugenics and sterilisation long before they became associated with Nazi rule, due to the number of staff in Tübingen's school of medicine who professed an interest in racial hygiene.[8]

Glimmers of Griesinger's unexceptional university career emerge from the papers he kept with him to the end of his life. Shares in a company that took him on as a student intern were among the documents hidden in Jana's chair, for example. But his time in Tübingen also left a physical inscription on his face – a scar that repeatedly caught my eye in photographs from his adult years. During his first term there Griesinger joined the Corps Suevia Tübingen, an elite right-wing duelling fraternity, a rite of passage for young men coming from conservative wealthy backgrounds. As I delved into the Corps' arcane rules, I realised Griesinger had not suffered an accident. After being injured by his opponent's sword, Griesinger deliberately obtained the *Schmiss*, or duelling scar, by putting salt in the wound to make a bigger scar and to appear more martial. His Corps portrait from July 1925 shows him wearing the Corps' distinctive bright-red visor with its black-and-white rim. I found the photo in the drawer at Jochen and Irmela's house that he had sent home to his parents. He was proudly displaying his *Schmiss*. During the ritual duels, students did not wear masks and were not permitted to move their feet. Flinching was strictly frowned upon.

Robert Griesinger's Corps portrait, 1925

A duel among Suevia Tübingen's Corps brothers, 1931

A booklet produced in 1931 to celebrate 100 years of Suevia Tübingen revealed that Griesinger was initiated into the Corps as its 881st member and was immediately known as Griesinger II.[9] Duelling made up only part of Corps life. From the moment Griesinger joined the fraternity, his daily routine took on a militaristic rhythm. Believing they were victims of the First World War, Corps leaders set out to enshrine the war and its lessons for the future as a central pillar of the group's activities. A large part of life at the Corps revolved around commemorative ceremonies for the twenty-six fallen and forty-nine wounded Corps brothers. Unfortunately for Griesinger, who had shown such a mediocre aptitude for sports in high school, sport was central to fraternity life. After the First World War it became a compulsory criterion of membership. Student fraternities were anxious that the Treaty of Versailles, which banned military conscription, would emasculate German men. In sport, fraternities saw alternative ways to instil in their members physical responsibility and national pride. On top of his daily fencing lessons, Griesinger did three to four hours of sport each week. He probably swam or did gymnastics, as these were the most popular activities, but it is also likely that he took part in standard team sports, such as football or fistball.[10]

Corps brothers of Suevia Tübingen had privileged access to the *Schwabenhaus*, an opulent four-storey rococo building next to the Neckar River, whose rooms were decorated with trophies, swords and deer antlers. When not in classes, Corps brothers headed to their clubhouse to sit and relax in the large braided café chairs of the coffee room, where they sometimes plotted revenge against the 'November Criminals', politicians who had stabbed the army in the back by signing the Treaty of Versailles. Members were expected to spend as much time as possible at the *Schwabenhaus*, even into the early hours. Alcohol was part and parcel of student life. As a marker of masculinity, the young men were expected to engage in heavy group drinking, and it was common for individual Corps brothers to drink a thousand litres of beer a year. Members were notoriously raucous at the nightly drinking parties that dominated fraternity life, so much so that the police were often forced to go to the Corps house, sometimes two or three times on the same evening, to try and restore calm.[11]

On top of his studies, membership of a Corps was an enormous time commitment, but it was one Griesinger enjoyed. In the 1920s he was the only member to hold all three positions of responsibility: speaker, secretary and cashier. That he appeared in the centenary history of the society is significant. The book is one of the few published sources that mentions Griesinger directly by name.[12] In his roles, Griesinger oversaw Suevia Tübingen's ban on Jewish students, which – given their absence from the university – had no practical implication. Control of these key positions afforded Griesinger privileged access to the Corps' former members, including Konstantin von Neurath, whose son, Konstantin Alexander, joined Suevia Tübingen at around the same time as Griesinger, and Hans von Watter. These contacts would prove invaluable when Griesinger later arrived in Nazi-occupied Prague, thanks to their important positions in the city. In Tübingen it gave him access to a close brotherhood that counted among its ranks the sons of some of Germany's most powerful families.

Thanks to a document in Barbara's possession, I learned that Griesinger swiftly befriended Gustav Albrecht, fifth Prince of Sayn-Wittgenstein-Berleburg, another law student in his Corps, who was later father-in-law to Princess Benedikte of Denmark. The men were close and probably frequented each other's homes during the holidays.[13] Some years later Gustav Albrecht even sent Griesinger a card with a photograph to mark the occasion of his wedding to Margareta Fouché d'Otrante. Barbara knew only that the man in the photograph was a friend of her father; she was unaware of his royal status. As chance would have it, one of my interviews with Barbara took place the week after the funeral of Prince Richard, Gustav Albrecht's son, an event that gathered together Europe's royal houses. Barbara had seen pictures of the funeral in the newspaper. When I revealed her father's close connection to Prince Richard's father, she became excited that she had this minor link with European aristocracy. Unlike his participation in the SS, it was the kind of information about her father that she was pleased to uncover.

Wedding portrait of Gustav Albrecht, fifth Prince of
Sayn-Wittgenstein-Berleburg and Margareta Fouché
d'Otrante, 1934

Griesinger was proud of his lifelong membership of the Corps
Suevia Tübingen, later documenting it in all his official papers.
Based on the Corps' motto, 'Fearless and Loyal', members pledged
to help each other for life, securing jobs and promotions where
possible for one another. Access to such a significant network would
prove eminently useful under the Third Reich.

During his degree, the ambitious undergraduate gained work experience in the offices of Kabelwerk Duisburg, an electric cable manufacturer.[14] Given that Robert's mother was from Duisburg, it is likely she was behind this placement. Wally Griesinger might also have provided the wherewithal for her son's first financial wager. Among Griesinger's papers hidden in the armchair was a bank statement showing that Griesinger had invested shrewdly, having accumulated 112,000 Reichsmark worth of shares in Kabelwerk Duisburg.[15] And he exposed his ambitious side in other ways. He was an earnest student and enrolled in summer courses at Munich and Göttingen universities to advance his legal training and develop new social networks. He also spent a term in Berlin at the Friedrich-Wilhelms Universität, known today as the Humboldt University. Coming from the provinces, nothing could have prepared Griesinger for life in vibrant Berlin at the height of the Golden Twenties. Traditional Tübingen had shielded him from the modern avant-garde trends in architecture, art and culture that were exploding in the city. Griesinger was probably put off by aspects of life in liberal Berlin, which conservatives likened to a modern-day Sodom and Gomorrah, because of the way it supposedly gave free rein to abortion, prostitution and homosexuality.[16]

Such dedication to his education and his future career was not reflected in his grades. Despite being taught by some of the finest legal minds of the era at Tübingen, Griesinger was an unremarkable student at university, just as at high school. I was able to uncover multiple sources on Griesinger's studies, ranging from the reports of his university tutors, to the actual scripts Griesinger wrote by hand under exam conditions. A rather stern archivist in Ludwigsburg frowned at me when I laughed out loud as I held one of Griesinger's exam scripts. Commenting on Griesinger's analysis, his professor had written that the young law student was 'full of hollow talk, without any knowledge'.[17]

After Griesinger returned to the south-west from his Berlin stint, he rented a room in a small guesthouse run by two unmarried sisters in their mid-forties, Paula and Bertha Wacker. The guest-house was probably one of the few places in Tübingen where

Griesinger interacted with women of his own age. During his spell in Tübingen there were fewer than 300 female students, who made up less than 10 per cent of the 3,500-student body.[18] But, unusually, Paula and Bertha Wacker rented rooms to young single women as well as men enrolled at the university, and they were all expected to take their evening meals together.[19]

As a student, Griesinger was not drawn to the Nazi party. During these Weimar 'Golden Years' the party was in the political wilderness. The Nazi student grouping, the NSDStB, founded in 1926, only became a real force on campuses across the country when the Great Depression struck in late 1929. In Griesinger's day, it was fraternity life and not political activism that dominated the male university experience.[20] By September 1930, four months after Griesinger left Tübingen, only thirty-five students had joined the party.[21] Nazism took hold of Tübingen's students only in autumn 1931, thanks to the dedication of Erich Ehrlinger, Martin Sandberger and Erwin Weinmann, student members of the SA (Stormtroopers), the radical paramilitary wing of the Nazi movement during its rise to power. Donning their notorious brown shirts, Ehrlinger, Sandberger and Weinmann adopted threatening methods to spread the Nazis' message to staff and students at the university. Griesinger later came to know them in the mid-1930s when the three men held leading positions in the SS and SD in Stuttgart.[22] In elections to the student council in July 1932, the NSDStB won half the seats, an emphatic sign of the Nazis' progress, but compared to results elsewhere, it was hardly a triumph.[23]

Griesinger's trajectory from Tübingen to the SS was unusual. Amid the thousands of university graduates who later forged careers inside the party machine, few had attended Tübingen. More than 80 per cent of SS members with a degree attended the universities of Leipzig, Munich, Göttingen and Heidelberg, with Leipzig being by far the most popular.[24] While his university experience exposed Griesinger to plenty of anti-republican and antisemitic discourses, it had not granted him the networks for entry to the SS in the way it had done for thousands of others graduating from Leipzig and elsewhere. In 1930 other doors remained open for

Griesinger. Even as the Great Depression hit, it was still not inevitable that he would become a Nazi.

Griesinger scraped through his degree. He passed the first set of state law exams (*Referendarexamen*) in spring 1930 with a 'below satisfactory', the second-lowest possible grade. But it was enough to grant him a place as a junior lawyer.[25] Aged twenty-three in May 1930, Griesinger returned to his parents in Stuttgart to begin his legal training. The cityscape had changed during the five years that he was away, as architects such as Paul Bonatz constructed their eclectic designs amid the city's late-Gothic churches and castles. Works to build a new train station, which had begun in 1914, were finally completed in 1928. A year before the station opened, seventeen of Europe's most famous avant-garde architects converged on Stuttgart for the opening of the Weissenhof Estate, among the most important model-family home exhibitions in twentieth-century Europe. Modernist designs flourished in Stuttgart in the late 1920s, as villas, apartments and school buildings sprang up across the city. The Tagblatt-Turm, the city's first skyscraper, was built and became home to the offices of the Stuttgart daily newspaper, the *Stuttgarter Neues Tagblatt*. The municipal indoor swimming pool, then the largest in Germany, opened in 1929.

Adolf and Wally Griesinger took part in their own building project during the expansion of the city, leaving their apartment on the Alexanderstrasse in 1926 to move to an imitation antebellum mansion on a hill in the south of Stuttgart that overlooked the city. It was to this new and unfamiliar location on the Auf dem Haigst that Griesinger settled in 1930, and in which Jochen and Irmela still live. Upon his return from Tübingen, Griesinger immediately embarked on two years of practical legal training to prepare him for the second set of state law exams (*Assessorexamen*). For a part of this time he worked as a legal intern in Esslingen, a town ten miles east of Stuttgart, where he gained insight into the functioning of state and municipal administration. A report on Griesinger by his superior in Esslingen showed him to be very able and practical as he went about his work. It stated that Griesinger's appearance and manners were 'impeccable'.[26]

During spring 1931 Griesinger managed to secure sixty-two days of leave to write his doctoral thesis, which he submitted to the law faculty at Tübingen in August. Twenty-seven libraries around the world hold a copy of Griesinger's PhD. Most are in Germany, though one duplicate made it as far as Tokyo. His advisor, August Schoetensack, was a venerated authority on criminal law, whose expertise was later used by the Nazis. During the Third Reich, Schoetensack was a member of Hans Frank's Academy for German Law, a legal think-tank that served to transform German law codes in line with Nazi ideology. In January 1935 Schoetensack sat on the commission for a prison law that agreed on procedures to render imprisonment more arduous, such as by shaving inmates' hair and detaining in dark cells prisoners who required disciplinary action.[27] Working under Schoetensack's guidance, Griesinger's thesis investigated usury and profiteering in German criminal law. The title included the loosely antisemitic term for extortion, 'Wucher'. But despite writing about usury, the oldest antisemitic stereotype, Griesinger's fifty-three-page thesis, which granted him the title of doctor, did not discuss Jews, either directly or indirectly. His analysis followed a standard approach for the era, which involved digesting an area of law and making recommendations for legal reform.[28]

Faced by the bland legalism of Griesinger's dissertation, I wondered how the wider world appeared to him at this formative moment. The short commute to Esslingen gave him time to catch up on current affairs. His newspaper of choice would almost certainly have been the same as that of his parents, the conservative *Süddeutsche Zeitung*. During the first few months of 1931 the national campaign to decriminalise abortion – and the paper's opposition to it – dominated its headlines.[29] Large numbers of women were seeking to terminate their pregnancies during the harsh economic climate. It is estimated that throughout the Depression one million women in Germany had an illegal abortion.[30] Mass protests to repeal Article 218 of the Criminal Code, the law that criminalised abortion, began in February 1931. The campaign against Article 218 received immense coverage in the national press, as women were encouraged to write letters to left-liberal newspapers detailing their experiences of abortion.[31]

The abortion debate was just one of many important issues confronting the German population. Griesinger's attempts to launch a career in the early 1930s took place against a backdrop of economic disaster and a crisis of governance, in which no party could secure a majority of seats in the Reichstag to form a single-party government. Beginning in late 1930, Chancellor Brüning of the Centre Party introduced austerity measures by increasing taxes, cutting government expenditure and reducing salaries. His response proved harmful to the economy and led to price increases and severe unemployment. It was a time when some of the brightest young graduates found themselves laid off, rather than being taken on: yet another setback for Griesinger's 'war-youth' generation.[32]

More so than any other party, the Nazis benefited from the dire economic situation. Nowhere is this clearer than in the elections to the Reichstag in September 1930. Whereas in the previous elections of May 1928 the Nazis were Germany's ninth leading party, they finished two years later as the second-largest party.[33] Despite this groundswell of support, in 1930 voters in Württemberg bucked the national trend and did not rush to vote en masse for Adolf Hitler. Unemployment rates remained far lower than in the rest of the country, especially in the heavily industrialised regions. Württemberg was still predominantly agrarian and was made up of small-scale farmers, craftsmen and artisans who specialised in the manufacture of furniture, clocks, toys, harmonicas and accordions.[34] The local economy had managed to resist the onslaught of the Great Depression until 1932.[35] The people of Württemberg, historically wary of external power, were proud of their Swabian regional identity and institutions, leading many to mistrust the Nazis' centralising ideology. In Germany's third-largest state the Nazis had failed to make inroads.[36] In 1930 most voters in Württemberg would not have seen Nazi posters, slogans or rallies, nor did they hear activists' speeches.[37] That summer Griesinger was probably not scared by the prospect of unemployment and economic deprivation, which might have impelled him to vote for the Nazis. In conservative Württemberg he still had his pick of established nationalist, anti-Weimar right-wing parties from which to choose.

In the two years that followed, the Nazi party enjoyed an astonishing reversal of fortunes in Württemberg. As the consequences of the Great Depression seeped into the south-west, and thanks to the efforts of a well-organised team of local leaders, the party was able to actively recruit new members. Within two years party membership increased fivefold. With 430 local branches, the number of card-carrying Nazis was increasing steadily.[38] As the economic situation worsened, people across all layers of society, from the upper classes right down to some workers, saw the Nazis as a viable alternative to ineffective Weimar politicians. Parties on the right that had previously acted as a bulwark to the Nazis disintegrated. In 1932 the Nazis became the most popular party in Württemberg, securing 30.3 per cent in the July elections to the Reichstag.[39]

People are often surprised to discover that the Nazi party did not storm to power on the back of mass popular support. Four months after the elections in July 1932, more than two million voters had deserted the party. Even though the Nazis gained more votes than any other party, only one-third of the German population voted for them in the country's last free elections before Hitler took power, while in Württemberg the figure was just one-quarter. Griesinger was probably not among them. Many who for the first time had supported the party in July were dismayed by Hitler's refusal to serve in the Cabinet, when offered the chance in August 1932 by President Hindenburg.

In January 1933 former chancellor Franz von Papen struck a deal with Hitler that awarded the Nazis the chancellorship and two other positions in government. Von Papen became vice-chancellor and all other government positions went to nationalist parties. In the spring of 1933 Griesinger was not yet a member of a single Nazi organisation, but – like so many conservatives who opposed the Weimar Republic and feared the spread of Communism – would have looked on approvingly at many of the Nazis' early actions. For someone of Griesinger's background, a drastic solution was needed to counter the Communist menace. For years the German middle class had heard stories about the abysmal conditions in the USSR. As his own mother had once written in her diary, anything would have been better than living under Communist rule. 'We have to hold out against the Bolsheviks,' wrote Wally, fearing that Communism meant hunger and destruction.[40]

Her Communist panic was real. Having polled 17 per cent in the November 1932 elections to the Reichstag, the Communists were now the country's third party. In the aftermath of the Reichstag Fire, which the Nazis dubbed a Communist conspiracy, an emergency decree legalised the repression of political opposition. At this time Hitler had the support of Cabinet member Alfred Hugenberg, leader of the DNVP, the party that Griesinger probably voted for, who spoke of the need for 'draconian measures' to stamp out the Communist threat.[41] A few weeks later Hugenberg and the DNVP voted for the Enabling Act that suspended parliament for four years and gave the Cabinet almost unlimited executive powers.

The conservative attempt to control Hitler was a dismal failure. Thanks to a sustained campaign of violence launched against its enemies, the Nazis, within just six months of Hitler's appointment, had consolidated their grip on power. SA units took to the streets, terrorising and intimidating the party's real and imagined opponents. Across Germany the leadership of the Brownshirts gave orders to carry out illegal acts of violence against possible opposition, safe in the knowledge that there would be no consequences. The SA grew at a spectacular rate. In January 1933 the organisation had half a million members. Within a year, this figure had grown to almost three million.[42]

Among the main targets of SA brutality were German Jews, including Jewish judges and lawyers, whom they sought to purge from the legal profession. During March and April 1933 SA units stood at the entrance to courthouses across Germany to identify Jewish judges and lawyers and restrict them access. In some cases they famously entered the courtrooms, looking for Jews to beat up and throw out on the street.[43] A series of laws and decrees, designed to quash any opposition, swiftly followed. One can imagine how much changes to the law mattered to an aspiring lawyer like Griesinger. He would have carefully followed each of the amendments and paid particular notice to legislation affecting the civil service. He could not have ignored laws passed in April 1933 that banned Jews and political opponents from state and legal professions. Jewish women, such as the renowned Stuttgart lawyer Ella Kessler-Reis, were doubly persecuted for being Jews and for being women. In 1933 Kessler-Reis had her licence to practice revoked before even her male Jewish colleagues.[44] In the months that followed the Nazi seizure of power, Griesinger made a series of significant decisions that were to inform the rest of his life. It was make-or-break time for the young lawyer seeking to establish a career in an unprecedented political and legal landscape.

Republican institutions did not disappear overnight. In this early phase of life under Nazi rule, the daily routines of those Germans not immediately targeted by the new regime did not change drastically. Life went on, and many were willing to give a chance to the new government, which promised to curb mass unemployment, control runaway inflation and make Germany great again. In the first weeks and months under Hitler's chancellorship, market traders continued to set up their stalls each morning, farmers attended to their cattle and students sat their exams. Griesinger was among this last category. Everything he had worked towards for the past few years came down to the second set of state law exams (*Assessorexamen*), which took place over April, May and June 1933. He had to pass to become a lawyer. Given that he had never been the most promising of students, this was not inevitable. In their concise reference to the exam board, Hedinger, Lenckner & Drescher, the Stuttgart law firm where Griesinger worked, described him as a 'diligent' worker whose legal understanding was 'quite good'. It was hardly a glowing endorsement.[45]

Even in a town like Stuttgart, one that for so long had shunned the Nazi advance, local people now saw the party's brutal methods on the streets of their city. In March 1933 Dietrich von Jagow, leader of the Württemberg SA, was appointed as emergency Reich Commissioner for the state and swiftly launched a wave of terror against the regime's perceived opponents, arresting Communists, Socialists and Jews. Lacking sufficient prison space, von Jagow set up the Heuberg concentration camp 100 kilometres south of Stuttgart in late March. Heuberg received immense press coverage both at home and abroad. The Nazis encouraged journalists to visit the camp. Many of those who did so filled their reports with details of the correctional facilities at the camps, designed to 're-educate' prisoners and lead them away from Communism.[46] In these first few months of the new era, Griesinger might have found some of the Nazis' behaviour distasteful. Nevertheless, as an ultra-conservative eager to reduce Communist, Socialist and Jewish influence, and in order to restore Germany to its former glory, he would have gone along with their unusual methods of governance, especially since DNVP politicians continued to serve in Hitler's Cabinet. If he had any qualms about Nazi violence, he must have quickly pushed them aside.

In January 1933, when Hitler took power, the Nazi party had 1.4 million members. Thanks to the Nazis' success in the March elections to the Reichstag, by May of that year an additional 1.6 million people had signed up.[47] However, neither Griesinger nor his parents were among these sudden converts – or 'March violets', as they were contemptuously called by long-standing members. Even though the Nazis' electoral success and the passing of the Enabling Act suggested a permanence to the regime, nobody could have foreseen that, with just three Cabinet positions, the Nazis would shortly usurp total power from their conservative partners in government. In spring 1933 Griesinger still had not joined. The party restricted membership on 1 May, the week in which Griesinger had his three most important exams.[48] The twenty-six-year-old was living under his parents' roof and, for his staunchly monarchist father, as for most former officers, the Nazis continued to represent little more than a vulgar rabble, with Hitler, the lowly corporal, a mouthpiece of the hysterical masses.[49]

Griesinger qualified as a lawyer, passing his final exams with a characteristic 'satisfactory' mark on 20 June 1933. He was not disheartened by his unremarkable grade. Quite the contrary. A pass was all that was needed to join the Ministry of the Interior as a probationary lawyer. Griesinger carried his certificate with him everywhere for the rest of his life and it was, unsurprisingly, among the documents discovered in Jana's chair. After spending his summer in Giessen, he formally joined the Württemberg Ministry of the Interior on 11 September 1933 as a public official. On that same day Dr Robert Arnold Griesinger walked into the Stuttgart recruiting office of SS-Gruppe 'West' and signed up to join the organisation.[50]

As a newly minted lawyer and junior civil servant, Griesinger entered a transformed legal and political landscape. In June 1933 the DNVP's avowed monarchist and extreme nationalist leader, Alfred Hugenberg, resigned from the Cabinet. By the middle of July the Nazis were the only legal political party, the others that remained having been either dissolved or banned. In the space of just six months, Griesinger and millions of Germans had gone from living in a pluralist democracy to living in a one-party state. Because joining the party was no longer an option, Griesinger needed to find other ways to show his support – opportunistic though it was – for the Nazis. As a highly educated man, he was fortunate. His profession afforded him entry to the Nazi Lawyers' Association (Bund Nationalsozialistischer Deutscher Juristen), and his pedigree made him eligible for entry into the SS. He joined both.

Griesinger stepped out of studenthood and into adult life marked by perhaps the two most striking things about him: the facial scar that announced his embrace of Suevia Tübingen's elite masculine codes, and membership of the SS.

The SS was a highly complicated organism of the Nazi state, which cannot be reduced simply to a homogenous group of 'men in black coats'. Despite all that has been written about the SS, today's historians still know far too little about how the organisation functioned and how low-level members navigated their day-to-day lives.[51] No book has ever been written on a low-ranking, regular SS officer:

these Nazis have vanished from the historical record.[52] While academics have studied in some depth the SS's Main Offices in Berlin, such as the Reich Security Main Office and the Race and Settlement Main Office, and have shifted attention to some of these organisations' more radical personnel, most popular histories have generally focused attention on the Armed SS (*Waffen-SS*). It is a tactic that, as Griesinger's case study reveals, is grossly misleading, for it has resulted in most people conflating the regular *Allgemeine SS* (the General SS) with its more fanatical branches. Piecing together Griesinger's trajectory to shed light on where low-level SS members came from, personally and professionally, before they donned the infamous uniform enables us to question some of our most ingrained historical images.

To join the SS in September 1933 was not the same as joining in 1937 or 1941. The organisation's structures changed over time. In the early to mid-1930s there were numerous reasons that led men to join the SS. Just as some were ideologically committed to its cause, thousands of young men coming from the 'war-youth' generation used the SS as a channel for career advancement. Many were impressed by its elitist nature, especially its uniform. For example, when one Rudolf Hofmann was thrown out of the organisation in Bavaria for financial irregularities, his brother Franz immediately signed up – simply because he was drawn to the now-discarded uniform.[53] Some young men displayed no interest in joining the SS, even when presented with the opportunity. At a recruitment event at a college in the town of Heilbronn, just north of Stuttgart, one student who did not wish to enlist was seen escaping through a bathroom window.[54]

The SS was founded in 1925 as Guard Detachments (*Schutzstaffel*) consisting of several ten-man unit bodyguards to protect Hitler and other Nazi leaders from political opponents. Created at a time when the Nazi party was firmly in the political wilderness, the SS could only muster nine men in the whole of Württemberg for Hitler's first visit to Stuttgart, in December 1925.[55] When Himmler was appointed *Reichsführer-SS* in 1929, the organisation had between 250 and 300 men. The expansion of the SS in the years that followed, and the role it came to play under the Third Reich, was entirely down to Himmler, who sought to cast his SS men as the racial elite of Nazi society, coming from 'the best human material that we still possess in Germany'.[56] Himmler introduced the principle of racial selection as a key membership criterion for his SS men, whose principal role had evolved by this time to act as a disciplined security force, charged with maintaining order and crowd control at Nazi-party rallies and events. To prepare for this task, the men were expected to attend compulsory local meetings four times a month, undertake training drills and marches, sing military songs and meet up with neighbouring SS units.[57] Griesinger, like 90 per cent of all SS members, served in the non-military *Allgemeine SS* (the General SS) that was tasked with ensuring the security of the Nazi party, its leaders, and the rest of the German *Volk*. Members of the *Allgemeine SS* were distinct from the *Waffen-SS*, the *SS-Totenkopfverbände* Death's-Head Units (concentration camp and extermination camp guards), or the *Einsatzgruppen* (mobile SS killing units), with which the organisation's brutal methods of terror are commonly associated.[58]

The timing of Griesinger's recruitment in 1933 makes sense. As the organisation grew in prestige, so too did its membership figures. By June 1932, only three years after Himmler was appointed to lead the organisation, SS membership had expanded to 41,000 men. In the months that followed the Nazi seizure of power, membership of the SS surged. In October 1933, a month after Griesinger joined, membership of the organisation stood at 180,000 men.[59] The organisation's demographic also changed. Griesinger was one of a wave of men coming from the upper-middle class and the German social elite who joined the SS in 1933. As the organisation expanded in a changing Germany, working towards its goal of having a *Sturmbann* (SS Storm Unit) of 500–800 men in every town, it no longer sought to attract only Nazi ideologues and fighters. Griesinger joined at the very moment when the organisation was calling out for well-educated new recruits capable of assuming complex administrative functions.[60] The young men like Griesinger who were now joining the SS tended to be better-educated than the old fighters who had joined the organisation earlier: 28 per cent of these new recruits had even obtained doctorates.[61] Men from the middle and upper classes who looked down on mass movements were attracted to the SS elite guard, as their rigorous discipline provided a stark contrast to the street rabble and revolutionary intentions of the SA. Famously, members were expelled if they were caught carrying firearms, failed to turn up for training or fell behind in their monthly membership fees.[62] From starting out as a few select units of body-guards, the SS had evolved, by the time Griesinger joined the organisation, into a tight military-style hierarchy with SS Districts, Sub-Districts, Regiments, Storm Units and Companies that were in place across the country.

Dozens of archives spread out across south-west Germany, their collections spared Allied bombing, helped me to piece together Griesinger's early life in the SS and his moves across Württemberg as a junior civil servant. While in some archives I found only scraps of information on this transitional phase in Griesinger's life, in others I found – to my delight – full reports written about him by his superiors. More often than not the documents pointed in the same direction, revealing Griesinger's quasi-obsession with career stability and advancement in the civil service, whose structures remained largely intact in the years that followed the Nazi seizure of power.

Within days of becoming SS member no. 161,860, Griesinger headed to Urach, a picturesque medieval spa town in the beautiful Erms Valley, sixty kilometres south-east of Stuttgart, to take up his position as a newly appointed probationary legal official (*Gerichtassessor*).[63] Griesinger's office at the municipal administration was located in a fifteenth-century half-timbered house with painted red beams and flowerpots on every windowsill. His spell in this rural locality coincided with the introduction of some of Nazi Germany's grand projects for national renewal. For the whole of his adult life, the humiliating terms of the Treaty of Versailles had hung over Griesinger, and others from his background, like a dark cloud. He would have revelled in October 1933 when Konstantin von Neurath, Hitler's Foreign Minister and a Corps brother from Suevia Tübingen, put the wheels in motion to withdraw Germany from the League of Nations. It was a sign that the Nazis intended to rebuild Germany's military and diplomatic strength and restore national honour.

Wanting to know more about Griesinger's life in autumn 1933, I contacted Stefanie Leisentritt, a jeweller who, in her spare time, is also an accomplished local historian and author of a book on Urach during the Third Reich. Stefanie's research revealed that at that time the SS was non-existent in Urach, a small locality with fewer than 7,000 residents. SS units did not appear suddenly across Germany following the Nazi seizure of power. Indeed, in 1933–4 it was the SA, and not the SS, that commanded a heavy local presence in Urach. SA members met each night at the Falke tavern, just a three-minute walk from Griesinger's apartment on Wilhelmstrasse.[64] Griesinger was the first SS member to reside in sleepy Urach. There were no meetings or lectures to attend, and no SS newspaper to read. He would have dedicated most of his time to his new job and not to the SS. To play a role in Hitler's New Order and advance his career prospects, he needed to channel his ambition beyond Urach.

Six weeks after beginning his placement, Griesinger travelled to Munich to take part in a series of ceremonies to mark the tenth anniversary of the Beer Hall Putsch – a bloody shootout in November 1923 initiated by Adolf Hitler and 2,000 Nazis at a beer-hall cellar, in an attempt to overthrow the German government. Sixteen party members and four policemen were killed during the failed *coup d'état*. The ceremonies that took place in Munich in November 1933 marked Griesinger's first taste of active SS service. On the night before the main event, Hitler gave a speech in the famous beer-hall cellar that was transmitted across the city by loudspeaker. The all-too-familiar sound of the Führer could be heard in hotel bedrooms, while in Munich's streets the roar of his voice reached almost deafening proportions.[65]

The centrepiece of the occasion on Thursday 9 November 1933, Griesinger's twenty-seventh birthday, was the midday procession, where Hitler slowly led 2,000 men through the streets of historical Munich to the sombre beat of drums and funeral music. It was the same men who, ten years earlier, had taken part in the failed uprising. After the march, thousands of spectators attended Hitler's address in the main square. Like so many ordinary SS and SA men who had travelled to Munich, Griesinger was probably tasked with forming part of a cordon to keep at bay the crowds.[66] He would not have been kitted out in the black uniform of the SS, which had only just been introduced and was not readily available to lower-ranking members. He would have worn the organisation's original design, which was very similar to the clothing of the SA, with the same SA brown shirts and breeches, but with black caps and ties instead of brown, and their own distinguishable leather badges and black riding boots. Munich was a turning point in Griesinger's life. Far from being a peripheral dues-paying member, he was now a more active participant in the SS, who was prepared to travel some distance to signal his loyalty. He later realised the significance of his attendance at this historic event. Hoping to enhance his social and professional standing, he included it on his CV.[67] Within the space of only a few months, Griesinger had become a fully-fledged Nazi.

After just four months in Urach, an opportunity for career advancement arose in Tettnang, a quiet town by Lake Constance, close to the Swiss and Austrian borders. The *Landrat* (the representative of the state at the local level) had requested to go on leave and Griesinger agreed to replace him.[68] His work in Urach had until this point been deemed 'quite good' by superiors – as ever with Griesinger, there was plenty of room for improvement.[69] The young civil servant's transfer in early 1934 occurred at a challenging time for the regime. The euphoria that had accompanied Hitler's ascent to power was gradually subsiding. As prices continued to rise, most Germans felt the promised economic revival was unlikely ever to occur. On the week that Griesinger began his new job, Victor Klemperer, a Jewish professor of literature at Dresden Technical University, wrote in his diary that people were no longer as convinced 'of the everlasting durability of the present state of things'.[70]

To secure the position of *Landrat* was important. It was widely known to be a first real chance for ambitious civil servants to move up the career ladder. Despite being only a small town of 40,000 inhabitants, the position in Tettnang gave Griesinger his first experience of unmitigated power and influence, because the job involved ensuring the implementation at the local level of new laws coming from above. Tettnang's location as a border town meant that Griesinger would have had to be especially familiar with the legislation aimed at preventing Communists and Social Democrats from escaping into Switzerland. As *Landrat*, he was also charged with overseeing the development of the Nazis' new racial state. This was not as grand for Griesinger as it might at first sound: Tettnang was home to only seven Jews at the time, and it is doubtful he ever met one.[71] During his posting in the town, the marginalisation of Jews from the rest of the population had no practical consequences for the twenty-seven-year-old *Landrat*, whose career was rising steadily. Griesinger's training in Tettnang did, however, equip him with the new regime's mindset and language, when it came to dealing with Jews and other enemies of the Reich. These skills would later prove invaluable.

It was at this time that Griesinger was promoted to the next rung on the civil-service ladder, becoming a junior legal secretary (*Regierungsassessor*), while the Nazis tightened their grip on power. By the time he left Tettnang in autumn 1934, Germans lived under a total dictatorship. On 30 June, Hitler turned on his once-trusted comrades, the SA, in the Night of the Long Knives, after they began to threaten his power. Across Germany, SS forces murdered hundreds of SA leaders and other opponents of the regime. The SS emerged triumphant, at the expense of the SA, which was decimated. It is unlikely Griesinger took part in the violence that unfolded during the Night of the Long Knives, because most SS men learned only in the days that followed about what had occurred.[72] Fortunately for him, Griesinger had bet on the right horse. Throughout the summer of 1934 Nazi control intensified. On the death of President Hindenburg in early August, Hitler called a referendum to ask the German people to support the merging of the offices of president and chancellor. In an unfree election, he won by a resounding 88 per cent of the vote. As sole ruler, Hitler took on the title of Führer. In the weeks that followed, civil servants such as Griesinger pledged personal oaths of loyalty to him.

As Nazism infiltrated German society, Griesinger's participation within the party steadily increased. In Tettnang, he joined the NSV, the Nazi Welfare Organisation (*NS Volkswohlfahrt*), which was responsible for the Nazis' welfare and social-activist agenda. He also played a more active role in the SS and, shortly after his arrival, was promoted to the position of Section Leader (*Rottenführer*), a junior rank that came with some responsibility. In summer 1934 Griesinger led an SS unit for the first time (SS *Sturm* 8/10). He assembled his men close to the green banks of Lake Constance, wearing the new uniform of the organisation. The famous black tunic and peaked cap were by now widely available, although unlike concentration-camp guards, ordinary members of the *Allgemeine SS* with full-time jobs elsewhere did not wear the uniform every day to work. Griesinger and the men of his *Sturm* also had to pay for theirs.[73] It is likely that most of the SS men with whom Griesinger spent evenings and weekends were single. Despite the rhetoric on the duty of SS men to marry and produce four racially healthy children, low marriage rates afflicted the organisation. In 1936 only 30 per cent of SS men were married.[74] Just as he did with his participation at Munich in November 1933, Griesinger went to great lengths to play up the significance of his experience leading the *Sturm* in summer 1934, using it later to signal his natural leadership qualities and his early commitment to the SS.

At a time when Himmler and other senior SS leaders were attempting to mythologise the SS as an elite grouping, SS officers throughout the south-west were constantly reminded of the need to set an example to their fellow citizens. As often stated by Hans-Adolf Prützmann, leader of the SS for the south-west, a member's conduct, behaviour and appearance had to be beyond reproach. On every occasion that a member acted out of turn, Prützmann alerted each *Sturm* in Baden and Württemberg to the incident, to ensure that similar misdemeanours would not be repeated else-where. For example, in July 1934 Griesinger's *Sturm* in Tettnang was made aware that hitch-hiking was 'unworthy of an SS member'. Prützmann was unequivocal in his condemnation of the practice. He wrote that if he were ever to see or hear of an SS member attempting to hitch-hike, the person in question would be imme-diately fired from the SS.[75]

In towns close in size to Tettnang, SS gatherings took place usually on one or two evenings a week and lasted for up to two hours. Reports and timetables of meetings show the men taking part in a wide range of events: sports games against another local SS *Sturm*, marching sessions, singing lessons, learning first aid or listening to a presentation by an SS official from Stuttgart. At least one full Sunday morning each month Griesinger also took part in training drills that began at eight o'clock.[76] During his spell in Tettnang, he might even have taken part in local SS schemes around Lake Constance to help the prosperity of the local rural community and economy. On one occasion an SS unit built a new house for the widow and ten children of a member killed in an avalanche in January 1934. Neighbouring SS units came to watch when a repre-sentative from the SS Reich High Command (*Reichsführung* SS) presented the widow with the keys to the house at an official ceremony.[77]

In rural Württemberg in 1933–4 Griesinger engaged in activities typical of the *Allgemeine SS*. In 1934, for most of the organisation's 200,000 members, taking part in *Allgemeine SS* meetings and activ-ities was only a part-time pursuit. Thousands of businessmen, teachers, doctors and lawyers who carried out their SS duties, when called upon, were able to put the Nazi messages and propaganda they encountered in meetings to the back of their minds, at least temporarily, as they focused on more pressing tasks. If Griesinger's case is any judge, most members neither met the exacting standards demanded of them by their superiors nor lived up to the stereo-typical image of an SS officer – someone who was entirely dedicated to forming the elite of German society. In 1936, in preparation for an annual rally, twenty members of an SS troop spent an hour and a half peeling potatoes. At the end of the ninety minutes, they had successfully peeled twelve.[78]

After eight months in post at Tettnang, Griesinger was ready for a new challenge. At the end of September 1934 he took leave from the Ministry of the Interior and spent late that year and early the next in Paris and the south of England, to work on his language skills.[79] It was a strategic move. When he left Germany, Griesinger was advancing in the SS and was making steady career progress. He was on course to achieve further promotions in both. He would have been pleased by the first eighteen months of Nazi rule, characterised by the erasure of Weimar democracy, the obliteration of the left and the restoration of national pride. His trip was part of his long-term commitment to, rather than an escape from, his life in Hitler's new Germany.

Drawing on my experience as a historian of France, I visited all the relevant archival collections in Paris, hoping that Griesinger's name would turn up on a document, but it did not. He had not aroused sufficient interest among the French authorities to merit his own file. He stayed for just three months, and so did not need to register with the police or local authorities.

What did Griesinger do in Paris? He had a passion for art. I pictured him, with limited French, struggling to purchase a museum ticket or decipher the label of a portrait. And why was he in Paris anyway? His decision to learn the language was surprising. By late 1934 English was the Nazis' foreign language of choice. In English, Hitler saw the possibility for Germans to think as imperialists. He constantly denigrated French, proclaiming it the language of an 'exhausted' people, and one that was unfit to be taught in schools and universities.[80] Despite the Nazis' known aversion to the language, Griesinger later listed his 'fluency' in French on all subsequent CVs. He did the same with Dutch, despite only ever spending summer holidays with German-speaking relatives at his maternal grandfather's castle at Slangenburg in the Netherlands.[81] He clearly had a penchant for exaggerating his skills, in order to serve his ambitions. As his high-school reports revealed, Griesinger was not a natural linguist, constantly finishing bottom of his class in Latin and underperforming in English.[82]

In Paris he may well have mingled with like-minded Germans in the tenth arrondissement at the Taverne d'Hauteville, a pub serving German food and beer, which in the mid-1930s was the largest meeting place in the city for Nazi enthusiasts. Nazi social evenings were held every Friday night and attracted several hundred people.[83] Griesinger might even have struck up a friendship with French men and women who were sympathetic to Germany and German culture. Since the 1920s the German embassy in Paris was active in promoting cultural exchanges between young French and German students, bringing hundreds of Germans to spend time in the French capital. Scores of Franco-German groups and societies emerged during this time, and remained active following the Nazi rise to power. In 1934 there were so many joint meetings and ventures between French and German associations that French officials began to worry that their students were becoming receptive to Nazi ideas.[84]

We can also only speculate about what Griesinger did in the south of England in early 1935, after arriving from Paris.[85] From a financial point of view, life in England would not have been easy. The Nazis had limited the amount of currency that Germans were allowed to take out of the country to 2,000 RM, which wouldn't have lasted long in France or England. Unable to work because of his visa situation, Griesinger would have been forced to economise. An article in the *European Herald*, published a few months before Griesinger arrived, described the thrifty living of young German men in England, forced to cook for themselves and share bedrooms in guesthouses.[86]

If Griesinger perched in the corner of a shared room reading the English papers, news from Germany would have reached him: the progress of the Anglo-French talks on German rearmament and the reintroduction of conscription. If he behaved true to type in his new surroundings, he might have made one extravagant purchase. According to the *European Herald*, the 'first thing' a young German bought after arriving was a pipe, irrespective of whether or not he even smoked.[87] Griesinger's chances of romance were probably slim. According to the young German men interviewed in the article, English girls were found to be cold and wholly unapproachable, nothing like the girls back home.

When he returned to the Ministry of the Interior after his six-month trip, Griesinger immediately picked up the work he had left off, re-joining the merry-go-round of civil servants performing short-term stints of service across Württemberg. Next he was sent to Ulm, on the banks of the Danube, the third-largest town in Württemberg after Stuttgart and Heilbronn. Griesinger joined the local administration as a junior legal secretary on 1 April 1935, and for the next three months was second-in-command to the *Landrat*. Important changes to the rhythm of SS life had taken place during the period he was away. The organisation had launched *Das Schwarze Korps* (The Black Corps), an official weekly newspaper, to promote its worldview. Its readership was treated to articles justifying the regime's obsession with biology and antisemitism, and sections that promoted the racially healthy family.[88] *Das Schwarze Korps* had a larger readership in Ulm than elsewhere in Württemberg. The city was home to Oberer Kuhberg, one of Germany's earliest concentration camps, set up in November 1933 in an abandoned nineteenth-century fortress. SS guards were brought in to oversee the camp's 600 prisoners, made up predominantly of Communists and Socialists.[89] Griesinger's position as second-in-command to the *Landrat* would undoubtedly have exposed him to the appalling conditions that existed inside the walls of the fortress. It is impossible to know the sort of SS lectures, drills or other gatherings Griesinger would have attended in Ulm because, just as in other parts of the south-west, few records survive from the whole of 1935.[90]

In July 1935 Griesinger returned to Stuttgart to take up a position as a junior legal secretary at the Württemberg Police Department. Originally a luxury hotel, Hotel Silber became Stuttgart's chief post-office directorate after the First World War. In 1928, under the Weimar Republic, the Württemberg Police Department moved into the premises. For the young, ambitious lawyer seeking to secure a permanent and desirable position in the Ministry of the Interior, this was a step up. Soon after Hitler came to power, the Nazis began to take control of the state police agencies – and Württemberg was no exception.

On 9 December 1933 Himmler, already head of the SS and the Political Police Commander of Bavaria, was made commander of the Political Police in Württemberg. Himmler made changes to the police leadership in Württemberg, dismissing Dr Roller, the former deputy leader, and replacing him with Wilhelm Harster.[91] Roller's removal was out of the ordinary. Even though a significant number of men from the SS and SD took on new roles in the Political Police, no purge of the existing police ever took place. Committed Nazis formed only a small percentage of the organisation's work-force. Most police officials had risen through the ranks of the Weimar state police, ensuring continuity of personnel into the Nazi era.[92] By mid-1934 Himmler effectively controlled the functions of all police forces in Germany. In the first year of Griesinger's appointment at the Political Police, Himmler merged all the Political Police forces of the German states into a single unified organisation, which was henceforth known as the *Geheime Staatspolizei*, or Gestapo.

At the time of his transfer back to Stuttgart, Griesinger knew that competition for jobs was fierce and that there were far too many young graduates in law looking for work, without enough positions for all of them. In 1932, of the almost 13,000 legal apprentices and jurists eager to launch their careers, only 980 found positions in the legal profession.[93] Having secured a position at the Political Police, Griesinger was now firmly on course to climb the rungs of the civil service.

It was also around this time that he either began, or resumed, a love affair with Ingeborg Venzmer, the wife of Dr Gerhard Venzmer, a well-known doctor and the editor of *Kosmos*, a reputable science magazine. In July 1935 Ingeborg Venzmer happened to have her younger sister, Gisela, staying with her in the family house on the elegant Schottstrasse, in the north of the city, when Robert came to visit. This encounter changed the course of Griesinger's life.

Chapter VI

The SS Family

When they met, Robert was twenty-eight and Gisela was twenty-three. Both were finding their feet in Stuttgart during the third summer under the swastika. Gisela came from one of Hamburg's most distinguished families. Like Robert, she had also travelled outside Germany. When she was eighteen she had spent several months in England learning English, and as a child she had lived in Guatemala, where her father's brothers controlled Nottebohm Hermanos, a coffee producer that owned several plantations.[1] The company was led by Gisela's uncle, Friedrich Nottebohm, whose experience of internment during the Second World War and subsequent hearing at the International Court of Justice in The Hague has made his name renowned among specialists of international law.

The SS archives in Berlin gave me my first insight into Gisela. Curiously, the files did not refer to her as Gisela Nottebohm – the maiden name she had listed on documents that I had discovered in Prague, when I first set out to explore Griesinger's past. The woman who wanted to marry Robert Griesinger in October 1935 was called Gisela Grosser. This was because, at the time of their meeting, Gisela was married to somebody else. She had married Otto Grosser in Hamburg in 1931, aged nineteen, and was still married to him when Robert proposed to her on Saturday 7 September 1935. When Robert met her, Gisela was in the process of divorcing her husband because of the 'illicit relationships' Otto was having with other women.[2] Gisela described Otto's achingly long absences and his serial infidelity in her handwritten letters to SS authorities. In the second year of their marriage Gisela had tried to leave him, taking refuge at her parents' house in Liechtenstein, but Otto persuaded his young wife to return to Hamburg.

As I read the word 'Liechtenstein' in Griesinger's SS dossier, a tiny mystery was solved. Since first reading his papers, I had wondered about the relatives in Vaduz that Robert had visited in summer 1944, before returning to Prague. His SS file revealed that he had been visiting Gisela's parents, who had emigrated from Hamburg to Liechtenstein.[3] Gisela undoubtedly rued her decision to leave Liechtenstein in 1934 to give Otto a second chance. Once back in Hamburg, little changed. She was devastated when she discovered that Otto had been having more affairs. She left straight away, this time heading to her older sister Ingeborg's house in Stuttgart. The documents showed that she did not arrive alone. She was accompanied by her three-year-old son, Joachim.

The SS archives, which contained dozens of pages detailing the couple's relationship, did not reveal how Griesinger and Gisela first met. Fortunately, Jutta was able to fill in the gaps. Griesinger and Gisela's sister, Ingeborg, had been lovers when Gisela and little Joachim arrived in Stuttgart midway through 1935. Any feelings Robert might have held for Ingeborg vanished, so the story goes, as soon as he met her much younger sister. Gisela was beautiful, vivacious and fun. A photograph from this time shows her dancing on top of a piano. Griesinger was infatuated, and within weeks they were engaged.[4] Himmler's pressure on SS men to marry by the age of twenty-seven might have helped hasten the courtship. Already a year past the prescribed age, Griesinger may have felt it was in his best interests to settle down.[5]

Gisela first needed to secure a divorce, which was not easy in Nazi Germany in 1935. Only in 1938 did the Nazis relax divorce laws, to ensure that those wishing to remarry could produce more children in their new marital union.[6] In Robert, Gisela had luckily found someone who could help navigate the bureaucratic divorce process. Otto, a salesman, was no match for Robert and did not put up much of a fight. The Hamburg court ruled on 30 September 1935 that Otto was solely responsible for the breakdown of the marriage. In the weeks that followed, Gisela set about making a fresh start for her new life in Stuttgart. In preparation for her marriage to Robert, she buried every trace of her previous life as Frau Grosser.[7]

Ironically, Gisela's divorce was the only part of the wedding preparations that went to plan. SS officers were not free to marry whomever they pleased. The SS had passed an 'Engagement and Marriage Order' in January 1932 stipulating the requirements for all members seeking to marry, and over the next few years these became even more stringent. Himmler took a personal interest in ensuring that members of his elite order found spouses who lived up to his expectations; an SS officer was unable to marry without his direct consent.[8] To secure the future of the Reich, SS brides in theory had to be 'racially pure', have no hereditary diseases or illness and be able to bear at least four children. As a member of the SS since September 1933, Griesinger needed to obtain permission from the highest ranks of the organisation before announcing his engagement, let alone setting a wedding date. However, while the divorced mother might not have matched the ideal image of a virgin maiden worthy of marrying one of Himmler's SS supermen, in reality the ability for an SS wife to produce four strong healthy children took precedent.

Two and a half weeks after Gisela's marriage to Otto had been dissolved, Robert sent the couple's supporting evidence to the Main Office for Race and Settlement in Berlin, putting into motion the steps necessary to secure a wedding licence. An elaborate system was in place to test that Robert and Gisela were in good health, were descended from Aryan stock and that nothing was wrong with Gisela's fertility. Griesinger's request, in his wavy handwriting that was now so familiar to me, ended with the words 'Heil Hitler'.[9] It was the first time I had seen him write the words. It was impossible to tell whether he really meant it, or whether the expression was a routine salutation that happened without any reflection. By autumn 1935 'Heil Hitler' was firmly entrenched in everyday parlance and there were repercussions for people, especially those working in the civil service, who avoided using the term. Such new habits of self-presentation and expectation that were emerging in German society did not occur overnight. One low-ranking functionary was so self-conscious about using the greeting in his personal correspondence, that he kept quotation marks around 'Heil Hitler' for two years.[10]

Robert and Gisela were confident about the outcome of their marriage request. They were both in good health and Gisela, aged twenty-three and having already produced a healthy son, was seemingly fertile. Things did not, however, go smoothly. The drawn-out and invasive process interfered in Griesinger's career advancement and probably put a strain on the couple's relationship. It also exposed Robert's temper.

The SS demanded extensive proof to ensure that Gisela would be a worthy SS bride. They insisted on medical tests, photographs, the completion of lengthy forms and character references. They even wanted details about Otto, and asked Gisela to provide a copy of her former husband's birth certificate and details of his family.[11] On top of this, she also had to complete a full family tree going back four generations, in which she had to provide detailed information on her ancestors' illnesses and causes of death. A wedding could not go ahead without it, and the onus was on Gisela to deliver this material in its entirety. Should a single relative be omitted from the file, eyebrows would have been raised, leading to all sorts of speculation that the missing ancestor was not Aryan or suffered from a genetic illness.

Such strict controls that involved hours of paperwork could only tell the authorities whether anything existed in Gisela's lineage that might threaten the health or racial make-up of any future offspring with Robert. But it could not tell them whether she would be able to conceive again. After overcoming the bureaucratic hurdles, Gisela's body fell under scrutiny. As the progenitor of the next generation of SS leaders, tests were conducted on her to ensure she was able to produce healthy children. Such checks went far beyond a routine medical check-up at her local doctor's surgery. Gisela was subjected to a full examination by Dr Wilhelm Egloff, a fifty-year-old local orthopaedist, who was also a member of the SS medical corps and the doctor in charge of Griesinger's SS *Sturm*.[12] Before proceeding with the examination, Gisela signed away her right to doctor–patient confidentiality, granting Egloff the right to disclose his findings to the SS authorities. Decisions pertaining to her body were no longer a private affair. Egloff noted Gisela was petite (five feet four inches, and nine stone), with dark-brown eyes and 'simple' dark-blonde hair. Her skin was of an ivory colour and she walked without impediment. Crucially, he found nothing wrong with her hips or uterus and found her to menstruate normally. Egloff had a 'good' overall impression of Gisela. He noted that she was not pregnant, and that her future children would be desirable, from a *völkisch* perspective.[13]

With the physical part of the investigation complete, attention turned swiftly to Gisela's personality. She was instructed to name two people to comment on her character in the form of a written questionnaire. It was obvious, from the choice of names, that Gisela had little say on those selected. Robert handled the entire affair. Thinking it would make Gisela look favourable in the eyes of SS authorities, he chose SS Obersturmführer Walter Stahlecker, his fellow lawyer and then boss at the Gestapo, and Rottenführer Wilhelm Ströbel, an associate from the SS. The men had ten days in which to complete the questionnaires. Among the questions, the SS asked about the mental and physical health of Gisela's relatives, including whether anyone had committed or tried to commit suicide. Stahlecker and Ströbel were expected to conduct preliminary investigations before answering. In the event, both men found Gisela thrifty, reliable and fond of children. Ströbel noted that she was addicted to cleaning and that she was a good friend, albeit one who 'tended to dominate'. The two SS men ended the questionnaire by insisting that Gisela was an appropriate candidate to be an SS bride.[14]

All that remained was for the couple to send Berlin a selection of photographs of themselves. The authorities needed to confirm that their images matched the way Robert and Gisela described themselves in the forms, and to support Dr Egloff's findings on their physical appearance. As I turned to look at the images, I was wary of how personal or private these images might be. I had heard stories of couples having to provide images of themselves wearing only underwear or bathing suits. Fortunately, the files did not hold any explicit photographs or locks of hair, items that some couples submitted to the authorities.[15]

Like thousands of future SS brides, Gisela dressed up for the occasion. Her dark-blonde hair was parted at the side and she appeared elegant in her lace dress. She realised the importance of making a good impression for the authorities. In one full-length outdoor photo, she stood alone in front of a house. Another photograph showed Robert standing in exactly the same spot. The shots must have been taken seconds apart. I imagined Robert positioning Gisela in front of a window, instructing her to look into the lens and stand straight, without smiling. He might even have advised her on how to arrange her feet and hands. Once satisfied, he would have handed her the camera, before resuming the exact position she had just left. The act might possibly have occurred the other way round, with Gisela arranging the choreography. Ordinary Nazi couples across Germany played out scenes such as this thousands of times throughout the 1930s.

Robert and Gisela's attempts to marry occurred at a point when popular support for the Nazis was at an all-time low. In late 1935 and early 1936 it was still possible for some Germans to exhibit their dissatisfaction towards the regime. During the 1930s episodes of popular unrest arose that threatened to upset the Reich's delicate social order. The winter of 1935–6 was one such moment. Nazi rearmament policies had taken on a new lease of life in March 1935, when Hitler reintroduced conscription and established an air force. Spending on raw materials, essential for rearmament, had strained the Nazi economy. For the first time since taking office, the Nazis were unable to guarantee a suitable standard of living

The photograph Gisela Grosser submitted to the Main Office
for Race and Settlement to secure a marriage licence, 1935

for the bulk of the German population, who were steadily becoming
disenchanted.[16] At exactly the time that Robert and Gisela were
planning to build a life together, wages were suffering and the cost
of living was beginning to spiral rapidly. The Reich's Food Estate
was almost in disarray, as shortages reached crisis levels. Butter,

The photograph Robert Griesinger submitted to the Main Office for
Race and Settlement to secure a marriage licence, 1935

eggs and pork were practically nowhere to be found as the government, aiming for autarky (economic self-sufficiency and independence), refused to import agricultural products. The scarcity of
goods dominated conversation. In the same week that Robert and
Gisela applied for their marriage licence, radio messages were

transmitted aimed at German housewives, ordering them not to spend selfishly and to serve the nation by not sending their husband's hard-earned money abroad.[17] In this atmosphere, many questioned the government's capability of steering the ship out of dangerous waters. In early 1936 reports in Berlin showed the absence of the 'Heil Hitler' salute in the streets.[18]

As dissatisfaction reigned across Germany, Robert and Gisela had their own problems to deal with. Something had gone horribly wrong with their marriage application to the SS authorities. On 16 January Griesinger sent an urgent telegram to Berlin to enquire about its status. He was quick to inform officials that, 'for professional and personal reasons', the wedding was planned for the following week.[19] Within hours, officials at the Main Office for Race and Settlement had rejected his request. SS officials had an enormous backlog of marriage applications that required attention.[20] The rules were the same for everyone, and the Berlin authorities were not going to speed up the process at the demand of a mere *Rottenführer* from far-away Swabia.

Over the course of the two weeks that followed, Griesinger entered into an intense correspondence with officials. He sent messages to Berlin at least once a day, stating that his application needed 'to be hurried' and asked for 'immediate permission'. When his appeals were denied, he daringly responded that the wedding could not be postponed. In some of his letters his tone was angry. In others he showed signs of desperation. In one heated letter, Griesinger had written 'very urgent' four times at the top of the page. Uncharacteristically for someone so well educated, this letter was full of spelling mistakes.[21] Perhaps Griesinger's desire to settle down with Gisela prompted his incessant writing. It was also possible that Gisela was already pregnant with Robert's child. Griesinger would not have been the only SS member to find himself with a pregnant fiancée. In early 1936 Himmler was irate at the large number of SS members submitting requests for marriage to women who were already pregnant.[22]

But in fact Griesinger's urgency was entirely careerist. His appointment at the Ministry of the Interior was up for review at the time, and he believed putting himself forward as married, rather than single, would help his career prospects.[23] Griesinger was in luck. A week after receiving notification that he would become a permanent member of the Ministry of the Interior, the SS granted Robert and Gisela permission to marry. After having waited four months to complete the vetting process, February 1936 was truly a time to celebrate. Within a week the young couple married at the Gedächtniskirsche, a Protestant church in the north of Stuttgart, only a few minutes' walk away from the Venzmers' house.[24]

Like the overwhelming majority of SS members, including 80 per cent of the leadership, Griesinger was born a Protestant.[25] SS men were expected to leave the church upon joining the elite organisation. Officers who married in church ceremonies were known to have been mocked by other members of their unit.[26] While no evidence suggests that Griesinger was religious, he might have consented to a church wedding on Gisela's insistence, or to show deference to his parents and future in-laws, who might have preferred a religious wedding for tradition's sake. Gisela wore a white dress on the day. Robert, unlike so many of his comrades, did not get married wearing his SS uniform. He chose not to, out of respect for his father, who made little secret of his disdain for the SS. And unlike the more zealous members of the SS, Robert did not take out an advert to announce his wedding in *Das Schwarze Korps*, the national SS newspaper.[27] His closest SS comrades knew about the wedding, having either been invited to the ceremony or having been present to welcome Gisela to their *Sturm* during her initiation as a new SS bride.

*

'Do you remember him?' I asked Barbara, Griesinger's youngest daughter as we sat in her living room looking at old photos. She shook her head. 'I don't remember him at all.' Barbara was five when her father died. Six months after my first meeting with Jutta, I had arranged to meet Barbara and her husband, Fritz, at their home close to Nuremberg. Only two people were waiting on the platform as the train pulled into Heilsbronn station. Fritz sped towards me and greeted me excitedly. He was a short, slim man in his early eighties, wearing a blue plaid shirt. Barbara was a couple of steps behind and was more reserved than her lively husband. She bore some resemblance to Jutta, but she did not look like their father. Barbara had short white hair and light eyes, which were covered by a thick pair of glasses.

Fritz and Barbara's house was in the middle of a row of small post-war houses, each having its own distinctive façade, with different-sized ornaments and plant pots. Inside, I paused to look at a picture that hung on the wall. Unlike at Jutta's house, which did not have any images of Griesinger on display, here a large portrait of Robert as a little boy was unmissable. As I sat down, Barbara placed a handful of old photos on the table to show me.

Robert and Gisela's wedding day lunch, 11 February 1936.
From left to right: Wally Griesinger, Hermann Nottebohm,
Gisela, Robert, Harriet Nottebohm, Adolf Griesinger. The girl
on the bottom left is Ingeborg Venzmer's daughter, Marion.

She also handed me her parents' wedding book (*Familienstammbuch*), saying it was all she had from her father. As in so many families, Robert and Gisela's papers, heirlooms and objects were separated after their death and divided haphazardly among their children.

Barbara told me she had been very sick during the war. 'I had tuberculosis and deforming bones: I spent a lot of time in bed.' When she spoke, her voice was quiet, soft and vulnerable. As a result of her early illnesses, she has enormous gaps in her childhood memories. She knew her father only from pictures and stories that she had heard. But even these were few and far between.

I decided to ask her about what she termed 'the almost unbelievable story' of the chair, and if she had a theory about how the documents came to be hidden inside. 'I think it was him,' she said calmly. Ever since Jutta had written to her informing her of the discovery, Barbara had had time to think up a scenario that made sense to her. She and her husband had read up on what it was like to be a German in Prague in May 1945. They were under no illusions about the dangers Griesinger faced. Barbara described a scene in which a scared and frantic Robert was in the house on the day of the Prague Uprising. Wanting to hide his identity papers and his uncashed stocks-and-shares receipts for his family, he somehow opened the cushion and placed the documents inside. But she thought he must have told someone where they were – 'he couldn't have just put them there', without telling anyone. In Barbara's mind, the concealment of the papers had to stem from a rational decision.

The wedding book was a small tome of just a few pages, listing details of Griesinger's marriage to Gisela in February 1936 and the birth of their children. 'Their marriage was the product of many months of hard work,' I remarked as I turned the pages, remembering the stacks of papers I had sifted through in the SS archives when I followed Robert and Gisela's efforts to marry. 'The SS did not make life easy for your parents.'

Fritz swiftly leapt in. 'I think you mean the Nazi party,' he said, visibly startled upon hearing mention of the SS.

'No,' I replied, before turning to Barbara. 'Your father was an SS member. Please say you knew this detail already? I presumed Jutta would have told you.'

Silence. Barbara and Fritz looked at each other across the table. Fritz promptly got up and walked round to put his hand on Barbara's shoulder. I looked on and felt I was an unwelcome addition to this intimate act. I was an unfamiliar person, bringing them disturbing information about their family. They were clearly finding difficult the dual process of grappling with this revelation and responding to the stranger sitting across from them.

'This is a surprise,' Barbara said finally. 'When you say the SS made life hard for my parents, what did you mean exactly?'

I handed Barbara some of the documents I had discovered in the SS archives. They included the letters Griesinger had written to the SS authorities requesting permission for his marriage to Gisela to go ahead. Fritz attempted to turn a negative into a positive, seeing the lengthy process as proof that Griesinger intended to fight to marry the woman he loved.

'It was amazing he stuck by Gisela,' said Fritz, nodding his head as he read his father-in-law's letters. 'When he saw the difficulties, he could have walked away and left her, but he did not. In this respect, he was an honourable man.'

Fritz was partially correct. Other SS members did break off their marriage applications because of similar technicalities.[28] I admired Fritz for wanting to try to smooth things over. Throughout our time together, he was the chattier of the two. A man who appeared much younger than his eighty years, Fritz often interrupted discussions of Griesinger to inject anecdotes of his own, ranging from his own childhood memories of the war, to his love of dogs, bicycles and caravan holidays. Barbara's sentences were crisp and thoughtful. Only occasionally did she ask a question. This was her first opportunity to learn actively about her parents and her family history, and she was trying to make sense of the various strands that, when brought together, produced a formidable image of a man she did not know, but whose presence had hung over her for more than seventy years.

Barbara remained silent as she sat reading her father's letters. I asked her whether she had ever seen her father's handwriting before. 'Yes,' she said, 'but not often.'

'Do you feel anything when you see it?'

Barbara looked down again at the page. 'Somehow he is a stranger to me.'

★

Gisela and Robert's wedding took place midway through the ten-day 1936 Winter Olympics that were held in Bavaria. The Nazis saw the Winter Olympics as a dress rehearsal for the summer Games, which were to take place in Berlin later in the year. With the eyes of the world upon them, the new regime could not afford for anything to go wrong. At a time when the Nazi leadership was seeking to strengthen and rebuild the country, it was vital to develop and maintain diplomatic relations with other world powers.

In February 1936 Hitler had not yet embarked on an expansionist or aggressive foreign policy. Once he did, he gave little consideration to what the world thought of his domestic agenda. But in early 1936 international opinion mattered to Hitler. Around the time of the Games he refrained from violent antisemitic speeches, and the party saw to it that the antisemitic violence that marked the regime's first two and a half years subsided. While racial laws against Jews remained in place, a lull in anti-Jewish outbursts ensured a period of relative order and restraint until early 1938. Even when a Croatian Jewish medical student assassinated Wilhelm Gustloff, leader of the Swiss branch of the Nazi party, two days before Hitler officially opened the Games, the Nazi leadership expressly banned antisemitic demonstrations and rallies, and Hitler toned down his rhetoric in his speech at Gustloff's funeral.[29] The Nazis could not risk the consequences of violent antisemitic attacks in front of the thousands of foreigners who had travelled to Germany.

With 650,000 people in attendance, Bavaria was packed to capacity with tourists sleeping in hotel corridors and bars, eager to watch the twenty-eight-nation tournament.[30] It was crucial to maintain the new Germany's image as a welcoming, peaceful nation. In the build-up to the Games, traces of antisemitic propaganda disappeared. In January officials removed antisemitic billboards on the 'Olympic Road' connecting Munich to Garmisch-Partenkirchen – the two villages where the Games were held – with adverts for Coca-Cola swiftly taking their place. Printed notices across almost every village in Upper Bavaria stating that 'Jews are not wanted here' were promptly removed. So too were the warnings on speed-limit signs that gave Jews special exemption from keeping to the limits, fatefully enticing them to drive faster in hazardous conditions.[31] Germany's inclusion of the Jewish athlete Rudi Ball to represent the country in the ice-hockey team was widely publicised. The Nazis wanted the 500 foreign journalists to report back that earlier accounts of German antisemitism were grossly exaggerated. Covering the Games, US journalist William Shirer reprimanded scores of foreign correspondents who fell for the Nazis' trick.[32]

At the time of Robert and Gisela's wedding, public discontent with the Nazis had begun to dwindle. Hitler's personal intervention ensured the release of foreign exchange for imports, which went some way towards improving the cost of living. Added to this was the jubilation that accompanied the German reoccupation of the Rhineland in March 1936, when 10,000 soldiers restored full German sovereignty to the territory, in violation of the Treaty of Versailles. Hitler's popularity immediately surged. By summer 1936 a combination of increased employment and the reappearance of consumer goods at affordable prices put an end to popular irritation against shortages.[33]

Robert and Gisela began their married life together in a changing Germany, and the contours of their social world closely followed those of the Gestapo and the SS. By this point Griesinger had been working alongside some of the most notorious Nazis at the Gestapo for seven months – though at the time the organisation was still known as the Württemberg Political Police. Post-war legal sources from the Nuremberg Trials shed light on the Griesingers' social networks at the Hotel Silber, which would have been helped by Griesinger's university connections. Fellow Gestapo lawyers Walter Stahlecker and Rudolf Bilfinger, each the son of a Protestant pastor, had studied law at Tübingen. Bilfinger was in Griesinger's cohort, whereas Stahlecker was a few years ahead. While in custody after the war Bilfinger was interviewed by Lieutenant-Colonel Smith W. Brookhart Jr, a rock-jawed criminal lawyer and the son of a Republican senator from Iowa, who was already experienced at interrogating dozens of leading Nazis.

Brookhart's notes from his interrogation sessions with Bilfinger reveal that the men in Griesinger's bureau, each of whom subscribed to a Protestant-nationalist worldview, were more than just colleagues. They forged lasting friendships and enjoyed outings with their wives and children away from the Hotel Silber. Gisela would have been expected to befriend the wives of the four other lawyers, who often socialised without their husbands.[34] In the summer of 1939 Stahlecker named his daughter Gisela. Despite their organisation's sinister and secretive reputation, Griesinger and his colleagues led unremarkable, public-facing lives. Each of these ordinary Nazis – even Stahlecker, the head of the Gestapo in Stuttgart – was easily traceable. As I sat in Stuttgart's city archives and scrolled through the dusty public city directories from 1936 and 1937, I had no trouble finding the men's home addresses, phone numbers and the names of their neighbours.

At the Hotel Silber Griesinger's work covered all areas of Gestapo business. Civil servants entering the Gestapo from the government administration had the power to distribute orders to police detectives without ever having been one.[35] Griesinger kept up to date with the passing of new laws and made them known to detectives across Württemberg. Due to the sensitive nature of the Gestapo's work, its agents had to choose their words carefully. Compromising information was not put in writing. Officials who received Griesinger's letters were expected to read in between the lines. For example, in a study of 19,000 case files compiled by the Gestapo of Würzburg, which represents one of only two surviving local collections in the whole of Germany, not a single document mentions the torture methods carried out by the Gestapo on suspected opponents of the regime. They do not even refer to torture by its official name, using instead the description 'intensified interrogation', which left little to the imagination of local police agents.[36]

The Württemberg Gestapo had exercised its ruthless tactics for more than two years when Griesinger joined in summer 1935. Initially the Gestapo focused its attention principally on the regime's political opponents, the Communists and the Social Democrats. In

the years 1933–5 the organisation, aided by regular informers, infiltrated the Communists' and Social Democrats' clandestine organisations, learning about their structures, branches and members
and, eventually, smashed them apart. Round-ups and incarcerations
followed, forcing leaders and activists into exile abroad. Lilo
Herrmann, the mother of a small child, was among the last of
Stuttgart's Communists to be captured. In late 1935 Stahlecker
ordered the arrest of the twenty-six-year-old, who was detained for
passing on plans of German rearmament to contacts in Switzerland.
Herrmann was incarcerated in Stuttgart for eighteen months, where
she endured harsh interrogation. She was found guilty of treason
and was guillotined, becoming the first woman to be executed by
the Nazi regime.[37]

In the absence of material, it is impossible to determine
Griesinger's involvement in tracking Lilo Herrmann and the three
other members of her Communist cell during the autumn of 1935.
But he was, at the very least, indirectly involved in their capture.[38]
In Stuttgart, Griesinger was a bureaucrat who could ignore the
human consequences that his work had on its victims. Though he
did not participate in the more brutal aspects of the Gestapo's
work, such as physically interacting with detainees and taking part
in the interrogations, he was nonetheless responsible for measures
that it carried out. The orders to bring in suspected enemies of the
state for questioning had his fingerprints all over them. He would
have been all too aware of what happened to thousands of men
and women in the torture cells beneath him, as he typed away at
his desk in the Hotel Silber.

Much of the success of the Gestapo in conducting arrests and
incarcerating opponents stemmed from the aura surrounding it.
Stories of brutal police raids and interrogations circulated rapidly
as the Nazis clamped down on their political opponents. Barely a
month after taking power, the Reichstag Fire Decree of 28 February
1933 made it possible for police forces to arrest Communist and
Socialist suspects arbitrarily and hold them in 'protective custody'.
Without the means to cope with the increased number of prisoners
in existing penitentiaries, the Nazis set up concentration camps in

which to intern their political opponents. Dachau, the first concentration camp, was created in March 1933 just outside Munich. By April 1933 officials in Württemberg had sent 1,902 Communists, Socialists and trade unionists to the Heuberg concentration camp. By the end of the year the camp held 15,000 prisoners.[39] Throughout 1933 it is estimated that 100,000 perceived leftist opponents were arrested and detained in Germany.[40]

By the time Griesinger joined the Gestapo in summer 1935 people in Germany were familiar with its ruthless tactics, and believed the propaganda concerning the extent of the organisation's reach and powers. Not only was it thought that the Gestapo encompassed an 'army' of spies, but also that it had an extensive network of paid informers in place who, as trained agents, were the organisation's eyes and ears in every restaurant, train carriage and street corner. In reality, things were not as they seemed. The 200 employees at the Hotel Silber lacked the manpower to monitor properly the activities of the almost three million inhabitants of Württemberg. Instead, just as elsewhere in Germany, suspects were brought to the Gestapo's attention by denunciation. As some locals denounced their neighbours out of envy, others willingly supported the exclusion of people from the so-called *Volksgemeinschaft* or racial community. Some were so scared of the regime that they denounced friends, neighbours and sometimes relatives to prevent their own arrest and interrogation at the Hotel Silber.[41]

It was only after local sections of the Communists, Social Democrats and trade Unionists had been smashed that the Gestapo turned its attention elsewhere. Jews and other perceived asocial elements – including homosexuals, Freemasons, Sinti and Roma (then known as Gypsies) – became targets. Griesinger's appointment in summer 1935 coincided with this new phase. Within weeks the Nazis passed the infamous Nuremberg Laws, which defined who was a Jew and set into law a series of measures that aimed to exclude them from German social, economic and cultural life. While before summer 1935 reports against Jews were handled by the local party or the SA, the publicity surrounding the Nuremberg Laws ensured that from autumn 1935 onwards the secret police was called upon to investigate Jews' perceived illegal acts.[42] From this point on, surveillance on the 8,000 Jews living in Württemberg increased drastically. Officials at the Hotel Silber gathered and analysed information about Jews, tracking their daily movements and networks. It fell to the Gestapo's legal specialists, such as Griesinger, to make the Nazis' anti-Jewish position and decrees known across the region.

His mother's newspaper clippings and the intense anti-Jewish environment at Tübingen suggest that Griesinger's position on Jews was indistinguishable from that of Stahlecker, Harster and the other lawyers at the Gestapo, and from associates at the local SS and SD, with whom he also interacted. One of the Gestapo lawyers, Rudolf Bilfinger, who had joined the Nazi party even before the Beer Hall Putsch in 1923, came from a family that included a number of notorious antisemites. His uncle, the influential lawyer Carl Bilfinger, once famously threatened the editor of a journal that unless it sacked its Jewish co-editor, he would no longer write for them.[43] The ferocious antisemitism of the men within Griesinger's immediate circle, almost all of whom came from upper-middle-class Protestant families, was beyond doubt.[44] Only a few years later, during the Second World War, most of these men, who had started out as ordinary Nazis before working their way up the party hierarchy, murdered hundreds of thousands of Jews when they led killing squads in the east.

Among the surviving reports that Griesinger drafted in the weeks following his engagement to Gisela are two with the coded heading 'No. 5'. Because so few of the Gestapo's archives have survived, it is only in the last few years that historians in Stuttgart have established that this was the code for Jewish Affairs.[45] One report detailed the channels necessary to prevent non-Aryans from transferring their property abroad illegally, while the other banned Jewish artists from having pseudonyms or stage names that supposedly disguised their Jewishness. In May 1937, four months after becoming a father, Griesinger sent out a report stating that there had been appalling violations of the law forbidding sexual relations between Jewish guests and Aryan employees (*Rassenschande*) at Jewish hotels, sanatoria and pensions. He asked the police to investigate. A few months later he sent another report affirming that it was illegal for Aryans married to Jews to fly the national flag.[46] His instructions were sent to police across the region, irrespective of whether the area had any Jewish inhabitants.[47]

During his time administering Jewish Affairs at the Gestapo, Griesinger was probably involved in a legal case concerning a twenty-year-old Jewish architectural student that threatened German-American relations. The affair began in the basement of the Hotel Silber, when, in late 1936, Stahlecker's men arrested Helmut Hirsch, an American citizen, and brought him to Griesinger's place of work for interrogation, after the student was suspected of attempting to kill the influential Nazi Julius Streicher, Gauleiter of Franconia, at the Nuremberg Nazi Party Rally Grounds. Despite the American government's efforts to save his life, Hirsch was the first American citizen executed under Nazi law.[48]

Griesinger's work at the Gestapo rendered him a significant link in the chain of the Nazi police state. He was good at his job and was written about in favourable, albeit not glowing terms by his bosses, who supported his dossier when he was up for promotion in spring 1936. 'A very good worker', 'diligent' and 'reliable' were some of the words used to describe him. They also wrote that Griesinger had never been a member of a political movement or party.[49] Despite not being a member of the party – a moratorium on accepting new members remained in place between 1933 and 1937 – Robert was promoted from a junior legal secretary to a senior civil servant (*Regierungsrat*) after just a year in the job.

Away from the Gestapo, Griesinger continued to participate in the SS. By the time he returned to Stuttgart in July 1935, the SS had evolved into an important piece of state apparatus. It was no longer the same burgeoning and exploratory organisation that Griesinger encountered during his professional stints in Urach and Tettnang. Rather, it had undergone intense restructuring, which led to changes in the leadership and the creation in January 1935 of an SS Main Office (*SS-Hauptamt*), the primary command centre for the organisation. After the Main Office was set up, the SS became more centralised and bureaucratically better organised. Its tasks expanded, which gave the organisation a renewed purpose. In the years that followed, it continued to evolve.

After the SS broke away from the SA, following the Night of the Long Knives in early summer 1934, Himmler organised a thorough 'house-cleaning' to weed out new members whose behaviour he considered anathema to the interests of the organisation. By 1935, 60,000 men had been removed, accused of an array of breaches that included alcoholism, homosexuality, inadequate physique, questionable racial or political backgrounds and even simply a general lack of commitment to the SS.[50] Griesinger was not among those excluded. During the two and a half years that he worked at the Württemberg Gestapo, SS Rottenführer Robert Griesinger was a regular contributor to his SS *Sturm*. Under the leadership of SS Sturmführer Steidle, *Sturm* 1/Mo/10 met every Wednesday and Friday evening for two hours, first at Wörthstrasse 26 on the site of a former chocolate factory and later at Königstrasse 1, both in central Stuttgart. They also met once a month on a Sunday.[51]

Even though the SS in Stuttgart destroyed all its records in April 1945, it remains possible to get an idea of what went on at a typical SS meeting, thanks to the existence of surviving records from the SS in Karlsruhe, the largest city after Stuttgart that also fell under the auspices of the SS Main District South-West (*SS-Oberabschnitt Südwest*). Just as in secluded Tettnang, urban meetings involved indoor shooting, marching, singing and exercise. When Griesinger met his unit on a Sunday at the *Morgenfeier* (morning celebration) – the Nazis' alternative to church services – the meeting was neatly choreographed into four parts. In one such meeting, members first heard Beethoven, Wagner or Grieg performed by a local SS orchestra. Second, they listened to a reading of a classic text of Nazi ideology, either Hitler's *Mein Kampf* or Alfred Rosenberg's *The Myth of the Twentieth Century*. In the third part, members first listened to a forty-five-minute lecture on a subject relating to the positive aspects of the SS, before turning to discuss race-blood and heredity, SS wives and party ideology. Finally, the meeting ended with another musical performance or song.[52]

Beyond the bi-weekly meetings at their *Sturm*, SS members in Stuttgart were also required to participate in a host of other activities across the city. Attending evening lectures was one such obligation. It is likely that Griesinger attended a 1936 talk on links between the *Wehrmacht* and the SS, given by Erasmus von Malsen-Ponickau, the chief SS officer in Stuttgart, at which all senior SS members were present. In his lecture Malsen-Ponickau, the former police chief of Nuremberg, spoke of the SS as the natural successor to the heroic German soldiers of the First World War.[53] Lectures were not the only space in which the First World War was invoked: the memory of the war was brought up at every opportunity. Adolf Laux, a member of Griesinger's *Sturm*, even founded a local SS group to ski in summer, in honour of Stuttgart's fallen soldiers.[54]

The physical protection of senior Nazi officials at party meetings and rallies remained a core feature of SS activity, and Griesinger will have shared these duties. When leading figures visited Stuttgart, uniformed members of the *Allgemeine SS*, such as Griesinger, acted as auxiliary policemen, guarding doors and forming human cordons to line the streets to shield them from political opponents. Unlike 1925, when the SS in Württemberg failed to muster ten men to protect Hitler, by the mid-1930s SS leaders were able to deploy hundreds of men to uphold the safety of guests. On the occasion of the visit to Stuttgart of Wilhelm Frick, Reich Minister of the Interior, and Rudolf Hess, Deputy Führer, it fell to Ludolf-Hermann von Alvensleben of the local SS to organise the security measures. Alvensleben, a radical Nazi who in 1939 murdered a relative he thought associated too much with Jews and Poles, arranged for 100 SS men from Stuttgart to be present at the airport alone, and for a further 400 to guard key buildings in the city centre during the men's visit.[55] Even though documentation does not survive, it is probable that Alvensleben's security plans went even further for the visit of Hitler in April 1938.

SS wives, meanwhile, were expected to contribute to the elite SS 'community of kinship' (*Sippengemeinschaft*). Upon marriage, an initiation ceremony took place to welcome an SS wife. When a couple had a baby, a similar initiation, which replaced Christian

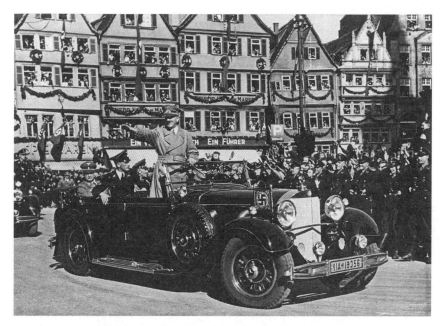

Adolf Hitler's visit to Stuttgart 1 April 1938

baptism, took place for the newborn. Thereafter, to cultivate a sense of belonging and understand their new community and responsibilities, SS authorities encouraged members' wives to attend SS family nights (*Sippenabend*). A family night was divided into two parts. The first part, which was more ideological, involved a speech on the SS as a 'community of kinship' or a visit to a museum. The second part was more informal. SS men and their wives were encouraged to bond with other SS families through discussion, singing and dancing.[56] Other events were also open to members' families and friends, and some of them had little to do with SS ideology. Instead these social gatherings were geared to appeal to the highly educated background of the typical SS member. In January 1936 the SS sub-district for Stuttgart, *Abschnitt X*, organised a Beethoven recital at the majestic Liederhalle concert hall in the city centre as part of *Winterhilfswerk*, the Nazis' Winter Relief drive. The evening performance showcased the SS's cultural and artistic mission in all its glory. It featured some of the most popular musicians of the day, including the conductor Rudolf Schulz-Dornburg and the distinguished tenor Karl Erb. Such grand public celebrations were places for ordinary members and their wives to participate in, and build, the SS's 'community of kinship'. The Beethoven recital was scheduled for the day Gisela and Robert were supposed to marry, before complications with Gisela's forms at the SS Main Office for Race and Settlement led to the postponement of their wedding.[57]

The SS in Stuttgart's annual St Nicholas Day event on 6 December offered another opportunity for Robert and Gisela to mingle with other SS couples and their children. Fatherhood was central to the expanding SS community, and the SS man was expected to adopt multiple paternal responsibilities, which ranged from changing the newborn's nappy to pushing him or her in the pram. Each *Sturm* was even supposed to have one or more communal prams to provide to its members, with some decorated with swastikas and runes. For an SS man to show affection by holding or playing with his children was not seen as unmanly or in any way shameful. If anything, assisting his wife with domestic tasks and spending time with his children was the duty of a 'genuine man and a proper husband' and was to be encouraged.[58]

Robert and Gisela might have attended the St Nicholas Day celebrations in 1935 and 1936 with Gisela's son, Joachim, and from 1937 with Jutta. Along with the other women present, Gisela might have helped the *Pelzmarte* – the Swabian St Nicholas – distribute gifts to children, before listening to Malsen-Ponickau's speech to SS wives, reminding them of their important role as female members of the Nazi racial elite.[59] Sport remained as important as ever in the formation of the new SS man. The local SS branch in Stuttgart organised public sporting festivals at which members paraded and competed against other local teams and organisations. On one occasion 5,000 SS men, their wives and other visitors crammed into an arena in Stuttgart to watch a handball tournament in which the SS beat the local police 3–2 and a local SA formation 2–1. At an equestrian tournament, the SS won first prize in show jumping and dressage.[60]

Griesinger holding Jutta in his arms while visiting his
parents, *c.* 1939

Even though Griesinger needed to take part in the minimum
number of SS activities necessary to retain his membership, it is
unlikely that he went above and beyond this amount. Just as in
his work at the Gestapo, he did not want to stand out: he wanted
to conform. Whereas Alfred Filbert, an SS member in Berlin born
at the same time as Griesinger, who also had a doctorate in law,
achieved five substantial promotions in two and a half years,
Griesinger managed only two modest promotions in the SS
between 1934 and 1938.[61] Despite his connections at the Stuttgart

Gestapo and among the city's Tübingen alumni in the SS and its security and intelligence service the SD, by autumn 1938 Griesinger had only reached the non-commissioned rank of *Scharführer*. Unlike the other lawyers at the Stuttgart Gestapo, he was not recruited for a permanent position in the SD.[62] Such sluggish progress suggests he was lacking the desire to move up in the organisation. Griesinger was not an SS militant at this time. He was not tempted to relinquish his status as a civil servant and dedicate his life to the service of the SS. It is more likely that he recognised that the prestige of belonging to such an elite organisation brought him exciting potential for career advancement within the civil service. Legal matters at the Gestapo, and settling down to family routine with Gisela, took precedence in the life of this ordinary Nazi.

Changes in personnel occurred at the Gestapo in 1937, which affected Griesinger. Walter Stahlecker, Wilhelm Harster and Rudolf Bilfinger – among his three closest colleagues – left Stuttgart to take up positions elsewhere in the SS and Gestapo. Griesinger left the Gestapo and returned to the Ministry of the Interior in autumn 1937, months after joining the Nazi party on 1 May, the very date that the moratorium on accepting new members was lifted.

Because evidence does not survive, it is possible only to speculate on the reasons behind his departure from the Gestapo. Did Griesinger leave the organisation because he objected to its abhorrent tactics? It seems unlikely. Throughout his two and a half years at the Hotel Silber Griesinger epitomised the desktop perpetrator (*Schreibtischtäter*) who continued his work unfazed by its consequences. Had he opposed the brutal methods that were carried out, in part, as a result of orders signed in his name, he probably would not have lasted quite as long. It might be that he rubbed up one of his new superiors the wrong way, which led to his transfer. However, none of the earlier reports about him even hints that Griesinger might be insubordinate. He might have transferred to fill a gap in personnel elsewhere. Or perhaps he might have been affected by the loss of Stahlecker, Harster and Bilfinger, his core colleagues in the legal team at the Gestapo. Their replacements were neither natives of Württemberg nor did they attend Tübingen university.[63] Perhaps he felt it was the right time to move on.

After their wedding on 11 February 1936, Robert and Gisela moved into his parents' house in the south of Stuttgart. Six weeks later they moved into a rented house on Schottstrasse.[64] The Griesingers were already familiar with the street. Before they married, Gisela lived with her sister Ingeborg and her family at Schottstrasse 22. At the time of their wedding, Robert and Gisela owned few possessions. When Gisela appeared in Stuttgart in 1935, having left her husband behind in the marital home in Hamburg, she arrived with little. For his part, Robert entered married life straight from the comforts of his parents' house. In early 1936 the newly-weds needed to begin filling their new home with furniture to build their lives together, and receipts from a removals company showed that Robert and Gisela bought bed frames, tables, bookcases and other pieces.[65]

The acquisition of furniture came at some expense. Even though Griesinger earned more than most ordinary workers, civil servants did not have a huge amount of spending power in the mid-1930s. Their wages were badly hit by Chancellor Brüning's deflationary budget cuts of 1931, which were still in place in 1936.[66] However, Robert and Gisela were in luck. Not only did the couple come from families with considerable financial means, but the Nazis' introduction of a marriage loan in 1933, which was intended to increase the birth rate of racially pure Aryan families and reduce the number of women in the workforce, provided an additional source of capital to ease the pressure on newly-weds just starting out. This interest-free loan of up to 1,000 RM was paid to couples on the condition that the wife did not take up employment. For every baby born to the family, the debt was reduced by a quarter, ensuring that the loan was written off after the birth of the fourth child.[67] Rather than cash handouts, couples received vouchers with which to buy household goods and furniture. 1,000 RM, which today would be worth £17,600, was more than double Griesinger's monthly salary. If the newly-weds spent sensibly, they could stretch the loan quite far. In early 1936 the cheapest Siemens vacuum cleaner started at 69 RM, a decent radio cost 145 RM and a camera was around 125 RM.[68]

It is possible that among the Griesingers' new furnishings were items previously owned by Jewish families. All over Germany, the homes of SS officers and Gestapo agents became filled with the furniture left behind by Jews forced to emigrate, who had also had to sell their belongings in order to pay the exorbitant Reich Flight Tax.[69] At the time the Griesingers moved to the neighbourhood, around 100 Jews were leaving Stuttgart every month.[70] Yet records reveal that when the Griesingers moved in, their next-door neighbours were a Jewish couple: Fritz and Helene Rothschild.[71] It seemed incredible that Dr Robert Griesinger, SS officer and Gestapo employee, had Jewish neighbours, and so on a trip to Stuttgart I decided to visit the street where both families lived.

I began by calling Herr and Frau Schulz, the current residents of the Griesinger house on Schottstrasse.[72] I hoped to arrange a meeting to visit the house, but within seconds of Frau Schulz answering the phone, I began to regret my decision. 'We don't want anything to do with this sort of history,' she said, sounding quite angry. I tried to persuade her, telling her that I would not take any photos and that it would be a quick five-minute visit, but she refused outright to budge on her decision. 'We don't want to see our house appear in a book about the Nazis. It is simply out of the question.' As luck would have it, Herr Schulz arrived home at that very moment. I listened as Frau Schulz began to explain to her husband the purpose of my phone call, but the line went muffled as she put her hand over the receiver. I could make out strong words being exchanged between husband and wife. A few moments later, Frau Schulz came back on the line. 'You're in luck,' she said, a bite to her voice. 'My husband seems more willing than I do to meet you. Come over tomorrow at seven p.m., but remember, no photos.'

Schottstrasse was located on a northern hilltop overlooking Stuttgart. It was a sleepy residential part of the city, with just a handful of people in the streets and only a few vehicles on the roads, and it had avoided being bombed during the war. As I approached the street, it became clear that I was entering a more affluent part of Stuttgart. The large villas, and the cars parked in front, were far grander than any I had seen elsewhere. As I was early, I took the opportunity to walk around the neighbourhood. From the Griesinger house, it took under two minutes to reach the former residence of the Venzmer family at Schottstrasse 22, a striking modernist house with a white stucco finish in which Robert and Gisela first met.

I continued down a hill to look at the house on Gähkopf of Wilhelm Ströbel, Griesinger's associate from the SS, who had written a character reference for Gisela in which he suggested that she would make a good SS wife. As I stood outside, the neighbour asked if I was lost. I explained that I was interested in a former resident. Without prompting, the man asked if I was looking for a Jewish family. 'A lot of Jews lived in this area before the war,' he told me. I decided against revealing that I was looking for the home of a former member of the SS and continued on my stroll. Thanks to a recent initiative, current residents of the neighbourhood regularly remember the Jewish families who once lived on these streets. Today Stuttgart has hundreds of *Stolpersteine* (literally stumbling blocks), small metal plaques on the pavement outside a residence in which a Jewish family lived, before being deported. The shiny blocks record the names of the houses' former Jewish residents, the date they were deported and the location of their extermination. Eighty-nine *Stolpersteine* commemorate the deported Jewish residents in Griesinger's immediate area of Stuttgart alone.[73] On my walk I counted half a dozen within a stone's throw of his front door.

Griesinger's house on Schottstrasse was a single building that contained three separate residences. Together with the house next door, which was designed by the same modernist architect, Ernst Wagner, it stood out from the street's other structures. Painted somewhere between salmon pink and peach, it was built in the 1930s, much later than the neighbouring properties. Wagner's two houses were among the very last multi-family row houses constructed in Stuttgart. Multi-family houses with communal facilities, popular in the 1920s, did not sit well with the ideology of the Third Reich. As soon as the Nazis came to power, they set about dismantling cooperative housing projects, which for them epitomised Communism and decadent urban living, and looked instead to promote single-family dwellings that encouraged privacy. That Griesinger moved to Schottstrasse in 1936 suggests he was not too put off by the regime's stance on multi-family houses.[74]

As part of his design, Wagner paid homage to Stuttgart's proud local past by creating, on the wall that faces the street, a beautiful mural of the Grimm Brothers' 'The Seven Swabians' fairy tale. In September 1936 *Moderne Bauformen*, an architectural magazine, ran a special feature on Wagner. The article included a seven-page report, accompanied by twelve photographs, on his adjacent houses on Schottstrasse. Out of every building in Germany chosen as an icon of modern living, Griesinger's house fell under the microscope. Images of the houses' interiors shed light on the residents' style and tastes. One chair, located in the background of one of the pictures, caught my eye. It looked similar to the one containing Griesinger's documents.

Griesinger's house on Schottstrasse, *c.* 1936

When I arrived at Griesinger's marital home, it was a beautiful spring evening. Herr and Frau Schulz stood waiting for me at the entrance. Each time Griesinger opened his front door, he was greeted with a view of Stuttgart's old town, made up of its late-Gothic buildings and churches. He could also see the city's striking modern buildings, which had sprung up the decade before. As we stood on the doorstep, the Schulzes told me they had never heard of Griesinger. I asked whether there might be anything in the attic or cellar that belonged to any of the house's previous occupiers, but they insisted there was nothing.

The house's main habitable area was spread over two floors. Frau Schulz made it clear that I would not have access to the top floor, which contained the sleeping area, and she also reminded me not to take any photographs inside the house.

In the seventeen years they had lived there, the Schulzes had made their house on Schottstrasse into a beautiful home. A lot of thought had gone into decorating the space. Various vintage design pieces were arranged across the rooms. Handsome rugs covered the original wooden flooring. From the two large windows in the main living area it was possible to see the whole of Stuttgart. If there had been a ceremony in January 1937 to welcome the newborn Jutta into the SS-family community, it would have taken place in this very room. With the room filled with Griesinger's SS comrades, Robert would have made sure to abide by SS guidelines, which stated the importance of decorating the room in flowers and fir sprigs.[75] Remarkably, only the kitchen had undergone any significant building work since the time of the house's construction, and even here there seemed only to have been minor changes. Thanks to Herr Schulz's professional curiosity, I was able to see exactly how the space was arranged in the mid-1930s, for upon moving in, Schulz, an architect, acquired the house's original blueprints and floor plans. In advance of my visit, he had carefully arranged them on the dining-room table for me, in a corner of the room partially sealed off behind a glass frame – itself an original feature.

Unlike so many German homes in the 1930s, the Griesingers' house would not have had coal or wood piles taking up space in the kitchen or lying outside the back door. The plans showed that the house was equipped with central heating and a modern electric stove. There was a box room on the ground floor, which had probably been used as a maid's room. I also saw that alongside two bedrooms and an indoor bathroom and toilet, there was a designated children's playroom on the top floor. In total, the house had 150 square metres of living space. It was an ample amount for the growing Griesinger family.

Realising that my visit would last longer than the five minutes I had promised, Frau Schulz left us alone at the table. She returned a moment later carrying a bottle of locally produced Trollinger red wine and insisted on serving me some. We sat behind the glass frame and talked about the past, in the same space where once Robert and Gisela entertained guests. When I asked Frau Schulz whether she knew about any of her house's former residents, she admitted that she had not given them a moment's thought. As I asked the question, I realised that I had never sought to find out anything about the people who had lived in the end-of-terrace house in north-west London in which I grew up. How many of us give any consideration to the history of our homes? It is easy to disregard their past inhabitants, ignoring the fact that we stare at the same ceilings, cook in the same kitchens, touch the same handles and bannisters as previous occupants.

It was still light when the Schulzes led me to the back of the house and onto a small patio. Even though there was a table with a couple of chairs, Herr Schulz explained that they rarely sat there, because the sun was unable to reach the area. To enjoy the outdoors, the Griesingers had to traverse the patio and climb a stone path uphill for a few metres, leading into a long, narrow garden. I stood in the middle of the garden and looked down at the house, and at the whole of Stuttgart that I could see in the background. No real fence separated the gardens of the house's three residences; just a small hedgerow signalled the boundaries between the properties. From the garden, it was very easy to see into the adjacent garden and directly into their house. As I stood in what was once Griesinger's garden, I was hit by a sweet smell from the plum and cherry trees. The house plans showed that these were planted in 1935. Frau Schulz told me that in summer she makes cakes with the fruits that fall from the trees in her garden. Gisela probably didn't attempt to use the fruit for baking, because Jutta and Barbara had both told me that she was unable to cook and that she seldom tried. They said she found it unladylike, and out of keeping for a woman of her social standing.

A paved terrace of about thirty square metres separated Ernst Wagner's matching buildings on Schottstrasse. The house plans showed that the area, to which only the residents of both houses had access, served no practical function. Nevertheless, Herr Schulz told me that in summer he and his wife used the space as an extension of their patio to hold outdoor parties. With a steel balcony grille that gave way to views over the entire city, it was the perfect spot for a cocktail party. Robert and Gisela might have hosted guests in the same space. I later learned from their daughters that the couple enjoyed entertaining. Perhaps they did so in summer 1936, when they had reason to celebrate.

In early June 1936 Griesinger was called away to undertake his first spell of military service at the Wiblingen barracks, housed in a former Benedictine abbey in Ulm.[76] After the Nazis reintroduced universal conscription and military training in 1935, men like Griesinger who had been too young to serve in the First World War, but who by the mid-1930s were too old for regular conscription of one or two years, were expected to carry out a lighter programme of training for two or three months every year. Following their training, men in this cohort were assigned to new reserve divisions, where they would be used in a defensive or supportive role.[77] After completing his two-month spell, Griesinger returned to Schottstrasse as a Class II Reserve Non-commissioned Officer (*Unterführer*) in the 25th Infantry Division. The day of his return coincided with the opening ceremony of the Olympic Games in Berlin.[78]

In the two weeks that followed, German athletes won eighty-nine medals, including thirty-three gold – more than any other country. Hitler's showcasing of the new Germany on the international stage had been a triumph, and the whole country was gripped in a moment of collective euphoria. If they had organised a gathering for friends, the couple probably decorated the balcony with swastika flags and bunting, ensuring that it would all have been visible from the street below. Robert would have been very much aware that Block Wardens (*Blockwarten*) – low-ranking Nazis responsible for watching over an apartment block, or several houses in a street – were recording details of families who did not display sufficient support for the new regime.[79] On a personal and professional level, things could not be going better for the Griesingers. Even though SS newly-weds were not expected to conceive a baby in the two years after their wedding – SS chiefs having stated that the time should be spent on couples becoming acquainted with one another – Gisela was quick to fulfil her duty as an SS wife in the creation of child-rich families.[80] She fell pregnant after only three months of marriage. And in August 1936 Robert received his promotion to the rank of senior civil servant. Life seemed to be going well.

By the time I left Schottstrasse to take the bus back towards the centre of Stuttgart it was dark. My reflections on my evening with the Schulzes were interrupted constantly by the bus driver's sudden swerves as he sped down Lenzhalde's sharp corners. At each bend, all the passengers on board apologised for accidentally knocking into one another. After the fourth or fifth bend, people began to see the funny side and excused themselves with half-smiles. I thought of Griesinger standing on the bus, briefcase in one hand, the other tightly grasping a metal pole, trying not to make a spectacle of himself on his way each morning to the Gestapo.

In the days that followed, I could not stop thinking about how close the Griesingers and the Rothschilds lived, with only a wall between them, lives kept so separate by just a bit of plaster and wood. After passing the communal front lawn and terrace, the two families accessed their private quarters by individual front doors that were barely five metres away from one another. If the Rothschilds had a *mezuzah* – the small decorative case containing rolled-up parchment of scripture that many Jews nail to the right-hand side of their doorpost – then the SS member and Gestapo employee might have noticed it. From their back garden it would have been all too easy for Robert and Gisela to catch a glimpse of the Rothschilds, perhaps even lighting the Shabbat candles on a Friday night.[81]

I wanted to learn more about the family on the other side of the wall, who were racially undesirable, as stated in the law at the time. According to a database of victims of the Holocaust at Yad Vashem, Israel's main research centre and museum on the tragedy, Fritz and Helene Rothschild were 'Murdered in the Shoah'. It was possible that Griesinger played a role in the couple's demise. Sources I discovered in local archives enabled me slowly to piece together Fritz and Helene's life. Fritz was a veteran of the First World War, whose family had lived in south-west Germany for 200 years.[82] As a young man, Fritz worked at Rothschild Brothers Co., the family firm founded as a textile wholesale business in 1904 by his father and uncle. Rothschild Brothers Co. specialised in knitted womens-wear made from mechanical tricot fabric. In 1919 Fritz married Helene Rosenthal, who in April 1922 gave birth to their son, Hans Erich.[83] By the end of the 1920s the family business, now run by Fritz and his cousin Oskar, after the retirement of their fathers, was thriving. Fritz and Oskar then owned a four-storey factory that employed 150 staff. I tracked down Helga Rothschild, Fritz and Helene's granddaughter, who told me that the Rothschilds were active figures on Stuttgart's social scene, mixing with and hosting Jewish and non-Jewish friends alike. The pair enjoyed sport and were also involved in local amateur dramatics. Judaism played an important role in the Rothschilds' lives, as demonstrated by Fritz's work in the city's Jewish communal structures. Robert and Gisela would have heard and observed acts and rituals of Jewish life coming from next door. The Rothschilds kept a kosher home, a way of living that soon became a challenge under the Nazis, due to the ban on kosher butchering, and attached to their front door was a *mezuzah*.[84]

The Nazi seizure of power would devastate the Rothschild family. The antisemitic laws led Fritz's parents and sister to emigrate in

Helene and Fritz Rothschild *c.* 1930

1936. Fritz remained behind with Helene and Hans, their teenage son, and attempted to ride out the Nazi storm. Fritz could not have failed to notice that Hitler made exceptions to the racial decrees for veterans of the First World War, although these ended with President von Hindenburg's death. A fall in antisemitic incidents, coupled with Jewish uncertainty, confusion towards the Nazis' mixed messages and the unwillingness of nations to accept Jewish refugees, ensured that when the Griesingers moved in next door, the numbers of Jews emigrating was actually in decline: 23,000 Jews left Germany in 1934, and 21,000 left in 1935.[85]

Life did not improve for the Rothschilds, whose world was crumbling around them. Only a week after the closing ceremony of the 1936 Summer Olympics, the local authorities excluded Jews from outdoor pools and from membership of most Stuttgart clubs.[86] *Kristallnacht*, or the Night of Broken Glass, which occurred six weeks after the Griesinger family moved out of Schottstrasse, marked the moment when Fritz's problems spiralled out of control. The First World War veteran was caught up personally in the pogrom, when he was arrested by Griesinger's former colleagues at the Stuttgart Gestapo on 9 November 1938 and taken to a concentration camp. That night the Nazis arrested 878 Jewish men from Stuttgart – almost the entire Jewish adult male population. As was the case with 30,000 Jewish men across Germany, their only crime was that of being a Jew. What secured Fritz's release from the camp after three days was his position as head of an important weaving mill, as it was deemed vital to the national economy. He returned home to Helene a broken man. Over the weeks that followed, he faced daily threats and intimidation by local Nazis until, in early 1939, he was forced to Aryanise (liquidate) his company. After multiple failed attempts to emigrate to the United States and South America, the Rothschilds left Stuttgart for Paris in summer 1939.[87]

Fresh upheaval reached France within weeks. War broke out shortly after the family's arrival in the capital and eighteen-year-old Hans volunteered to join the French Foreign Legion, leaving his parents behind. In June 1940 France suffered a stunning defeat and signed an armistice with Germany. Remarkably Fritz and Helene – who did not speak French and who were without French citizenship – remained in Nazi-occupied Paris until they were arrested and deported to Auschwitz in May 1944, two weeks before the Normandy Landings.[88] They survived for as long as they did because of Fritz's job at the Reich Commissar for the Unilever *Konzern* (Sodeco), an official German organisation on the Champs-Élysées that had the monopoly on importing goods to France from French colonies on an industrial scale.[89] From the end of 1941 Germany began to feel the effects of the Royal Navy blockade. Experienced negotiators such as Fritz Rothschild were called in to ensure that oils, fats and other raw materials from French North Africa were brought across the Mediterranean to French ports and quickly sent on to Germany.[90] His work allowed families in Germany, such as the Griesingers, to get by with adequate supplies of butter, oil and soaps. It also helped to preserve the footwear of men in uniform, such as Griesinger, and other SS officers and soldiers, who rubbed fat into their boots to stop the leather from cracking and the stitching coming undone.[91] Fritz Rothschild's work was deemed so important that he and Helene were exempt from wearing the yellow star. Such a privilege was extremely rare. According to Heinz Röthke, chief of the *Judenamt* (Jewish office) at the German police in Paris, only twenty-six Jews in the whole of occupied France received exemptions.[92] When this protection ran out in February 1944, the couple spent several months in hiding in unused offices in Paris. In April 1944 they were two of 250 Jews apprehended in Paris.[93]

On 20 May 1944 the couple were among 1,200 Jews loaded onto cattle cars from the Drancy internment camp, which would take them to an unknown destination in the east. It was the seventy-fourth deportation train that left France during the Nazi occupation. The convoy entered Auschwitz on the morning of the 23 May. After almost twenty-five years of marriage, this was the last time Fritz and Helene ever saw each other; 61 per cent of the Jews on board Convoy 74 were gassed within hours of their arrival. Their number included fifty-seven-year-old Fritz. It did not include Helene. She was among the 247 women and 221 men selected to work in the camp. An SS doctor had made the split-second decision that Helene appeared healthy and younger than her actual age of forty-nine. Contrary to what was written on her Yad Vashem entry, Helene was not murdered in Auschwitz. She managed to survive the Holocaust.[94]

Once inside the camp, a Polish female prisoner marked Helene's left forearm with a tattoo, transforming her from Helene Rothschild into Prisoner A 5604. Robert and Gisela's former neighbour then spent eight months working at Birkenau. The women who arrived in Birkenau on Convoy 74 did a variety of jobs during their incarceration.[95] The more fortunate ones worked in hospital wards or sorted the clothes of the new arrivals, while others undertook debilitating physical work. Helene fell into this last category, working in the fields and on construction sites. For months she slaved away without adequate food, shoes or clothing, transporting stones and cement or working the land with pickaxes.

Helene was ill and weighed just seventy pounds on 27 January 1945, the day the Soviet Army liberated Auschwitz.[96] In an attempt to start afresh, she and Hans moved to London after the war. For the rest of her life she remained hazy about her life in occupied Paris and refused to speak to her grandchildren about Auschwitz.[97] She died in Wembley in 1983 – the same part of London and the same year in which I was born.

Chapter VII

Lebensraum

On either side of the wall that separated their residences in the mid-1930s, Fritz and Helene Rothschild and Robert and Gisela Griesinger took decisions on their family's future that had important consequences. After leaving the Stuttgart Gestapo in autumn 1937, Griesinger found his career taking an irregular turn. Given his background and the career trajectories of so many of his peers, one might have expected to see him taking a role at a Gestapo bureau in another part of the country or at a Nazi agency in Berlin, such as the Reich Main Security Office (RSHA). This was a common route for other ordinary Nazi lawyers.[1] Instead, according to his CV, Griesinger spent a year back at the Ministry of the Interior, before taking up a lectureship in agricultural law in autumn 1938 at the College of Agriculture at Hohenheim.[2]

On 30 September 1938, as most of the world, hoping to avoid another war, waited eagerly for the results of a meeting between Hitler, Mussolini, Chamberlain and Daladier in Munich, a removals van parked in front of the Griesinger and Rothschild residence. The Griesingers had packed up their entire house: they were moving to the countryside.[3] Relocation to Hohenheim seemed a peculiar career move, especially as Griesinger did not have a background in agricultural law. His CV did not chart the circumstances that impelled him to trade in his comfortable life, his idyllic house on Schottstrasse and his senior position as a *Regierungsrat* in the centre of Stuttgart for a job of little immediate significance in an obscure agricultural college in the country.

A day after Jochen and Irmela had entrusted me with Wally Griesinger's diary, I headed to Hohenheim to consult university archives in order to understand Griesinger's motivation for the move. Dr Ulrich Fellmeth, the university archivist, was standing in front of the eighteenth-century palace when I arrived. He was approaching retirement age, with white hair, a trimmed beard and small circular glasses. In his grey woollen fitted blazer, he reminded me of a German schoolmaster. Fellmeth promised to take me to the archives, but wanted first to give me a short tour of the palace to tell me a bit about the building's history. As we walked round the recently refurbished lecture theatres and classrooms, I told Fellmeth about my interest in a former member of the university's teaching staff. Griesinger's name didn't mean anything to him, but he said the university's archives from the 1930s and 1940s survived the Allied bombing of Germany. He was hopeful we would find something.

It was only in March 2016, when there were no longer any former faculty members or students alive to remember the Third Reich, that the university launched an inquiry to uncover the nature of its National Socialist past. Led by Dr Anja Waller, the project was expected to last two years and it would have complete access to university papers – something that I discovered was of marginal use.[4] In the aftermath of the war Hohenheim's archives, like so many others in Germany, had incriminating evidence about the Nazi activities of its faculty systematically weeded out and destroyed. Dr Waller's office felt like a crime scene. On one of her walls she had created a mural of all of Hohenheim's principal characters from the era. The names, party affiliations and other biographical information of the twenty-four faculty members she was most eager to investigate were written in large letters in black marker pen on separate pieces of white A4 paper. I recognised a lot of the names of the university rectors and professors, whose photographs I had seen adorning the university's walls an hour earlier with Dr Fellmeth. In an area of the palace reserved for important guests hung a portrait of Percy Brigl, under which was written 'Professor of Chemistry and University Rector', while in a back office only metres away, Dr Waller had written in bright pink the date that Brigl joined the SA and the Nazi party. Griesinger's name did not appear on Dr Waller's wall. This absence should not suggest that Griesinger was only a bit-part player in party-related activities at the university. The post-war destruction of so many archives, coupled with the fact that he was not later investigated for his involvement with the party, made it easier for his name to slip through the cracks.

Griesinger's dossier in the Hohenheim university archives revealed that he was a member of the prestigious college management team.[5] From 1938 until 1943 he was the third-most-senior member of the college, after the rector and the pro-rector. During these years he occupied a powerful position as head of the college council (Hochschulrat).[6] He probably revelled in having his own office and personal secretary in the eighteenth-century palace, which overlooked the beautiful botanical gardens.[7] As a member of the college management team, Griesinger was expected to live with his family in an area of Hohenheim palace reserved for professors and senior staff. It was this residency requirement that seemed the most likely explanation as to why the family moved from Schottstrasse. With two young children and the prospect of more on the way, the generous financial package would have made the relocation to the countryside easier.

Griesinger's decision to move to Hohenheim suddenly appeared less curious, and effectively ruled out any possibility that his transfer was borne out of opposition to the increasingly extremist Nazi programme. On the contrary, rather than a step back, it represented an important springboard from which Griesinger would, he hoped, be well placed to launch a glittering career in the Württemberg civil administration. By accepting the move to the countryside, Griesinger was following in the footsteps of other lawyers who had worked unassumingly in the palatial corridors of Hohenheim before an opportunity for career advancement elsewhere presented itself. Eduard Springer, for example, a Regierungsassessor at Hohenheim early in his career, went on to hold a string of senior government positions, before he became president of the Central Office for

Agriculture in the Ministry of Economic Affairs. Hohenheim was a fantastic career move for a young lawyer.

Despite his privileged position within the college, Griesinger, like all members of the management team, had to do some teaching for the college's 200 students. Teaching rosters showed that in the winter semester of 1938 Griesinger taught students German law on Wednesday and Saturday mornings for two hours, while in the summer semester of 1939 he taught agricultural law on Tuesday and Wednesday mornings.[8] Having seen the law modules he took as an undergraduate at Tübingen, and already being familiar with the nature of his work, first as a legal intern and later at the Gestapo, I knew that Griesinger was without any knowledge of agricultural law. I wondered how he fared teaching a subject that must have seemed so alien, to a group of students who were specialists in agricultural sciences and farm management and were already familiar with the undefined technical terms. It was no coincidence, I felt, that in the run-up to starting his new job at Hohenheim, Griesinger stopped showing up for work at his office in Stuttgart. He sent a sick note to his boss at the Ministry of the Interior on 19 September 1938, informing him that he was unable to return to work due to a high fever.[9] Rather than being bedridden, I imagined Griesinger sitting at home on Schottstrasse reading widely on agricultural law in the days before classes began.

Hohenheim was in a perilous situation before the Nazis came to power. The corrosion of the agricultural economy during the 1920s ensured that by the end of the decade the number of students studying agriculture was only a quarter of what it had been ten years earlier. The onset of the Great Depression in 1929 led to a further decline in student numbers, which threatened the institution with closure. The Nazis' interest and investment in agriculture couldn't have been timed better, and the results were immediate. Within a year of the new regime, student numbers had increased and the institution had recruited more staff. Rather than closing agricultural schools, the Nazis built more. It should come as no surprise that support for the Nazis' programme was high, among Hohenheim's faculty members.[10] Colleges and universities were fertile territory for Nazism to spread. Just as at Tübingen during the Weimar years, the overwhelming majority of German university teachers were sympathetic to conservative nationalism. Universities had not, as was later claimed, been taken over by a handful of Nazi fanatics who quashed academic independence.[11]

In this environment, a significant proportion of Griesinger's new colleagues had long-standing Nazi connections.[12] Almost all the professors were party members, and many had been members of the SA since the 1920s. Some were SS men. Hohenheim faculty members injected biological and nationalist components into their research specialisms, kowtowing to the racial and colonialist priorities of the new regime. They placed emphasis on *Lebensraum*, the Nazis' expansionist policy to create 'living space' for Germans in the east. In his inaugural speech as college rector in April 1938, Professor Erhard Jung, a renowned geologist and *SS Obersturmführer*, was unambiguous in his support for the new regime's imperial project, choosing as his title 'The importance of soil in the German resettlement of the East'.[13] Nazi officials looked favourably at the changing direction of scholarship at Hohenheim, rewarding the college with financial incentives from the Reich Food Estate (RNS).[14]

Thanks in part to the Nazi policy on agriculture, support for the regime was rampant at Hohenheim and unlike Stuttgart, where members of his SS *Sturm* lived in different parts of the city, the close-knit environment and living conditions at the Hohenheim campus created a space that encouraged greater SS interaction among ordinary Nazis. Such surroundings will have only added to Griesinger's desire to play a greater role in SS life. Now in a position of leadership, he would have wanted to fit in with the rector, leading professors and other senior university staff, many of whom were staunch Nazis. While in Stuttgart Griesinger's commitment to the SS was seemingly minimal, managing by 1938 only to reach the non-commissioned rank of *Scharführer*, his arrival at Hohenheim prompted more active participation in the organisation. Within six months he was given the honour of a commissioned SS rank in Hitler's birthday honour's list, becoming an *Untersturmführer* (junior storm leader). Less than two years later, while still at Hohenheim, he achieved yet another promotion.[15]

Griesinger's first test to display his Nazi credentials occurred within six weeks of joining the university. On the morning of his thirty-second birthday he woke up early. It was a Wednesday, one of his two teaching days. Neither the Griesingers nor anyone else in Germany knew then that the day – later known as *Kristallnacht* – would go down in history as among the most significant dates in the history of the Third Reich. It marked the transition from the economic, social and political exclusion of Jews, to physical violence unleashed against the Jewish population. On the night of 9 November 1938, male Jews in Württemberg and throughout Germany were viciously attacked as the SA, party members and Hitler Youth set fire to synagogues and wreaked havoc in Jewish homes and businesses, smashing windows and destroying furniture. Commenting on Stuttgart, Samuel W. Honacker, the US consul-general, described the measures carried out against the Jews in a report to the US ambassador in Berlin as 'unreal to one living in an enlightened country'. The Stuttgart fire service was especially willing to contribute to the destruction, helping to ignite the fire that set the synagogue ablaze and watching it burn, intervening only when the flames got too close to neighbouring houses.[16] Jews like Griesinger's former neighbour, Fritz Rothschild, were arrested and dragged to the Hotel Silber, before being sent on to the Welzheim concentration camp, forty miles north-east of Stuttgart, or to Dachau. In the countryside, buses transported SA men from one village to another, to wreak havoc. In Esslingen, a few miles from Hohenheim, Nazis stormed a Jewish orphanage, driving children out into the streets as they destroyed the building.

It is impossible to know where Griesinger was on the night of his birthday, but throughout the country some members of the SS who met that night to commemorate the fifteenth anniversary of the Beer Hall Putsch took part in the violence. Few in Württemberg spoke out against the atrocities, with most taking the view that Jews had only themselves to blame for the riots. Julius von Jan, a pastor serving in nearby Oberlenningen, was an exception and condemned the anti-Jewish violence a few days later in his Sunday sermon. Within a few days 500 Nazis from neighbouring towns and villages came to Oberlenningen and beat up von Jan, after which he was arrested and jailed.[17]

It has taken a long time to debunk the myth that universities were immune to Nazi ideology. From the late 1940s many academics who had been enthusiastic party members, or had offered the Nazis their expertise, were able quietly to continue their careers in the Federal Republic. All German universities were closed indefinitely in spring 1945 and were only permitted to reopen after the Allies had screened faculty members. Yet denazification failed miserably to root out former Nazis and was described as a whitewash by some historians. University professors, like many Germans, claimed during the proceedings that Nazism was something that had affected only a few fanatics, but otherwise received little support on the ground.[18] In the immediate post-war years there existed a collective amnesia in colleges and universities. Moreover, returning veterans, having been fed Nazi ideology during their deadly missions, came back to the universities, where they created a conservative environment.

Colleagues of SS Obersturmführer Professor Erhard Jung made sure to testify that Hohenheim's former college rector was an unenthusiastic party member, who did not push the party on anyone, and who spoke out when he disagreed with an aspect of policy.[19] In my own field of history, only twenty-four academics in the whole country were temporarily prohibited from re-entering the profession.[20] Their number included the scholar Günther Franz, who led a glittering post-war career, becoming rector of Hohenheim from 1963 to 1967. He had earlier been the model Nazi academic. Throughout the whole of the Third Reich, SS Untersturmführer Franz was an outspoken supporter of the Nazi project, serving on a number of SS cultural and scientific commissions. His fixation with *völkisch* ideas on race helped to shape and influence many of his historical interpretations on the sixteenth and seventeenth centuries. Franz dedicated his 1933 analysis of the Peasants' War of 1524–5 to Hitler. His book on the Thirty Years War, first published in 1940, has never gone out of print. After the war, most, though not all, of the overtly racist language was removed from subsequent editions of his work.[21]

Living on the Hohenheim college campus marked a whole new way of life for Robert and Gisela, who until the move were the epitome of urban dwellers. The living conditions were basic in the 1930s. Unlike their house on Schottstrasse, their new residence was without an indoor bathroom or toilet. A senior university administrator who, a few years earlier, lived in an apartment in the same building as Griesinger described his residence as 'primitive'.[22] No records remain that might indicate which rooms in the palace were occupied by the Griesingers, but Dr Fellmeth took me to several refurbished offices that he knew were once occupied by senior staff and their families.

As soon as we entered one of the offices, I knew we were in Griesinger's apartment. There was something familiar about the space. I sat at a desk and pulled out my computer to go through some of the photographs I had copied from Jutta. In one of the images Jutta, who could not have been older than two, was seated with her older half-brother, Joachim. Smartly dressed, Jutta was in a white dress and a white hairband, while Joachim wore a light-coloured shirt with a tie, and the children were playing on a rug on the floor with a toy rabbit. The picture appeared to have been taken in a bedroom, for in the background a dressing gown hung from a peg next to a slanting window. The window's unique angle, and its positioning on a slanting wall in a room with a low ceiling, had stuck in my mind. Jutta did not know where the photo had been taken. As I sat and examined the photo, I was in little doubt that quite by chance I was sitting in Griesinger's former living quarters.

The family was inexperienced at country life, yet upon their arrival they were expected to play active roles in this small rural community, where the people and the research-related discussions on *Lebensraum* and organic farming methods were entirely alien. Going back to Stuttgart was reserved for something of a treat or a day out. The large numbers of photographs of Robert with Jutta

Jutta and Joachim at Hohenheim *c.* 1939

as a toddler, taken in the garden of Adolf and Wally Griesinger's Stuttgart mansion on Auf dem Haigst, suggest that Griesinger returned often to visit his parents. Hohenheim's proximity to Stuttgart ensured that Robert and Gisela could enjoy time away from the children. Its accessibility by rack-railway to Marienplatz in Stuttgart in fifty minutes enabled the young couple to leave their rural hideaway to visit the city and catch an opera, a play or a film in the evening or at a weekend.[23]

One of the films showing in Stuttgart that autumn was *13 Stühle* ('13 Chairs'), a comedy starring the screen god Heinz Rühmann, in which he played the part of Felix Rabe, an impoverished hairdresser who travels to Vienna to claim an inheritance left to him by his recently deceased Aunt Barbara. Felix is mortified when, upon his arrival, he discovers that his inheritance amounts only to a collection of thirteen Biedermeier chairs, which he is immediately compelled to sell in order to pay for his ticket home. Having unloaded the collection to an antique dealer, Felix returns to his aunt's apartment where, on the back of a portrait, he finds a letter telling him that she has sewn her fortune of 100,000 RM inside the cushion of one of the chairs. By the time Felix returns to the shop, the dealer has sold all of the chairs to thirteen individual buyers. In the rest of the film, Felix and the antique dealer scour the city, searching for the chair that contains the fortune.

After its opening night on 11 October 1938, the film screened every day for two weeks at the fashionable Palast-Lichtspiele cinema in Stuttgart, one of the largest and more opulent of the city's cinemas, which stood on the site of the old Stuttgart train station.[24] Even if Robert and Gisela did not see the film, it was well advertised on billboards and in the local and national press: a large announcement on 11 October dominated the fourth page of the *Stuttgarter Neues Tagblatt*. The plot was common knowledge. I pictured Robert in Prague years later, in fear for his life amid the chaos that accompanied the Liberation in spring 1945. He finds himself clutching his identity papers in his hands, desperate for a hiding place, and remembers Felix's Aunt Barbara. He hides the papers in the chair and flees the house. It was an absurd but deeply satisfying idea. I set it aside and turned back to the archives.

Griesinger's move away from a position in the Nazi police or security services in autumn 1937 later proved critical in shaping his first years of war. In summer 1939 Stahlecker, Harster and Bilfinger – the men with whom two years earlier he had spent every working day – were called up as agents to serve in the SS Security Police. As part of this role, the men were responsible during the German invasion of the USSR for organising, and sometimes participating in, the murder of hundreds of thousands of Jews. Griesinger's position in Hohenheim on the eve of the war, which had nothing to do with security, ensured that his war was never destined to follow this route. Despite being given a commissioned SS rank in summer 1939, Griesinger was, at thirty-two, too old to join a specialist SS fighting unit. Instead he was conscripted into a regular *Wehrmacht* division.[25] The torture of mundane army life as a lowly soldier, deprived of a leadership position and with few possibilities for career advancement, plagued the ambitious lawyer and his initial experience of war.

Chapter VIII

Stavyshche

After quizzing Jutta for so long on matters relating to her family during our first meeting, it was my turn to talk. Jutta had waited patiently and had kept her part of our unspoken agreement to provide answers to each other's questions. She was eager to learn what I had found out about her father's personal and professional life. Over the course of an hour I shared many of my discoveries, ranging from details of her ancestors in eighteenth-century New Orleans, to Griesinger's participation in the SS and the nature of his job in Prague. As I was speaking, Jutta seemed enthralled as she carefully listened to every word, only occasionally interrupting to ask for clarification or to remind me how bad she felt about knowing so little about her father. She seemed content, perhaps even relieved, to hear these details for the first time. More than once she told me how I was filling in the missing pieces of her past. When I showed her an example of a professional letter that Griesinger had written, she said it felt unfamiliar, as though it was 'written by a *stranger*', a word that Barbara would also use to describe their father.

As soon as I had finished, Jutta began rummaging through a chest of drawers on the other side of the living room. Even though they were not on display, it seemed as though she had kept relics of her past after all. 'This is all I have from my father,' she said as she returned clutching a photo album. In the 1950s the then-teenage Jutta assembled the photographs and arranged them neatly, gluing them by hand onto the album's thick beige pages. Of the thirty or so black-and-white items, there were a handful of her father. Four of them took the form of a portrait, in which Griesinger alternated between wearing either an army uniform or a smart suit and tie. In a fifth photograph Robert stood in a muddy field, looking grimly at the camera, dressed in a military greatcoat and holding a horse by the reins, as team after team of men and horses trudged past in the background.

Griesinger in *Wehrmacht* uniform with one of the horses from the 25th Infantry Division *c.* 1939

In August 1939 Griesinger, still living in Hohenheim, was called up as a cavalry sergeant (*Wachtmeister*) to the 25th Infantry Division, made up of local men from the Stuttgart region. He was already familiar with some of the other conscripts, having come to know them during the annual military training drills since 1936 at the Wiblingen barracks. Like most Germans, Griesinger was probably unenthusiastic at the prospect of war, but was resigned to it, having cast his lot with Hitler and the Führer's quest for *Lebensraum* (living space). Griesinger's division was swiftly taken to serve along the famous Siegfried Line on the border of Germany and France.

When France and Great Britain declared war on Germany on 3 September 1939, two days after the Nazi state invaded Poland, the Franco-German border did not turn suddenly into a theatre of action. At that time most of the German army was in Poland, where it took part in brutal fighting. For the first nine months of Griesinger's war, life in the 25th Infantry Division was characterised by training, exercise and constant marching. Other than some occasional artillery fire, there was no actual fighting against the French. During these months Griesinger was bored and unsettled, missing the comforts of home and family. Records show that he desperately sought to obtain a transfer from his position as a cavalry sergeant to a more prestigious role. 'I am still waiting for the war to start for me.' he wrote impatiently in one letter from March 1940.[1]

With a large proportion of German men conscripted for military service in 1939, Robert's absence was not unusual. While he was away, Gisela lived with Joachim and Jutta in the family's living quarters at Hohenheim. She spent most of her pregnancy with Barbara surviving the unfamiliar aspects of country life without her husband. The absence of a kindergarten at Hohenheim made life for Gisela even more difficult. She no longer had her sister, Ingeborg, across the street on Schottstrasse to help her out with the children. Fortunately the children could play with and feed the chickens, sheep, pigs and other animals that roamed freely across the university grounds.

Barbara, like Jutta, ended up with photographs of her father in uniform, which she dug out to show me during one of our interviews. As I told her about her father's participation in the 25th Infantry Division, she shared a story about her own birth. In December 1939, pregnant with her third child, Gisela went into labour several weeks early. Word managed to reach Griesinger on the Siegfried Line, and he obtained leave to travel the 110 kilometres back to Hohenheim. He arrived just in time. 'He didn't stay long, but he saw me and I saw him,' said Barbara.

In May 1940 Hitler's order to invade France put an end to Griesinger's hopes of a move away from the front. 'Germans versus the French' – the game he had played as a child during the Great

Griesinger in *Wehrmacht* uniform *c.* 1939

War in Stuttgart – had finally become a reality. The five-week battle was a traumatic time for Griesinger and his comrades. Death and destruction were everywhere. Later accounts of the 25th Infantry Division mentioned the number of slain horses, still in harness with legs upright, whose stench revolted the soldiers. At one point the remaining horses were so exhausted they could not continue. Orders were given to the soldiers to push the carts until the horses had regained their strength.[2]

Fortunately for Griesinger, the campaign did not last long. The German army swiftly outflanked the supposedly impenetrable Maginot Line and, within just five weeks, the French army had surrendered. Fearing the enemy advance, millions of French civilians took to the roads in a mass exodus towards the south. Throughout the campaign German soldiers remorselessly plundered French homes from cellar to attic, taking valuables, clothing and food. In a letter to friends at home, one soldier in the 25th Infantry Division spoke of entering empty French houses and finding dinner laid out on the table; in some cases, the food was still warm.[3]

At the time of the armistice with France on 22 June 1940, Griesinger was stationed in the grounds of a confiscated chateau, close to the town of Bourges (Cher) in central France. After France fell, the men of Griesinger's division knew what lay in store next. 'Hopefully, we will get to England over the coming days,' wrote one member of the 25th Infantry Division in a letter home on 27 June. Victory against the British was the only thing on these men's minds – 'it's what we've been waiting for the entire time'.[4] Griesinger and the men in his unit practised drills, marches and other training activities, many of which took place in canals and in the River Loire, in preparation for the amphibious attack on Great Britain that German generals had called Operation Sea Lion.[5]

As Griesinger and the men of the 25th Infantry Division waited for the signal to launch the cross-Channel invasion, they made the most of their time in central France. German looting, which soldiers referred to euphemistically as 'organising', did not cease with the June armistice. In a context in which the Nazi state was orchestrating the sustained plunder of French industry and its economy, to the point where the country was almost on the brink of famine, some German soldiers justified their thefts by considering French goods ripe for the taking. Nevertheless, the Nazis also encouraged men to visit French shops to buy products for themselves and their families at home, as a way of helping morale.[6]

Acquiring French goods had a positive effect on the soldiers. In their letters home the men described their idyllic summer in Bourges. As Erich N. observed, 'the saying is true, they live like gods in France'. The men always had plenty to eat and drink and, if they hadn't pillaged the shops, they found items there such as soap, coffee and oil that were in short supply in Germany. One man even wrote that he and his friends 'often' shaved with champagne or cleaned their dishes with it. Some managed to acquire silk underwear, wool and other fabrics to send home to their wives, girlfriends and mothers. For some of these men it was their first experience of regular shopping, usually considered a 'female' activity.[7] To pass the time, the men of the 25th Infantry Division read books, wrote letters and played chess. For those who sought physical pleasure, a visit to a local Bourges brothel was a popular pastime. Without sufficient numbers of sex workers in Bourges to serve the needs of German troops, visits were limited to a maximum of ten minutes.[8]

To their surprise, the order to attack Britain never came. To launch a successful invasion, the German navy needed to transport troops, horses and equipment safely across the twenty-two-mile English Channel. To do so, it needed first to take control of the skies. Efforts by the *Luftwaffe* (German air force) to destroy the RAF over the Channel and the south of England in August 1940 were disastrous, and on 17 September Hitler postponed the invasion indefinitely.

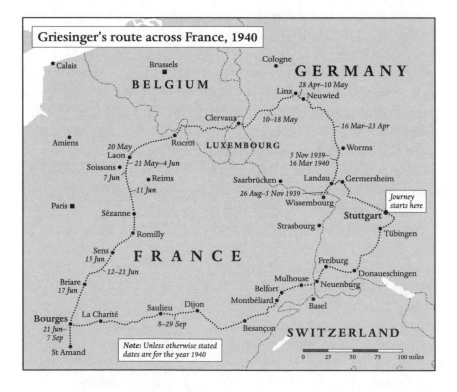

The 25th Infantry Division's route into France in 1940

Days later, the troops of Griesinger's division, in buoyant spirits after Germany's conquest of the Low Countries and France, left Bourges to make the long easterly march back to Stuttgart. News of the soldiers' triumphant return gave the city's residents something to look forward to. The first year of the war had hit the home front badly, bringing back memories of starvation and disease during the First World War. As food rationing and clothing cards were introduced in the summer and autumn of 1939, and meat, milk and eggs were in short supply, Germans became used to an unvaried diet of bread, potatoes and preserves, while Jews had even fewer options.[9] In October 1940 Griesinger's unit arrived in Stuttgart, to decorated streets lined with well-wishers. The men almost drowned in their cars because of the flowers and other gifts thrown by locals. Erich N. counted 678 cigarettes in his car.[10] With Operation Sea Lion still on hold, and no immediate plans for Germany to invade elsewhere, Griesinger was discharged on 21 October and swiftly resumed his position at Hohenheim, replacing Dr Otterbach, who had stood in for him during his absence.[11]

After a succession of lightning military victories, and having signed a non-aggression pact with the Soviet Union, Germany was the undisputed master of the European continent in the summer and autumn of 1940. With the United States steering clear of the war, most Germans believed that Britain could only hold out on its own for so long and would eventually ask Germany for a peace settlement. As German supremacy rapidly expanded, Griesinger was no longer content to remain in rural Hohenheim. Unlike in peacetime, when Griesinger's university position had benefited the young lawyer's career advancement, in 1940 a position in the administration in one of the Reich's newly conquered territories was far more of an indicator of upward mobility and brought with it the likelihood of rapid promotion. Out of the whole of Nazi-occupied Europe, Prague, located in the Protectorate of Bohemia and Moravia, was at the top of Griesinger's list.

Griesinger had good reason for wanting to relocate to Prague. Resulting from its position at the heart of Europe and its significance for Germany's war economy, the Protectorate was integral to the Thousand Year Reich. In addition, Griesinger had important connections in the city. Ever since the Germans first occupied the Czech lands in March 1939 the Protectorate had been under the control of the prominent Swabian Konstantin von Neurath, Hitler's former Foreign Minister and member of Suevia Tübingen, Griesinger's fraternity. Fulfilling his pledge to help his Corps brothers for life, Reichsprotektor von Neurath notoriously filled posts in his new administration with members of Suevia Tübingen and other Swabians. To head the important economics department in the occupied territory, von Neurath appointed Walter Bertsch, who had finished a PhD in law at Tübingen and in the early 1930s was, like Griesinger, a civil servant, slowly moving upwards through the Württemberg state administration.[12]

Over the summer of 1940 Griesinger put his Tübingen connections to good use. By early autumn a transfer to Prague appeared imminent. Walter Bertsch had assured Griesinger that he would recruit him to his economics department.[13] At this time Bertsch's department worked with food, agriculture, labour and pricing, to systematically transform the Czech economy to work for Germany. Work at the department involved ruthlessly closing Czech mines and factories, and coldly sending Czech workers to the Reich. In addition to its regular work, in the summer and autumn of 1940 the economics department was actively involved in the removal of Jews from the Protectorate economy. As Bertsch delivered public speeches outlining the importance of eliminating Jewish influence, his civil servants oversaw the expropriation of Jewish property, ensuring its confiscation and transfer to German ownership.[14] Given his dealings with Bertsch and his other contacts in Prague at this time, Griesinger was under no illusion that upon arrival in the Protectorate part of his work would involve the liquidation of Jewish property and businesses. As an experienced administrator of anti-Jewish legislation from his time at the Hotel Silber, he was ready for the task.

His transfer did not materialise, even though Griesinger received permission from his university and from the Württemberg Minister of Culture to move to Prague.[15] In late November 1940 his Corps brother Hans von Watter, County Councillor of Prague, informed him that von Neurath had halted indefinitely any further recruitment to senior positions in the Protectorate.[16] The decision had been made, and there was nothing further Griesinger could do to change it. His plans lay in tatters. Rather than settling down to an exciting new life in Prague, he spent autumn and winter 1940–41 back at rural Hohenheim, carrying out his professional tasks and celebrating the birthdays of both his infant daughters.

Life on the home front, marked by shortages and inactivity, was a devastating blow. Griesinger's insignificance to the Nazis' grandiose project of world domination was palpable. During this time he taught a class on agricultural law twice a week and continued his administrative work at the college.[17] Most of Hohenheim's academics had returned from active service, including those who were most active in the SS. As he settled back to life at Hohenheim amid the expectation of a German victory in the war, Griesinger resumed his activity with the SS. He may have thought that achieving a higher SS rank might strengthen his chances for a transfer to Prague, or even to Britain after the invasion, which – with some of the *Luftwaffe's* heaviest attacks coming in December 1940 – was seemingly imminent. Only a few months after returning from France, Griesinger, already a commissioned SS officer, earned another promotion on the occasion of the eighth anniversary of the Nazis' coming to power, from *Untersturmführer* (junior storm leader) to *Obersturmführer* (senior storm leader).[18]

During these months on the home front, important changes took place within the 25th Infantry Division. The regiment replaced its horses with motorised vehicles, and from then on was known as the 25th Motorised Infantry Division. Motorised divisions were the spearheads of the German army. As front-line elite combat units, they engaged in serious fighting and assisted tank units with their breakthrough operations. In the first half of 1941 Griesinger took part in regular training activities to become familiar with the new equipment.[19]

In early June 1941, after eight months away from front-line action, the 25th Motorised Infantry Division was mobilised and ordered to report to Stuttgart train station. The destination in late spring 1941 was completely unknown. Rumour was rife amongst the soldiers, with some believing they were headed to British India via the Khyber Pass. They were so convinced by speculation that some even bought language guides in Arabic and Farsi. An attack on Russia was the last thing on these soldiers' minds.[20] Ever since the signing of Hitler's non-aggression pact with Stalin two years earlier, many had thought it possible for the Third Reich to coexist alongside Bolshevism. Nevertheless, on 8 June 1941 Griesinger left Stuttgart with the 25th Motorised Infantry Division and headed east. The division arrived in Lublin, a town located close to the Soviet border, where they stayed for ten days and the men tried to take comfort from their new surroundings. In their letters home, they described the sights of the wheat and barley fields and the sound of bird song that filled the air amid the calm Polish forests. As some soldiers played tunes on the harmonica and others attended mass, most of the division tried to get some rest in the scorching June sun as they awaited the signal to advance.[21]

Since the 1960s relatives of soldiers who fought for Germany have donated thousands of letters that they received during the war to the Library for Contemporary History in central Stuttgart. The letters are arranged by military division, which made it easy for me to find scores of boxes marked '25th Motorised Infantry Division'. It was only after I opened the first box, full to the brim with letters on frayed and wrinkled paper, that my problems began. The letters were written in *Sütterlin* script, a style of handwriting that today is indecipherable to virtually all Germans below the age of ninety. Fortunately, help was on hand. Irina Renz, the friendly head archivist, sat with me and decoded letter after letter. After smoothing out the creases, she sometimes held a letter against the window to catch the light, when a magnifying glass did not suffice. Thanks to Irina, I was able to capture how the men of the 25th

Motorised Infantry Division perceived their new surroundings. This included their contact with the local Jewish population.

As they waited on the Soviet border, Griesinger and the other soldiers had the chance to observe the situation of Jews living in the Lublin ghetto. Often with *Wehrmacht* assistance, the German authorities targeted Poland's Jews for persecution from the moment they turned up in September 1939. At the time of Griesinger's arrival, 34,000 Jews, forced to wear a white armband with a blue Star of David, had for several months faced hunger, disease and overcrowding in the Lublin ghetto.[22] Polish ghettos were presented in Nazi propaganda as a preventative measure against Jewish disease and criminality.[23] Accordingly, the Jews' plight did not elicit any sympathy from the men of Griesinger's milieu. In their letters home to Stuttgart, the men of the 25th Motorised Infantry Division wrote descriptions of Jews in which they invoked common stereotypes that depicted the Jews as disease-riven parasites intent only on profiteering. 'A lot of Jews, a lot of dirt,' wrote Walter K. when conveying his new surroundings to his priest back in Württemberg. Hans S., a paramedic in Griesinger's division, did not hold back in letters to his mother, offering disturbing descriptions of Jews during the units' stay in Lublin. He wrote of an area 'swarming' with Jews wearing their armbands, and noted that nothing could better exemplify dirt than the Jews of Lublin, maintaining that they did not even need to wear the armband because their 'faces were so easily recognisable'. The pages of Hans's letter were worn and beginning to disintegrate. The faint blots and smudges on the cream paper suggested that the recipient reread the message multiple times after it was sent. Hans knew his mother would not be put off by his disparaging remarks about Jews. 'You can imagine what this place looks like,' he smugly noted, as he wrote of the Jews' continued efforts to racketeer in difficult times, comparing them to 'begging hyenas'.[24]

Only days before launching an attack on the USSR, it was commonplace for the men of Griesinger's division to consider Jews morally degenerate. Army ideology passed on to soldiers regularly conflated Jews with 'partisans', who, if left uncontrolled, would seek to sabotage the war effort against Germany.[25] During these final days in Poland, Griesinger and the other soldiers offered a social commentary on events that went on around them as they acted as deadly enablers to persecution. Even though at this time it was the German civilian administration, and not the *Wehrmacht*, that exerted control over the local population, the killing of Jews often occurred within soldiers' sight. Sometimes *Wehrmacht* troops even protected the SS as they executed Polish Jews.[26] Only a few days later, however, Griesinger and the other armed men of his division came face-to-face with Jews when they were advancing deep into Soviet territory. The situation was to be very different.

Just days before the invasion the men of Griesinger's division continued to have no idea why they were stationed so close to the Soviet border. Rumours circulated. Some of the men believed the USSR had granted Germany the right to cross Ukraine, in order to launch a surprise attack against the British troops in Palestine and Egypt. The soldiers who had purchased guides in Middle Eastern languages did not get a chance to test their newly acquired language skills. On 19 June 1941 military chiefs received orders about an imminent attack on the USSR. In the early hours of Sunday 22 June Hitler surprised the whole world by breaking his non-aggression pact with Stalin and invading the USSR in a large-scale *blitzkrieg*. To ensure total secrecy, the Nazi leadership even went as far as detaining the workers who printed and packed the thirty million propaganda pamphlets intended for distribution on the Eastern Front.[27]

Operation Barbarossa involved three million German soldiers, supported by 600,000 trucks, 3,648 tanks and 7,146 artillery pieces.[28] The 25th Motorised Infantry Division fell under the command of Army Group South, which was to spear through Ukraine and seize Kiev. After the panzer (armoured tank) divisions invaded, the task of the 25th Motorised Infantry Division was to provide them with direct support by protecting the flanks and rear of any penetration.[29] As soon as the men of Griesinger's division crossed the River Bug and began its rapid advance, they were involved in heavy fighting against Soviet troops. The *Wehrmacht* acted immediately with sheer brutality, using civilians as a human shield, coldly murdering civilians and butchering Soviet POWs who had surrendered. By early 1942 two million Soviet POWs were already dead. The *Wehrmacht* was also known to kill barbarically women in the Soviet army fighting to defend the motherland.[30] Despite the Soviets' heavy losses, they still managed to capture a large number of wounded German soldiers. Griesinger and the men of his unit witnessed what became of their unfortunate comrades as they made territorial gains. They saw the bodies of men who had been shot and then mutilated, some with their genitals cut off.[31]

It took only a few days for Griesinger's unit to reach Lutsk and Rivne in western Ukraine, the first principal towns on the road to Kiev. During the few hours they spent in those towns, as a reprisal for the killing of a German officer in the Jewish quarter of Rivne, men from Griesinger's unit rounded up and shot 150 Jews and burned their houses to the ground. They tried to kill even more, but were prevented by orders from above.[32] Alongside the shootings, the men also took part in acts designed to devastate and humiliate the local Jewish population. In one incident, a Jewish resident was forced to carry a broken statue of Lenin's head through a crowd of jeering soldiers of the 25th Motorised Infantry Division, some of them holding wooden clubs in their hands.[33]

Within the space of just a few days, some in Griesinger's unit had transformed from being *Wehrmacht* soldiers and enablers of terror to becoming unruly killers. The men knew they would not be reproached for murdering Jews. "Guidelines for Troop Behaviour" issued to forces at the beginning of the invasion gave *Wehrmacht* soldiers the authority to shoot 'bolshevist agitators, guerrillas, saboteurs and Jews'.[34] Some men in Griesinger's unit empathised with, and acted on, what lay at the crux of this order. 'Bolshevism has to perish,' wrote Helmut D. in a letter home within days of the reprisals in Rivne, while a few weeks later Hans S. told his mother about 'uncomfortable situations you shouldn't even think about'.[35]

As a commissioned officer in the SS and a former Gestapo employee imbued since childhood with extreme *völkisch* nationalism, Griesinger needed little convincing that Jews were the enemy of the German people. Nevertheless, anti-Jewish persecution that Griesinger might have witnessed, heard about or even engaged in before the war functioned on a different scale from what occurred as he lingered in Poland and, later, as he entered the USSR. Griesinger could not have ignored the fact that the regime's ferocious campaign against the Jews – hitherto discriminatory and violent, but not murderous – had taken a new turn. The Guidelines for Troop Behaviour had given this ordinary Nazi licence to kill.

If by summer 1941 Griesinger was himself not already a killer, then he had gained experience of mixing in the company of mass murderers. The killings of Jewish civilians carried out by the 25th Motorised Infantry Division and other *Wehrmacht* soldiers remain among the least-known aspects of the Holocaust. For decades after the war it was believed by the German public, and even historians, that front-line infantry divisions such as Griesinger's, generally behaved well towards the civilian population – including Jews – as it fought heroically against the Red Army.[36] Blame for mass murder was consigned to the *Einsatzgruppen* and *Sonderkommando*, the specialist police and security battalions, who arrived in a town or village after the *Wehrmacht* had already passed through. The sole aim of the police and security battalions was to protect the *Wehrmacht* by murdering supposed saboteurs and enemies of the state. It is therefore fascinating that as we follow Griesinger's division's eastward advance, the distinction between conventional warfare at the front and a war of extermination at the rear begins to disappear.[37] The men of the *Einsatzkommando* and *Sonderkommando* units were frequently called close to combat zones at the front, where they mixed with *Wehrmacht* troops. Reports sent by *Einsatzgruppe C* that accompanied Griesinger's division even commented on the *Wehrmacht* soldiers' increasing interest in the executions.[38] In 1941 Walter Stahlecker, Griesinger's former boss at the Stuttgart Gestapo, headed the mobile killing unit *Einsatzgruppe A* and wrote in one report that cooperation with the *Wehrmacht* was 'extremely close, one might even say warm'.[39] If they did not take matters into their own hands, *Wehrmacht* troops were significant accessories to murder. They captured and detained Jews for the killing units, safeguarded the security services as they carried out the executions, and supplied them with the logistical and administrative apparatus to complete the task.[40]

After learning from military sources that Griesinger's division had taken part in the execution of Jews only days after entering the USSR, I took out a large map of Ukraine and placed it on my dining-room table. Using coloured drawing pins, I began to plot the route that the 25th Motorised Infantry Division took to Kiev in July 1941, putting in pins to mark the towns along the way: Rivne, Novohrad-Volynskyi, Zhytomyr. At the back of my mind I had an ulterior motive for wanting to know Griesinger's precise route through western Ukraine. It even had a name: *Stavyshche*. That was the name of the small shtetl, sitting among several lakes, in which Israel Pougatch, my mother's grandfather, was born in 1903.

For hundreds of years generations of my family were born and died in Stavyshche, where their lives were marked by cycles of religious teaching, political oppression and, at times, pogroms and abject poverty. In 1907 Israel's father Tsudik, relocated his young family from Ukraine to settle in the East End of London. Tsudik left behind his parents, Chaïm and Chana, and three younger siblings: a sister, Rayza, and two brothers, Zelman and Moishe.[41] He never saw his family again. His mother, Chana, was a victim of the massive 1919 pogrom in Tarashcha. The fate of the others was unknown. It had never occurred to me to find out what became of the Pougatch family that remained in Stavyshche after Tsudik left.

My pursuit of Griesinger prompted me to ask questions about my own family, just as I had been quizzing Jutta and Barbara about theirs. Like them, I had been avoiding such questions. Other people's families were more interesting, and came with fewer strings attached. But now I had a reason to look into my family's past. I was asking questions about the Pougatch family for the first time, in order to learn more about Griesinger. At least that is what I told myself.

I called my maternal grandmother to see whether she knew anything about her grandfather's sister and two brothers. She did not. 'I retain vivid memories of going to visit *Zaydeh*,' she said, as she cast her mind back to the late 1930s. 'I remember watching him write the letters he used to send to Ukraine, and touching the responses he received back. It was the only time I ever saw writing in Yiddish.' According to my grandmother, Tsudik Pougatch's letters were usually about finding ways to help his family. 'His relatives would ask for money and he sent what he could,' she said as she looked at an old photograph of him. But my grandmother knew more than she thought. She remembered the Pougatch family did not emigrate west. They remained in Ukraine on the eve of the war. 'The war cut off all communication between Tsudik and his family. After that, there were no more letters.'

After leaving Zhytomyr on 18 July, a direct road leading east to Kiev lay before the men of the 25th Motorised Infantry Division. As I studied the map, continuing to mark Griesinger's route with pins, it looked increasingly likely that the unit avoided Stavyshche, located 150 kilometres south of Kiev. But just as the division approached the eastern outskirts of the city, it suddenly changed course and, for strategic reasons, headed south. Soon there was no doubt at all. In the last week of July 1941 Griesinger's division passed through the district of Tarashcha, home to a handful of shtetls and villages that included Stavyshche. In the days that followed Tarashcha's occupation by the *Wehrmacht*, professional killing squads were brought in to murder the district's entire Jewish population.

For a fleeting moment in July 1941, amid the 'crazy thunderstorms' and the noise of *Luftwaffe* aeroplanes overhead, Griesinger looked out on the district of Tarashcha and experienced the same sights and sounds that for centuries had provided rhythm and familiarity to my ancestors' everyday lives.[42] As they travelled in the rain between the villages, replete with small, single-storey dwellings, the men of the 25th Motorised Infantry Division saw the vast pine and oak forests that dominated the countryside, in which children went to play hide-and-seek and pick berries.[43] They also passed the purple lilacs sprouting from bushes at the entrance to the villages, and the many lakes dotted around the valley in which my ancestors bathed and washed clothes. Each time Griesinger

approached a new village, the roads were cleared of the inhabitants' carts, which were moved into the fields outside or shoved to
the sides of the roads. The division spent several days in the district
of Tarashcha, where it prepared to launch an attack against the
Soviets who blocked the route ahead. Griesinger's unit could not
advance as swiftly as planned, because the roads were soaked,
following torrential downpours. Letters sent home during this time
often got wet, causing the ink to run and rendering them only
partially intelligible for the recipient on the home front. The attack
was delayed several times, as it proved impossible for the troops
and heavy machinery to continue along the road south, which had
disintegrated into muddy slush and swamp.[44]

Even if Griesinger did not personally round up and execute my
ancestors and other Jews, he was in close proximity to their killers.
He would have known their faces, if not their names. In places
such as nearby Zhytomyr, the 25th Motorised Infantry Division
arrived in the town on the same day as killing squad *Sonderkommando*
4a. When this *Sonderkommando* unit orchestrated a public hanging
of Jews in the town during the weeks that followed, not only were
Wehrmacht troops present, but reports indicate that many soldiers
shouted, 'Slowly, slowly' to the hangman, as they sought to take
photographs of the gruesome spectacles. Many of these 'execution
tourists' even sent the film rolls back to Germany for processing,
where the images would have been seen by developers and by any
of the soldiers' wives who went to collect the photographs.[45] If
the Pougatch family was still in Stavyshche at the time of the
German arrival in July 1941, they only had months – if not weeks
– to live.

The Holocaust in Tarashcha began with the German military
occupation, which forced Jews to live in designated buildings and
ordered them to wear white armbands marked with the Star of
David. The *Wehrmacht* also introduced forced labour and forbade
Jews from buying food at the market.[46] During summer 1941 1,000
Jews of Tarashcha were forced onto carts and transported a short
distance to a nearby forest, where they were murdered by German
killing squads and their Ukrainian accomplices. The victims were

not simply 'Jews'; they were neighbours and friends of my ancestors, people with whom they had played and studied as children.
Some might even have been relatives. Years later a local Ukrainian
recalled that some of the Jews were not killed instantly and were
instead thrown alive into the pits. Even after the ditches were filled
with mud, the 'earth moved for several days'.[47] While there is no
way to know if Griesinger was involved in the atrocities that took
place in Tarashcha, charting his proximity to mass murder shines
a spotlight on the actions of many of the three million German
soldiers who invaded the USSR. These men lived for the rest of
their lives with the knowledge of what they had witnessed or
participated in, allowing a silence surrounding the *Wehrmacht's*
slaughter of Jews in Ukraine, the Baltic and parts of Russia to
pervade millions of German families.

After leaving Tarashcha, the 25th Motorised Infantry Division
continued on to Kiev in excellent weather conditions. Improved
circumstances also led to changes in the way the men crafted their
letters home. As we sat together in the Library for Contemporary
History, Irina Renz ploughed through the August letters with ease,
without the need for a magnifying glass. After the deluges of July,
the well-rested and well-fed men wrote longer letters in better
handwriting. By August, as the rain cleared, Griesinger's division
progressed along mud-free roads as they pushed back the Red Army
and occupied towns and villages, many of whose Ukrainian inhabitants considered the Germans to be liberators from Bolshevik
tyranny. Some even greeted Griesinger and the other troops with
offerings of bread and salt.[48] Among those celebrating the Germans'
arrival was the local ethnically German *Volksdeutsche* population,
who had lived for generations in Ukraine and numbered almost
400,000 in 1939. Hans S. wrote that in one village the *Volksdeutsche*
ascended, bearing gifts to the men of Griesinger's division, which
included cheeses covered in enormous leaves.[49]

During summer 1941 fighting against the Soviets was sporadic
and interspersed with long periods of leisure time. 'We don't even
deserve our salary,' wrote Willy F. in a letter home, and he duly
noted that the situation was 'not as dangerous as you might think'.[50]

The men of Griesinger's unit spent time lying around, washing clothes and waiting for something to happen. Hans S. wrote home about the songs he played on the piano. Other soldiers attempted to play music on the banduras, mandolins and other traditional Ukrainian plucked string instruments, left behind by locals who had fled east. There was even time for the soldiers of the 25th Motorised Infantry Division to take part in a competitive football match with Hungarian troops who were in Ukraine fighting alongside their Axis partners.[51]

Without exception, the men discussed food in their letters home. During the rapid advance in July they grumbled about the scarcity of fresh food. By August the division's intense travelling had subsided and the soldiers had an opportunity to prepare and enjoy their meals, usually with plundered ingredients, as they made their way towards the Dnieper River. Here the men wrote of drinking good hot coffee, and enjoying Japanese tuna and tea with lemons. More than thirty years later, as some of the men of the 25th Motorised Infantry Division put into writing their wartime experiences, they recalled the month of August 1941 with great affection, going so far as calling it 'paradise'. They described a week spent on an island in the Dnieper River overflowing with plums and honey, and remembered picking apricots and driving through fields of melons. All this occurred in the fertile fields of Ukraine, bread-basket of the USSR, which, according to Hitler, would eventually produce food for the rest of the Reich. Summer 1941 was a time marked by bonding, manly rituals and camaraderie, as the men of Griesinger's division swam together and used grenades to kill fish. In the August heat – more 'like Africa' than Ukraine, wrote one soldier – the men preferred to spend the nights sleeping outside in tents.[52]

Even though Robert and Gisela's correspondence from August 1941 does not survive, it is likely that his letters charted similar experiences. At this time the difficulty of raising children on the home front, coupled with Robert's absence, meant that Gisela seldom strayed far from the university. On 6 August it was more convenient for her to travel from Hohenheim to nearby Esslingen than to

The 25th Motorised Infantry Division's route into
the USSR in 1941

go into Stuttgart to renew her driver's licence.[53] Even though she
was not going away for more than a few hours, Gisela still made
sure to dress carefully for the occasion, putting on earrings and a
pearl necklace and wearing an elegant dark polka-dot blazer with
light-coloured spots that covered a white lace blouse. She might
even have sent a copy of the photograph to Robert on the Eastern
Front. On the same day Gisela went into the office of the district
administrator in Esslingen and pressed her ink-stained thumbs onto
her new driving licence, Walter Stahlecker was in Riga, where he
headed the mobile killing unit *Einsatzgruppe A*. On 6 August
Griesinger's associate, not content with arbitrary shootings or ghet-
toisation, penned a document that called for a 'radical' solution:
the complete extermination of Jews in the USSR.[54]

Gisela's driving license, 1941

The euphoria of the 25th Motorised Infantry Division ended with the advance on Kiev that began on 12 September 1941. German forces encountered fierce resistance when they attempted to prise the Ukrainian capital from Soviet control. Despite eventually capturing Kiev, victory came at an enormous cost. German divisions suffered heavy losses, with more than 20,000 men killed and tens of thousands of soldiers wounded. The week of 12–19 September was the bloodiest and most deadly of Griesinger's war, as gunfire, carnage and explosions lasted several days. Griesinger was among the wounded, hit in his right thigh on 19 September, the day Kiev fell.[55] As he lay on a makeshift hospital bed, medical staff cut open his blood-soaked trousers. With his thigh exposed, he was probably given injections of morphine to stop the pain, as doctors sought to remove the bullet that had shattered bone and torn up muscle. His injuries were so severe that they ended his experience of front-line combat on the Eastern Front. It took him months to recover.

In the days that followed, Griesinger learned about the atrocity at Babi Yar, the largest single massacre of Jews during the entire Second World War, which took place in Kiev on 29 and 30 September 1941. The collusion and participation of the *Wehrmacht* ensured such a high number of victims. On the morning of 29 September the Jews of Kiev were forced to assemble close to the city's main cemetery, from where they began the short walk to the Babi Yar ravine. *Wehrmacht* soldiers lined the route; there was no chance of escape. In just a couple of days at Babi Yar, 33,771 Jews were shot in the neck on the edge of the ravine. News of the enormity of the massacre, on a scale never previously seen, spread quickly throughout the *Wehrmacht* and the city. With soldiers writing about the scenes in their letters home, the bloodbath was not even an open secret.[56]

Despite the initial frustration he felt while serving on the Franco-German border, Griesinger's experience in the *Wehrmacht* had not been a disaster. Even though he was eventually wounded, he had not, like so many of his comrades, been killed or captured by the enemy. Instead he returned to a military hospital in Stuttgart, proud of what he had achieved at the front. Not only was he promoted from *Wachtmeister* to lieutenant during the course of the campaign, but he was also decorated with the Wound Badge for spilling blood for his country, and received the Iron Cross, both 2nd and 1st Class, for bravery in combat. His superiors also put forward his name to receive the Infantry Assault badge.[57]

Griesinger left the east in 1941, before the severe Russian winter, which turned out to be the coldest European winter in the twentieth century. Amid sub-zero temperatures, German soldiers who remained were poorly equipped to continue offensive operations. Hitler's hopes for a rapid victory did not materialise, and German soldiers experienced four years of ferocious warfare. But none of this was foreseen at the time Griesinger sustained his injury. With the USA still out of the war in autumn 1941, he returned to Stuttgart confident that a German victory was only a matter of time.

In the weeks and months that followed, Griesinger made it his mission never to return to the front line. Armed with a distinguished war record that would be a credit to any of the Third Reich's offices or institutions to which he sought to apply, he attempted, even before being released from hospital, to obtain a transfer to a prime administrative position in one of Germany's newly conquered territories.[58] Despite his wounds, Griesinger had not lost any of his earlier careerism. His letter to the authorities was printed on his own embossed letterhead.

Griesinger's sustained contact with Berlin in the hope of securing an administrative position in the east occurred at a critical moment. Only days before sending his first letter, the United States had entered the war on the Allies' side after the Japanese attack on Pearl Harbor on 7 December 1941. In the week he was preparing his application to transfer, Griesinger might have spared a thought for his American cousins – especially Dunbar Christ, a father of three young daughters living close to New Orleans, who was only a few years older than him. Christ's grandmother Mathilde and Griesinger's grandmother Lina had been sisters. Over Christmas 1941 and the weeks that followed, Griesinger waited anxiously for news of a transfer.

At the time Germans were living through their third winter of war. With the Nazi leadership having bargained for a short war with the USSR, food stocks on the home front were in a precarious state by January 1942, with more and more provisions being sent east to feed the German army. A short time later, the government made drastic cuts to the food-ration allowance, ushering in a diet in which bread and potatoes accounted for 90 per cent of the daily intake. Women spent more time waiting in shop queues for bread, whose quality had deteriorated to the point where people in the south began to complain of digestive problems. In some cases wealthier women were able to offset hunger, at least temporarily, by finding food on the black market. Intense rationing had a calamitous effect on the public, sparking comparisons with the debilitating conditions during the 'Turnip Winter' of 1916–17. Within a week of the decision to reduce rations, the SD reported that it was the worst single blow to civilian morale thus far in the war.[59]

It was during this time that Griesinger's mother, perhaps while looking through old boxes, rediscovered the diary she had kept during the First World War. Then in her late fifties, Wally reread her words of more than twenty years before, when, as a young mother with a husband away at the front and two children with her at home, she agonised over Germany's prospects for the future. By early 1942 two and a half years of war, coupled with news trickling out of Russia, reminded her of those tense bygone days. Wally once again picked up her fountain pen and began to write her thoughts. She turned over the cream page from her previous entry, written on 11 January 1920, and in blue ink in the middle of the next side wrote the words, 'The Second World War. 1939– '. In her short entry of just three paragraphs, Wally wrote of her disapproval of the ongoing war against the Soviet Union. 'What are we doing in this strange country?' she asked, as she wrote of the precarious situation during the harsh Russian winter, 'It is like 1812 all over again', making an explicit comparison to the failed invasion of Russia by Napoleon's Grande Armée. As she conveyed the freezing conditions and the indescribable violence unleashed upon – and not by – German troops, Wally was building up to her key sentence. 'Do we really want to follow Hitler to India?' she wrote, revealing her doubt in the Führer and questioning his war in the east. In a regime that criminalised all criticism, Wally must have known, as she put these words onto paper, that she was committing treason. The entry occupies the last page of her diary. She may have written more, but at some point the following nine pages were cut from the binding.[60]

Griesinger did not resume work following his release from hospital. He spent the best part of 1942 convalescing in Hohenheim as he waited patiently for a transfer to an occupied territory. His lack of promotion in the SS suggests it is unlikely that he committed greater time to SS activities. The local branch of the organisation no longer met as frequently. Most of his SS colleagues had not returned to the university since the launch of Operation Barbarossa. In some instances, their teaching and administrative replacements were not even party members.[61]

By late 1942 Griesinger was just about well enough to resume work. An administrative position had opened up in the Protectorate. The transfer that he longed for had arrived, and it would seal his fate. He would never return from Prague.

Chapter IX

Beer Bottles

When Griesinger arrived in the city of a hundred spires, on 8 March 1943, he will have been full of optimism for his life there, and fully aware of what his duties would entail at his new job at the Ministry of Economics and Labour, the government agency responsible for transforming Czech industry to serve the Reich. Gisela stayed behind in Hohenheim with the children, from where she diligently organised the entire family's move. They joined him in Prague three weeks later.

During my first visit to the Czech capital, as I spent the mornings looking for documents and the afternoons querying chairmakers and antique dealers in the city's Old Town, I began to piece together fragments of Griesinger's life in wartime Prague. Unlike Germany, where so many archives were destroyed at the end of the war, the Czech National Archives in Prague hold the complete records of the Reich's Ministry of Economics and Labour. The archive even retains detailed paperwork relating to the moving costs of its personnel to Prague, right down to the very receipt that Gustav von Maur's furniture-removals firm issued to Griesinger. After packing the family's smaller belongings into thirty-three crates and boxes, and larger items into a furniture carrier, Gisela signed the inventory on 30 March, allowing von Maur's men to transport everything by rail to Prague. Some of the Griesingers' glass possessions smashed on the journey, a matter that Robert made sure to complain to the firm about.[1]

The three-storey villa that Griesinger rented for his family was a grand house in a comfortable neighbourhood. As soon as Gisela and the children arrived in Prague on 9 April, the family moved into their new accommodation. Griesinger had used the weeks prior to their arrival to find the suitable family home, which was not a difficult task. Many Czechs seeking to take advantage of the influx of Germans with large salaries moving to Prague vacated their residences and either moved in with relatives or into houses in the country, as a means of generating income. Griesinger found the perfect residence at 749 Zitekstrasse in the affluent suburb of Bubeneč.[2] This area had been home to a significant middle- to upper-class Jewish population, which by the time of the Griesingers' arrival had vanished in its entirety.

Griesinger saw in Bubeneč the possibility to settle down and plant roots. In 1943 it was home to a large number of German officials and their families working for the Reich. Signature villas with large gardens, built in the 1920s and 1930s, were spread out over Bubeneč's wide tree-lined streets, which contained an attractive array of boutique shops and leafy parks. Today it is mostly diplomats and their families who live in this quiet area. When I tried to visit the Griesingers' former house, there was nobody home. I left a note for the current owner in the postbox, asking if I could come back another time. The current owner refused my request. They gave the same reason that I had heard before: they did not want their house caught up in a story involving the Nazis.

Griesinger would have known a large number of German officials who lived in Bubeneč. Walter Stahlecker moved to Prague in 1939 when he was made head of the Security Police for the Protectorate. After he was deployed to Oslo, his wife, Louise-Gabrielle, and their four young children remained in the city. The Stahleckers lived on Kastanienplatz, two streets away from the Griesingers. A number of Griesinger's colleagues also lived in the area. Walter Bertsch lived with his wife, Margot, and two sons at Bubentscher Strasse 22, around the corner from the Griesingers. Hanns-Martin Schleyer, who in 1977 was famously kidnapped and murdered by the Red Army Faction, also lived on Bubentscher Strasse with his wife and son. Griesinger would have known Schleyer through his position at the Central Association of Industry in the Protectorate. Schleyer's agency coordinated daily with the Ministry of Economics and Labour in overseeing the growth of Czech industry.[3]

Griesinger might have met Adolf Eichmann in the city, through his connection to Stahlecker. Eichmann's Czech-born wife, Vera, also lived in Prague during the Occupation. Stahlecker and Eichmann had been friends since 1938, when Stahlecker was Eichmann's direct superior at the Central Agency for the Emigration of the Jews in Vienna. From 1940 Adolf and Vera Eichmann lived apart, as Adolf worked in Berlin, where he headed the Central Office for Jewish Emigration from the Reich. During the war he made weekend visits to his wife and three sons, who lived in a luxurious villa at Molischstrasse 22, located on the opposite side of Bubeneč from the Griesingers. Unlike the home of Robert and Gisela, who rented their property from Dr Karel Brabenec, a high-ranking Czechoslovak government official, the Eichmann villa had been seized from Rudolf Fišer, its Jewish owner, against his will.

For the Griesingers, Prague was safe and peaceful and seemed a world away from the Allied bombs descending over Germany. RAF aerial assaults, which for much of the war had spared the South West of the country, became a sudden worry at the very moment the Griesingers left Germany. The introduction in spring 1943 of new radio-guidance systems had made targeting more accurate. In the week Griesinger left his home town, the RAF dropped around 500 bombs and over 58,000 incendiary devices on the south of Stuttgart, killing more than 100 people and injuring almost 400.[4] In Prague, the brutality of the Occupation against the Czech people also contributed to the sense of calm in the city. As the Griesingers settled into their happy new lives, the local Czech population lived in constant fear of Nazi terror. Even though repression in the Protectorate did not reach the same level of intensity as it did in countries with large resistance movements, such as Poland or Yugoslavia, from the outset of the Occupation German officials set in place an excessively brutal system designed to outlaw opposition to Nazi rule.[5]

From the spring of 1939 German military figures with fixed bayonets, police and undercover security agents patrolled the streets of Prague. Much of the task of setting up and coordinating security fell to Walter Stahlecker, Griesinger's former boss, who was appointed Commander of the Security Police and Security Services in the Protectorate in summer 1939. As he had done five years earlier in Stuttgart, Stahlecker laid the foundations for the police state to flourish in the Czech lands. Throughout late 1939 and into 1940 he set up a network of security offices whose purpose was to clamp down on illegal groups and resistance cells. Using the Hotel Silber as a model, he set up the offices of the Prague Gestapo – including its torture cells – in the Petschek Palace, which employed a staff of 1,000 workers. The Prague Gestapo thrived under the leadership of Hans-Ulrich Geschke, who, like Griesinger, started his undergraduate degree in law at Tübingen in spring 1925.

The first major crackdown against the Czech population came in autumn 1939. Following the killing of student leader Jan Opletal at a demonstration, thousands of Czech students turned up at his funeral, which soon turned violent. Days later, on 17 November, the Gestapo began raiding students' homes and dormitories in Prague and Brno. As the Nazis executed nine members of the Committee of the Czech Students' Union that morning, 1,200 students were rounded up and sent for incarceration at the Sachsenhausen concentration camp. When they arrived, their heads were shaved and they were made to wear prisoners' uniforms.[6] The terrified students spent the next few years interned, hungry and cold, in appalling conditions. The anniversary of 17 November later became International Students' Day, in memory of those killed and imprisoned. In the weeks that followed the arrests, the Germans closed down all universities, initially for three years. As Nazi officials took over the Protectorate's government departments, forced Czech farmers off their land, attacked Czech culture and imposed tight censorship laws, they also launched a campaign against political opponents and resisters, whom they could arrest without warrant and convict without trial. After two German customs officials were killed in March 1940 in Domažlice, the Nazis retaliated by rounding up 100 of the town's inhabitants and deporting them to concentration camps in Germany.[7]

The appointment of Reinhard Heydrich as Deputy Reich Protector on 27 September 1941 made the lives of millions of Czechs even more miserable. On taking up his role, Heydrich set out to crush the will of the Czech people. He let it be known that the penalties for people caught listening to foreign radio or participating in the black market would be severe. Known as the 'hangman of Prague', Heydrich imposed a state of martial law to crack down on resistance activities, which had grown spectacularly over the summer. In June 1941 Communist resisters had distributed 377 pamphlets across the Protectorate. By October of that year the number had increased to 10,727.[8] Heydrich's reign of terror was marked by mass arrests, incarcerations and the setting up of summary courts. Within three days of his arrival in the Protectorate, the new courts sentenced to death ninety-two Czechs, and sent hundreds more to Gestapo prisons. During winter 1941-2 these prisoners, together with hundreds of other victims of Nazi terror, were thrown onto trains that transported them to concentration camps, where they carried out slave labour in gruelling conditions. Beatings, hunger and fear of death marked the rhythm of camp life for slave labourers.[9] The Nazis also homed in on black marketeers, whom they accused of subverting the economy. Czechs caught selling goods on the black market were sent to concentration camps. Sometimes the consequences were even more severe. In late 1941 a Brno court sentenced to death two men accused of selling two pigs on the black market.[10]

Of the 1,299 Czechs who were sent to the Mauthausen concentration camp in Austria, only 4 per cent returned at the end of the war.[11] SS guards executed most Czech prisoners in 1942, in retaliation for the assassination of Reinhard Heydrich. On 27 May British-trained Czechoslovak paratroopers Ján Kubiš and Jozef Gabcík had ambushed the Deputy Reich Protector as he made his way through Prague in an open-topped car. When Gabcík's gun jammed, Kubiš launched a grenade at Heydrich's car. The flying shrapnel wounded Heydrich, who died a week later of sepsis. Heydrich's assassination led to some of the most intense reprisals of the Second World War, which all but crushed any possible resistance. In the weeks that followed, the Germans raided 5,000 localities, arresting 3,180 people and sentencing 1,344 to death.[12] In Lidice, where villagers were falsely connected to aiding the assassins, all the men of the village were shot, while the women and children were deported to concentration camps. On 24 October 1942 in Mauthausen 135 Czech women, who had supposedly helped the parachutists, had their heads shaved, before being marched in the snow to a cellar, where they were beaten by SS guards. After being told they were to have a medical examination, each woman stood in line and waited her turn to enter the 'consulting room'. In reality, the women were lining up to be executed. They were led into the room at two-minute intervals, where they were shot.[13]

Just as elsewhere in the Reich, the SS in Prague was responsible for security and policing. It led many of the reprisals taken against the civilian population. Before his assassination, Heydrich had increased the intensity and scope of the SS, which meant that at the time of Griesinger's arrival the organisation was more powerful in the Czech lands than the army. Prague alone had 7,000 full-time SS men stationed in the centre and its periphery. As the SS requisitioned the Charles University Law School as its headquarters in 1939, the *Waffen-SS* moved into the Adolf Hitler barracks in the centre of the city.[14] For the citizens of Prague, it was not possible to walk past an important building without seeing SS guards standing in front. Even though by spring 1943 the spate of violent reprisals against Czechs had calmed down, the SS, under the command of Dr Erwin Weinmann (another contemporary from Tübingen and Stuttgart), was still shooting 150 people a week.[15]

Griesinger would quickly have noticed that the SS presence was not confined to the streets and that, rather, it was ingrained in the office culture of the Protectorate. According to witnesses, senior officials at Griesinger's ministry were emphatically pro-Nazi. Some took pleasure in denouncing Czech colleagues to the authorities.[16] Most of Griesinger's colleagues were SS members. Minister Bertsch was especially high-ranking, holding the position of *SS Brigadeführer*.[17]

Gustav von Schmoller, who as one of the five lawyers in the economics branch of the ministry was among Griesinger's closest colleagues, was also an SS member. He was one of a number of Germans who used their time in Prague as a springboard from which to launch an illustrious post-war career. After the war, von Schmoller was the West German ambassador to Sweden.[18]

During his time in the Protectorate it was Griesinger's work at the Ministry of Economics and Labour that proved more decisive than his position in the SS in earning him the status of a Holocaust perpetrator. Even so, advancement at the ministry hinged on being a part of the SS or SD, although there was no need to be an especially active member. Unlike at Hohenheim, where he received two rapid promotions, in Prague Griesinger was never promoted from the rank of *Obersturmführer*, while countless others were.

In Prague, German newspapers listed party activities that were open to all Nazi party members. Whole sections of *Prager Abend* and *Der Neue Tag* contained details of upcoming events. At some gatherings, such as party film events, attendance was optional. Newspapers made clear which events, such as participation in rallies, were compulsory.[19] Just as in the SS, Griesinger probably played a minimal role in party activities and meetings in his new city, due to the constraints of his job, which took up most of his time. From his 1944 passport, discovered in Jana's chair, it was clear that travel throughout the Protectorate and even beyond, sometimes for extended spells, was central to his role.

Griesinger fared better in adjusting to life in Prague than did his colleagues who left Germany for administrative posts in newly acquired territory in Lithuania, Belarus or Ukraine. Not only was life in the city described as tranquil by German visitors, but Prague was also grounded in German history, culture and intellectual life.[20] Its baroque architecture would have felt familiar to the Griesingers. Grandiose plans to Germanise the Czech lands continued under Heydrich. In May 1942 he launched Prague's Culture Week, hoping the injection of German art, music and literature, at the expense of Czech and Jewish culture, would transform Prague into one of the Reich's leading cities. He also put in place an ambitious architectural and road-design plan to render Prague the gateway of the new Nazi Empire into the Balkans and the Occupied East.[21]

Spring 1943 was an important moment for Griesinger to begin his job as head of Section WIC (production and management) within the economics wing of the Ministry of Economics and Labour. Shortly before his death, Heydrich catapulted Walter Bertsch, the department's head, into the new Protectorate government as Minister of Economics and Labour. Bertsch's inability to speak Czech ensured that from the moment of his appointment, meetings of the Protectorate's Czech government were conducted exclusively in German, a move that undermined any semblance of governmental autonomy. Alongside Bertsch, Heydrich also promoted to senior management positions those of his supporters with strong Nazi pedigrees. He hand-picked Erich von Wedelstädt and Wilhelm Dennler, who had worked for him at the *Reichsprotektor's* office, to lead the Economics and Labour divisions respectively. Griesinger arrived at a ministry whose senior officials had proved their worth and loyalty to Heydrich. It was an agency shaped in the Hangman's image. The twenty-five leading men of the Ministry of Economics and Labour, of which Griesinger was one, were all in their mid- to late thirties and had obtained doctorates at leading German universities.[22] Within weeks, Griesinger's stints working in remote parts of Württemberg, as he advanced up the career ladder, were a distant memory. Even his move to Hohenheim had paid off handsomely.

As an area rich in natural resources and heavy industry, the Protectorate was key to the Reich in an era of total war. Bertsch's Ministry of Economics and Labour existed to seize Czech assets and ensure that the entire Czech economy worked exclusively for Germany. Among its many responsibilities, the ministry also had the power to close existing Czech industries deemed non-essential for war. As a result of ministry intervention, shoe factories in Zlín suddenly began producing V-1 and V-2 rockets, as well as tyres for the *Wehrmacht*.[23] The ministry could also rely on a close working relationship with the Gestapo to force Czech workers to comply with demand production. Ernst Gerke, who replaced Hans-Ulrich Geschke as leader of the Gestapo in Prague, earned the title 'executioner' because of the brutal methods he used to discipline workers. Gerke's Gestapo agents ruthlessly hunted down and murdered in cold blood those Czech workers whose behaviour, they believed, threatened production. The Gestapo wasted little time engaging with workers' demands. When a group of fourteen miners from the Krimich mine at Tlučná failed to show up for work one Sunday, Gerke ordered the execution of one of them, while the others received a sentence of forty-nine years' imprisonment. In August 1943, four months after Griesinger arrived, 400 workers at the Bohemia-Moravia Engine Factory went on strike. Within three hours the Prague Gestapo had executed the strike's four leaders and sent fourteen others to hard labour. Work at the factory resumed promptly.[24]

As a *Regierungsrat* at the ministry, it fell to Griesinger to respond to legal matters related to production, from the heavy industries of glass, metals and stone products, down to the light industries of rubber, leather and tobacco.[25] Gleaning the papers of the Ministry of Economics and Labour, most of which survived the war, I began to get a sense of Griesinger's daily routine. One part of his job involved keeping up to date with new orders and decrees coming from Berlin and published in the *Deutscher Reichsanzeiger und Preußischer Staatsanzeiger*, the Reich's official daily newspaper, which set out new administrative regulations. Griesinger scoured the *Reichsanzeiger* to see whether instructions had been passed that fell within his remit. In the event they did, it was up to him to determine how to legally introduce or adapt existing legislation for the specific needs of the Protectorate. He often left Gisela and the children for long stretches, sometimes lasting weeks at a time, to travel across the Protectorate, holding meetings with local economics groups, speaking to employers of small and large businesses and visiting mills, mines, factories and other sites of production, many of which, given the importance of heavy industry, had SS troops stationed at the entrance.[26]

Some of the cases that landed on Griesinger's desk might seem surprising, when considering the war economy of the Protectorate. I came across letters from February 1944 that went back and forth between Griesinger and local representatives from glass and brewing industries about the shortage of beer bottles. Unlikely as it might seem, the issue was of the utmost importance. By early 1944 breweries in the Czech lands, responsible for delivering beer to the *Wehrmacht* and the *Waffen-SS*, struggled to find enough bottles to meet their targets. At a meeting in early February, Griesinger learned that there were only six to seven million beer bottles in the Protectorate, a figure down from twenty million in 1939. Since the outbreak of war, glass manufacturing had been geared towards weapon production. For the good of the war effort, Griesinger needed to ensure that every single beer bottle got reused, and he sought to punish companies and ordinary civilians that did not recycle. He was particularly vexed with Bulgaria – the 'only country', according to Griesinger, 'not to return bottles'. In early 1944 a beer bottle, its weight, cost and wholesale distribution took on new meaning and engulfed Griesinger's daily interactions, as he met with financial representatives of glass and beer companies, arranged visits to a galaxy of breweries and warehouses and compiled reports.[27] Curiously enough, Griesinger found himself performing similar tasks to Fritz Rothschild, his former Jewish neighbour in Stuttgart, who worked for the war economy hundreds of miles away in Paris.

From the moment the Protectorate was created, the Germans took advantage of cheap Czech labour. By the end of the war almost half a million Czech workers had been torn from their families and sent to work for the Reich. Displacement of forced labourers occurred at different stages of the war. By 1941, 140,000 Czech labourers were enforcedly working in Germany and Austria.[28] As the war went on and Germany suffered heavy losses on the Eastern Front, demand for Czech workers increased. A law passed in November 1942, only four months before Griesinger's arrival in Prague, made it compulsory for all Czech men born between 1918 and 1920 to work in Germany for the armaments industry.

The Ministry of Economics and Labour was responsible for sending Czech workers to German and Austrian mines, farms and factories. During his first year in Prague, Griesinger played his part in transporting 75,000 Czech men and women to join hundreds of thousands of forced workers from across occupied Europe to work for the Reich.[29] The Germans treated the workers, who were classed as Slavs and therefore inferior, worse than those mobilised from western Europe.[30] In Germany, hungry and exploited Czech workers spent their time living in filthy camps, where they performed back-breaking manual labour. Functioning for little pay, they worked for a minimum of ten hours a day, chiefly in agriculture and the metal industry, repairing roads and carrying out other menial tasks.

In most cases Czech workers did not receive training to operate dangerous machinery. Amputations and other accidents occurred time and time again, leaving Czech workers screaming on the blood-stained factory floor. Hundreds of miles from home, workers lived in constant dread of German terror. Just as workers were sent to disciplinary camps if they spent too long on their coffee breaks, courts meted out harsh sentences to male Czech workers found fraternising with German women.[31] At the Steyr works in Hütte Linz foremen took pride in taking away and violently beating 'lazy' Czech workers, whom they later brought back to the factory floor to serve as examples of what would happen to idle labourers.[32] The fear of what might happen if they were to step out of line weighed heavily on the minds of Czech workers. After being over-heard making a defeatist remark, one female Czech worker at an armaments factory near Berlin was so scared of the consequences that she took her own life.[33] Night-time was especially difficult. Workers were too scared to go to sleep, knowing that Allied bombers had their sights set on German factories and industrial areas. Even if they were fortunate enough to survive the bombing, they were forced to clean up the debris.[34] Overall, more than 3,000 young Czech workers died in Germany during the war, while thousands more suffered psychological trauma or were left permanently disabled.[35]

At the very moment Griesinger sought to establish his presence at the ministry, demand for labour was at its highest. One element of his job was to recommend the closure of certain Czech industries, sometimes with the intention of sending its workers to Germany. In summer 1944 he homed in on the phosphate-rock industry in order to, in his words, 'make more workers available' to send to the Atlantic coast, where the Todt Organisation was constructing roads and military coastal defences.[36] Griesinger was only just getting started. The speed with which he closed companies and redistributed labourers to German factories made him deeply unpopular with the Czech population. The National Archives in Prague contain pages of documents that point to Griesinger's heavy-handed methods when it came to liquidating glass, carbonate-mineral and ceramic-stone and earth companies. Anton Beran, owner of a carbonate-mineral company in Prague, was so angry with what he considered Griesinger's improper behaviour in the takeover of his company that he even wrote an official complaint about him in May 1944 to the highest authority in the land, Karl Hermann Frank, Secretary of State of the Protectorate. According to Beran, Griesinger was nothing more than a dishonest trickster, who had lied about the number of tonnes of carbonate minerals that Beran's mines were producing in order to cheat the Czech industrialist out of the company that he had spent ten years building up.[37]

When Griesinger first attempted to join the Ministry of Economics and Labour in 1940 he knew that part of the job involved active discrimination against the country's Jews. Upon his arrival in the Protectorate in spring 1943, Jewish life in a country that produced cultural greats such as Gustav Mahler and Franz Kafka was almost at an end. As was the case elsewhere in occupied Europe, the Nazis passed antisemitic laws in the Protectorate, prohibiting Jews from property ownership, a series of professions and entry to public places. From the outset of the Occupation, the Nazis subjected Jews who had lived in Bohemia and Moravia for hundreds of years to poverty, persecution and humiliation. Shunted out of public life, Jews also suffocated under the weight of heavy restrictions, entitled as they were to fewer food and clothing-ration coupons than their non-Jewish neighbours. Jews who were scared, cold and hungry tried desperately to get by as the noose began to tighten.

From early 1941 unemployed Jews were conscripted throughout the Protectorate for forced labour, where they often worked in debilitating conditions, earning less than their Czech counterparts. Part of the responsibility for deploying Jewish workers fell to Walter Bertsch's office. Fearing that local Jewish officials might sabotage the allocation process, in April 1941 Bertsch ensured that it was his office and *not* the Jewish community that decided where, and in what conditions, Jews were sent away to labour.[38] Persecution continued throughout that year. In September 1941 the Germans forced Jews in the Protectorate to wear the yellow star. A short time later the Ministry of Economics and Labour saw to it that Jews were prohibited from buying leather goods, due to shortages.[39] From the end of 1941 a camp-ghetto was set up at Theresienstadt, forty miles north of Prague, to confine all the Jews of the Protectorate prior to their deportation. In their final months in the Czech lands, Jews incarcerated at Theresienstadt lived in abysmal conditions. Disease and starvation were so rife in the overcrowded ghetto that the death rate became comparable to concentration camps such as Dachau and Buchenwald. For many prisoners the sight and sound of the funeral cart, as it made its way laden with wooden coffins along the ghetto's streets, became part and parcel of camp life.[40] The Holocaust eviscerated Czech Jewry. In 1939 there were 118,310 Jews in the Protectorate. In addition to the 26,000 Jews who had managed to emigrate, 72,000 Jews had been deported to camps and ghettos. By late 1944 only 6,795 remained.[41]

Just as they had done in Stuttgart in 1936, the Griesingers moved to an area that only a short while earlier had been home to a vibrant Jewish community. At the time the family arrived, just a few thousand Jews in the Czech lands remained outside Theresienstadt's walls. These Jews would have interested Griesinger. In 1943, 64.9 per cent of the non-interned Jews, most of whom were in mixed marriages, were forced labourers who worked constructing roads, in mines or performing farmwork for the German war effort. By

1944 this had risen to 83.3 per cent.[42] Some Jews, with the help of the Czech population, were in hiding outside the ghetto, but the consequences for their rescuers were severe, if discovered. In October 1943 theatre critic Marianne Golz, the leader of a resistance cell that sheltered Jews, was beheaded in Prague after the Nazis uncovered her activities.[43]

Griesinger appeared in the Protectorate long after most Jews had been purged from social and economic life or deported. Even so, as an employee of a ministry charged with deploying Jewish forced labour until spring 1945, he still played a direct role in the Holocaust in Bohemia and Moravia. As overseer at the ministry for cement and brick production, Griesinger controlled the destiny of the Jewish labourers who slaved away in these sectors. From his office in Prague hundreds of miles away from their sites of work, he was on occasion called on to decide their fate. Any worker about to be transferred from a mine or a brickyard needed first to have Griesinger's authorisation. In September of 1944, for instance, he was instructed to transfer to Prague – and almost certain incarceration in Theresienstadt – a company of Jewish forced labourers in the cement and brick industry.[44] No evidence in the near-complete archives of the Ministry of Economics and Labour suggests that he ignored this instruction.

Having finally arrived in Prague, Griesinger was in no hurry to leave it. Reading box after box of Griesinger's letters and reports that he produced during two years there, I got the sense that he loved his job at the ministry and the responsibility that came with it. His attention to detail bordered on fastidiousness. He revelled in the respect that the position afforded him. Prague had given his life a new passion and purpose. His zeal and professionalism at performing his tasks and obtaining results did not go unnoticed by his superiors. By 1944 the Protectorate was outperforming the rest of the Reich in its industrial production.[45] In Prague his efforts finally reaped the praise that for so long had eluded him. Reports from this time described Griesinger as a 'good and loyal worker'. In December 1944 Minister Bertsch put Griesinger's name forward for the sought-after War Merit Cross (2nd Class without Swords),

as someone who had served the ministry with 'great merit'. Only
two months later Bertsch attempted to promote Griesinger within
the ministry.[46] However, the course of the war put an end to his
long-awaited promotion.

At the time of our first meeting, Jutta was in her late seventies,
having been born in January 1937. She could not remember anything
of her life before Prague. Her earliest memory was of Barbara
nestling in Gisela's arms during the train ride there in spring 1943.
She was sure that her older half-brother Joachim, then aged ten,
did not travel with them. Written sources call into question the
accuracy of Jutta's early memory. Not only do Czech archives reveal
that Joachim was on board the train, but they also show that Robert
paid extra for three-year-old Barbara to have her own seat, to avoid
having to sit on her mother's lap.[47]

I asked Jutta to tell me what she could about the house on
Zitekstrasse. She remembered the number of storeys, the garden
on a hill that led down to the street, the sound of trains entering
and leaving the nearby railway station. Memories soon began to
flow. 'There were two people in the house who took care of us,'
said Jutta, happy to recall this detail that she thought she had
forgotten. 'A man who was the chauffeur and the gardener, and a
maid who cooked and looked after us. We spent a lot of time with
her.' Jutta remembered that in the evenings the children usually
ate dinner with the maid in the kitchen, her parents dining together
elsewhere. The family's after-dinner routine was always the same:
as Gisela went to light a cigarette, Robert turned on the record
player to relax to classical music. Only rarely did Jutta see her father
smoking. She remembered that her parents listened often to Verdi's
music, when she had to be silent. It might seem fanciful that a
seven-year-old could distinguish Verdi and recollect it seventy years
later, but I trusted Jutta on this detail. Herbert, Jutta's husband,
had been a violinist at the Tonhalle, Switzerland's leading orchestra.
'I know every Verdi,' she said with confidence.

Jutta shared other details of domestic life in Prague. As befitted
their backgrounds, her parents were long accustomed to having

domestic staff in the home. 'I never saw my father in the kitchen and my mother couldn't cook,' said Jutta. She recalled that her parents often hosted dinner parties during the war. She remembered the beautiful – non-uniform – clothes worn by the guests, but was unable to recall the names of any of her parents' friends. Even though the children did not attend such dinners, their presence was a highly choreographed ritual. In something akin to the 'So Long, Farewell' scene from *The Sound of Music*, Joachim, Jutta and Barbara would be summoned in their best clothes to bid goodnight to their parents' guests, before being led back upstairs by the trusted maid. 'Everyone made such a fuss, it was awful. It was like something from Jane Austen,' Jutta said, cringing as she relived this memory from childhood.

When I asked her whether she could remember any celebrations at which her father was present, Jutta thought for a moment. 'I can remember a Christmas. It must have been in 1943 or 1944.' She had an image of Robert standing next to a big tree covered in lights, with presents surrounding the base. She remembered him handing each daughter a package that his mother, Wally – 'Omi Haigst' – had sent from Stuttgart. 'Our grandmother had given us each a doll. Mine was pretty and extremely large, but Barbara's was very small: it wasn't nearly as nice. Nevertheless, I had no interest in mine. I desperately wanted hers instead.' Jutta explained that this was not an isolated incident. Rather, as the girls grew up, Wally constantly showed her preference for Jutta, Robert's firstborn child, who closely resembled a Griesinger. She was tall and slim with dark hair and dark eyes, whereas Barbara was fairer and looked more like her mother. 'It was always the same. I always got the nicer, more expensive presents. I couldn't understand why I was somehow more special than my sister. I hated it all my life.'

It took only some gentle probing for Jutta to remember more of her father's distinguishing features and character traits from her early life in Prague. She remembered that Griesinger regularly had nosebleeds. The only time she recalled seeing her father in his underwear was when he had a nosebleed in Prague. 'Throughout my childhood, he was always very smartly dressed. I never saw him without a tie. On this occasion, I remember seeing him coming out of the bathroom and calling for my mother. I watched as she put cold towels around his neck.' I asked at this point whether Jutta believed that her parents had a loving relationship. She remembered being raised in a house full of affection. The sound of the English word 'darling', used by both parents to speak to the other, was a constant presence in her childhood. So too were her parents' nicknames, Gisi and Robi.

Her father liked animals and had always kept a dog as a pet. For Jutta, one memory in particular provides real insight into Robert's character. On a hot summer day in 1943 or 1944, as the family was walking in Prague, their small miniature Schnauzer, whose name Jutta could not recall, noticed another dog on the other side of the street and suddenly dashed towards it. As it jumped into the road, it was struck by a car and lay helpless in a pool of blood. As the rest of the family looked on, crying and screaming in horror, Jutta's father rushed out into the road, removed his beige linen jacket and picked up the dog. He promptly marched the whole family to a vet. By the time they arrived, her father's jacket was soaked in blood. Jutta remembers his spontaneity on this occasion as being typical of Robert. 'That was what my father was like,' she said. 'When he had an idea about something, there were no questions. He didn't ask my mother, he just acted on it.'

As party and SS events became less of a priority for Griesinger in Prague, he strengthened his connections with Swabia and Tübingen University, hoping it would improve his social standing. Many of the Tübingen graduates that Reichsprotektor von Neurath hand-picked for management positions in the Protectorate had worked in similar positions in the Württemberg state administration. Eighteen Swabians were appointed to posts deemed 'important' for the day-to-day running of the Protectorate.[48] The familiar sounds and faces of Prague's large Swabian diaspora would have eased Robert and Gisela's adaptation to life in the city. So too would Griesinger's membership of Suevia Tübingen, his student fraternity. Having in the 1920s performed the roles of speaker, secretary and cashier of Suevia Tübingen, Griesinger was known to many of his Corps brothers in Prague, enabling him to take advantage of an extensive social network.

Throughout the entire period that Robert, Gisela and the children lived in the Protectorate, they were completely separated from the local Czech population. In Prague the Griesingers joined an elite social circle (*Gesellschaft*), enabling them to take part in an array of activities, music, artistic and other forms of entertainment laid on for Nazi officials and their families. During the war Prague had one of the finest entertainment scenes anywhere in occupied Europe, rivalled only by Paris. Cinema was especially popular. The city's 111 cinemas thrived during the Occupation, with audiences doubling in size to take in new German films.[49] As was the case with cinema, Prague's many theatres and music auditoria had a packed programme for each season. Knowing the importance of theatre to German public morale, Goebbels spent more money on theatre than he did on propaganda itself.[50]

The Griesinger family benefited from a series of official directives intended to improve the day-to-day lives of Germans in the Protectorate. From 1939 vast sums were set aside for strengthening Germandom, many of which were aimed directly at German children. In 1941 and 1942 German officials requested nine million Reichsmark from the central fund for Germanisation in order to construct brand-new German nurseries, kindergartens, libraries, cinemas and other cultural and educational initiatives. Robert and Gisela did not have to struggle to find a place at a local German kindergarten and primary school for their children, where there would be no possibility of their meeting any Czech children. At a time when the Nazis set out to Germanise Czech children and re-educate them separately, the number of German primary schools rose steeply during the Occupation, from 130 to 333.[51]

Griesinger charted his daily life in the letters he sent to his parents in Stuttgart. In Prague the family was healthy and well nourished. Until the end of 1944 there was always plenty to eat, and Griesinger

Barbara (third from left) and Jutta (fourth from left)
at school in Prague, c. 1944

was able to send packages of food home to his parents.[52] German
citizens like the Griesingers had priority over Czechs when it came
to shopping. Reich citizens were able to get first pick of supplies
in the shops, before doors opened for Czechs at ten o'clock. They
were also eligible for extra rations. It is little wonder that Germans
referred to the Protectorate as the 'land of smiles'. To add to their
meagre allowance, Czech residents of Prague took to growing
vegetables in public spaces. The Griesingers would have seen potatoes being grown in parks and cemeteries as they walked through
the city.[53]

   Like all German families at the time, the Griesingers' contact
with the local population was limited to their domestic help. I was
eager to discover more about the maid Jutta remembered. Someone
skilled at needlework had ensured that Griesinger's documents
remained inside that chair for seventy years, and the maid seemed
the most likely candidate by far. After a vigorous search in the
Czech archives, I was able to uncover her identity. Going back even

Joachim, Jutta, Gisela, Robert and Barbara with the family dog in
Prague, 1943

before the war, Czechoslovakian police kept meticulous notes on
every residential property, logging the names of each person and
the dates they moved in or out of a house or apartment. The
National Archives in Prague contain millions of property 'arcs' –
long sheets of paper with the address written at the top, under
which is recorded in chronological order every former resident – but
because of confidentiality laws, the arcs are inaccessible to
researchers. After I discovered their existence via a tip-off, I spent
several hours trying to persuade archivists to grant me access. My
request was repeatedly ignored until one archivist, presumably
wanting to be rid of this pushy British researcher, agreed to show
me the arc of Griesinger's house.

On the day the Griesinger family arrived in Bubeneč, Maria N.,
a twenty-eight-year-old housekeeper from Pilsen, moved into the
house with them. Her tenure with the family did not last long. On
6 July 1943, after just three months in service, she left the Griesingers'
employment. Maria was replaced the very same day by Anna K.,

a thirty-one-year-old maid from the Moravian village of Střílky.[54] *Der Neue Tag*, a daily newspaper in Prague, carried on its back page adverts seeking or offering work. There, just two weeks before Anna arrived in the Griesingers' villa, was an anonymous notice offering a position for a housemaid (*Hausmädchen*) with cooking skills.[55] If Robert and Gisela did advertise for their maid, this would have been one of the most promising places to start. Given the importance to her job of oral communication, the Griesingers must have been satisfied with the new maid's spoken German.

Anna was fortunate. Employment for a German family allowed her to avoid being sent to work in a German factory, a fate that befell tens of thousands of Czech women. She stayed in the Griesingers' house until 16 May 1945, eleven days *after* the Prague Uprising against the Germans began.[56] Believing that Anna might hold the key to solving the mystery of the hidden papers, I tried to uncover more about her.

She was in her mid-thirties and unmarried when she moved away from Bubeneč. Given that she was childless in spring 1945, coupled with her age, I thought it unlikely she went on to have children. I was wrong. Only ten days after leaving Griesinger's house, in what must have been among the first ceremonies to take place following the liberation of Prague by the Red Army, Anna married Josef K., a barber. Less than three months later, in mid-August 1945, she gave birth to a daughter, Magdalena. Anna had been pregnant with Magdalena since the end of 1944. She experienced the normal signs of pregnancy while living under Griesinger's roof – signs that, even amid the upheaval of the final months of the war, could not have escaped the notice of her employers. Additional records confirmed that by 1950 Anna and Josef had had a second child, a boy called Miloslav.[57]

From 1950 until 1983, when their trail in the archives ran cold, Anna and Josef lived in an apartment close to the Old Town in Prague on Dlouhá Street, just a couple of minutes' walk from Celetná and Králodvorská, the site of the furniture store where Jana first laid eyes on the armchair.[58] When I went to inspect the property on Dlouhá Street, the K. family name was still listed at the entrance as one of the building's residents. Within a few days I found myself speaking on the telephone to Anna's daughter, Magdalena, who was wary of my interest in her mother. She couldn't understand why anyone would be interested in the life of a maid. The conversation became easier after I explained Anna's significance to my research. Magdalena did not want me to send her a photo of the armchair. 'I can't know anything about it,' she said. She laughed when I said she might recognise it. I hadn't thought my idea absurd. In adulthood and even old age, when prompted, people can often recall objects from their childhood – a piece of furniture, an ashtray, a childhood toy – that they have not thought about for decades.

Magdalena admitted knowing little about her mother's life during the war. She was aware Anna had worked as a nanny, knowing that she had once even worked for a Jewish family, but claimed not to have known that a German family had employed her mother during the Occupation. As we spoke, Magdalena provided some useful insights into her mother's life, telling me that Anna spoke excellent German, a gift that would have played a central role in securing employment in the Griesinger household. She knew that alongside looking after the children in her charge, Anna also cooked and did the family's laundry. 'Sewing was not her forte and she was not a particularly good seamstress.' So it was unlikely Anna had helped sew Griesinger's papers, which ended up undetected for seventy years, into the chair. Had she been responsible for the act, the threads would have come undone in no time. And because Magdalena did not remember the lullabies her mother sang to her as a child, it was impossible to know the sounds that Joachim, Jutta and Barbara heard as they fell asleep in Prague each night.

As we discussed the Nazi occupation, Magdalena insisted on her father's wartime patriotism and his contempt for the enemy. I wondered how the vehemently anti-German Josef reacted to his girlfriend's presence in the home of a Nazi official, especially one who played a role in deporting Czech workers to German mines and factories. Just then Magdalena told me there was something burning in the kitchen and she had to go, a ploy used by grandmothers all over the world for generations to get off the phone. It was to be the only contact I had with her.

Over the summer and autumn of 1944 the Allies began to liberate the European continent with intense speed. By the end of the year the Red Army in the east, and Allied forces led by British and US troops in the west, had pushed back the retreating *Wehrmacht* thousands of miles. Despite such seismic events elsewhere in Europe, the Griesingers' settled life in Prague continued well into 1945. As the Allies closed in on Germany from all sides, did Griesinger have any inkling that time was running out for the Third Reich? If he had done, he might have prepared better for afterwards, perhaps transferring some of his investments to neutral Liechtenstein, where he had familial connections. He even had the opportunity to do so. The stamps in his passport show that on 21 July 1944, just weeks after D-Day and only a day after the German generals' failed attempt to assassinate Hitler, Griesinger took the family on holiday to visit his in-laws in Liechtenstein. Before leaving Prague, Robert and Gisela would have known about the plot at the Wolf's Lair in East Prussia. Word of the failed attempt had gone out on the radio the previous evening.

By the morning of 21 July, Hitler took to the airwaves to address the German nation, in which he cited Claus von Stauffenberg, a family friend of Griesinger's from childhood, as the person who placed the bomb and who had since been shot. Arrests and executions followed swiftly throughout the Reich, reaching even senior military officers involved in the plot in Prague, who a day earlier were planning to arrest all leading SS and party officials in the Protectorate. Von Stauffenberg's mother, Caroline, an old friend of Wally Griesinger, was promptly arrested and held in solitary confinement until the end of the war.[59]

Not only did the plot's failure reveal that Hitler continued to enjoy the support of senior military personnel, but it also instilled in the German people a renewed belief that Hitler was invincible. Concurrently German propaganda continued to give hope to the civilian population about the war in the east and the development of new *Wunderwaffe* (Wonder Weapons) that would soon defeat the Allies. Scared of Nazi reprisals and of future Bolshevik terror, the nation was prepared to fight to the end. Well into 1945 most Germans turned a blind eye to the grim reality, believing instead messages of hope that they heard from the party, government and army officials and others whom they trusted. In early 1945 an elderly lady made her way to an appointment on the other side of Königsberg as bombs exploded around her. After arriving on time at the hospital where she was due to have surgery to treat varicose veins, she was urged by hospital staff to flee the doomed city. Their advice was met with a piercing response: 'the Führer won't let us fall to the Russians; he'd sooner gas us,' she said. Even those mistrustful of state propaganda could not fathom the possibility of defeat and tried to go about life as normal, in a deluded hope that the inevitable could be avoided.[60]

If Griesinger had sensed the impending fall of the Third Reich, he could have remained in Liechtenstein with his wealthy in-laws or, through loyalty to Bertsch and the ministry, he could have left his family there while he returned to Prague. But they returned as a family to Prague in summer 1944. Until spring 1945, when events took a sudden change, he was not ready to contemplate that the end was in sight.

'When I first saw these stamps, I couldn't understand it,' said Jutta, looking at her father's passport. She couldn't understand why the family left the safety of Liechtenstein. She knew that if they had stayed, the course of their life could have turned out so differently. Jutta and I discussed the possible reasons that led them to return to Prague: the belief that Germany would still win the war; the safety of Prague compared to Stuttgart; the sense of pride and achievement that Griesinger took from his job in the Protectorate. I could tell, however, that Jutta was still puzzled by it.

Barbara also struggled to come to terms with her father's decision to return the family to Prague at the end of their summer holiday. 'Why didn't he stay? Why didn't he stay?' she kept muttering to herself. This decision, probably given little thought when it was made, seemed to affect Barbara more than any of the other things we talked about. Had they not returned, the Griesingers would not have been one of the millions of German 'incomplete' families (*unvollständig*). The death of her father in 1945, and her unhappy childhood in the suburbs of Zurich, could have been avoided.

I asked Barbara whether she wanted to stop the interview. We had by then been speaking for several hours. It was a hot summer day and we were both tired. 'Don't go. Not yet. I am finding it all very interesting,' she said softly. 'I don't have any memories,' she continued. 'It's like I'm reading a story or a history book.'

Chapter x

The Man on the Bahnhofstrasse

By early 1945 living conditions in Prague had worsened. As the Allies prepared their final advance, the land of plenty was on its last legs. Restaurants had run out of food and shop windows lay bare. Residents of Prague were under the swastika for their sixth winter, living in bitterly cold homes, due to restrictions on gas and electricity. Gone were the days of music and theatre. Performances ended in November 1944, with cast and crew assigned to the war industry. While some semblances of normalcy, such as Prague's postal service, continued to function until the very end (eight-year-old Jutta had even sent her grandparents a letter on 17 March 1945), other certainties of everyday life fell apart. In addition to the hunger, confusion and fear for the future, the Griesingers would have breathed in the stench from the piles of rubbish left uncollected at the side of the streets, because the bin men's services had been deployed elsewhere.[1]

On 14 February 1945 sixty US aircraft dumped 152 tonnes of bombs on Prague, in what was later discovered to be a costly navigational error – the American pilots claimed afterwards that the German city of Dresden had been their intended target. It was the first time Prague experienced an aerial attack, in a raid that killed 701 people, all of whom were civilians. The public was so unprepared that many people hid in cellars that caved in on top of them when the bombs fell. As late as the 1970s, bodies were still being discovered in parts of Prague.[2] Jutta was personally caught up in the bombing as she made her way home from school by herself, when the air-raid siren went off shortly before midday. The noise did not worry her. The walk to her house on Zitekstrasse took under ten minutes; and besides, the siren had gone off countless times over the past couple of years without anything ever happening. There was no reason to think this time would be any different. As she passed the train station, Jutta recalled looking up and seeing an aeroplane. 'It was flying so low I felt I could touch it,' she told me. 'When the bombs began to fall, I felt paralysed, like a mouse before an elephant.' She watched, motionless, as the bombs hit freight trains loaded with straw in the sidings, which immediately caught fire. Fortunately a man who saw the explosion from his window ran outside and grabbed her. 'He carried me quickly into his house. I can still remember the red-checked shirt he was wearing.' Jutta told me that to this day she is petrified of fire, and seeing a burning fire remains one of the few things that evokes childhood memories.

With the Allies getting closer by the day, Nazi Germany put in place defence measures to prevent the advance and to protect the civilian population. Griesinger joined a *Volkssturm* unit, a civilian militia founded in late 1944, into which were recruited men deemed too old or too young for regular army service. It was the Third Reich's frantic last hope of averting defeat.[3] When in early April 1945 the Red Army launched an offensive on Bratislava, capital of the Nazis' puppet state of Slovakia, evacuations of Germans from the Protectorate to Germany began. Such relocation of the population was restricted to Reich personnel's wives and children and to Sudeten Germans. As an employed male worker of the Reich, Griesinger knew he had no choice but to remain in the city until he received his orders to evacuate. The consequences were severe for anyone attempting to flee before this time.

He decided against taking the risk, investing his energy instead in arranging for a truck driver to take his family to his in-law's house in Liechtenstein, where they would be safe. Gisela and the children joined millions of German families who in spring 1945 were heading westwards, towards areas of the Reich that were still free of Allied control. They probably took to the road at a similar time to Walter Bertsch's wife, Margot, and their two children, who left Prague to seek sanctuary with Bertsch's sister in Stuttgart on 4 April 1945.[4] In advance of the Griesingers' departure, Robert and Gisela even took precautions about what to do if partisans or Allied aeroplanes opened fire on the truck.

Jutta recalled the flight from Prague as a sort of adventure. 'They dressed us in green dresses and capes. We knew that if the truck stopped suddenly, which it did, we needed to jump out and stand upright behind the trees.' Sitting at her kitchen table seventy years on, Jutta raised and pointed her hands in different directions. 'We even had to pretend to turn into a tree.' Amid the excitement of this, she did not think for a moment that she would never again see her father. In April 1945 German children in Prague continued to believe in a final victory, even if their parents did not.[5] Joachim, Jutta and Barbara probably thought it was only a matter of time before Hitler set in motion his grand plan and the family would be reunited.

I listened in silence as Jutta recounted the story of her final farewell to her father at the end of the garden path, and of her family's escape. The narrative she had pieced together from partial memories was not that of an adult observer, but that of an eight-year-old girl, half-fearful, half-excited, perhaps experiencing as a tall tale what would otherwise have been too frightening to face. By the time Jutta reached safety with her mother and siblings, she and Barbara had come close to dying through illness and malnourishment.

After leaving Prague, the journey to Gisela's parents' house in Vaduz should have taken only a few days. Instead it took six months. Jutta remembered that as night fell in the first phase of the journey, the driver parked the vehicle in secluded woodland. The family spent the nights sleeping outdoors on the back of the truck, while the driver remained undercover in the front section. She vividly recalled the aeroplanes flying overhead as she tried to sleep. The final three months of the war marked the pinnacle of the Allied bombing assault, in which, on average, 1,000 people were killed by a blast every day.[6] During this time the US 15th Air Force dropped bombs on Bohemia and south-east Germany, an area that could not be avoided, when travelling from Prague to Liechtenstein by road. It took the Allies just over twenty minutes to drop 1,825 tonnes of bombs on Pforzheim, a town in south-west Germany, setting off a lethal firestorm that killed 17,600 people – at the time the worst raid on a German city.[7]

Despite the dangerous conditions, everything seemed to be going according to plan. The truck had managed to cross into Germany and was headed south. Soon, however, the group ran into trouble when, somewhere in the Bavarian forest, the driver refused to continue onwards. He told Gisela and the children that it was too dangerous for him to drive on. Jutta recalled that he abandoned them, weary and undernourished, at the side of a road. Gisela had no way of making it to Liechtenstein. She and her three small children were stranded in Bavaria. Gisela set up shelter that first night on the edge of a wood. Not anticipating a long journey after leaving Prague, she had only brought along enough dried food to last a few days. She did not know how long it would be until they could obtain more sustenance, and immediately set about rationing the few remaining items.

Jutta retained clear memories of that first night alone in the woods. As she was playing too close to the small gas cooker in which Gisela was preparing *Spätzle*, she accidentally knocked over the pot, causing the dumplings to fall on the muddy earth. Each family member quickly scrambled on their knees to pick the tiny pieces from the ground and brush off the dirt. Like the sight of fire, this is another episode from the journey that Jutta relives often, even in old age. 'Whenever I make *Hörnli* [a traditional Swiss pasta] I picture the scene as clearly as if it were yesterday,' she said. 'We had to pick it up. We had nothing else to eat.'

The Griesingers were just one of millions of refugee families who, in March and April 1945, took to Germany's packed roads to flee the bombings and the Soviet advance. Allied bombs had turned historical German cities into piles of rubble and had destroyed the country's railways and bridges. Electricity was cut and, with near-complete collapse of the phone, telegraph and postal systems, there were few means of communication. As the Nazi state disintegrated around them, Gisela, Joachim, Jutta and Barbara made their way on foot across Bavaria towards the Swiss border, where they encountered thousands of sick, tired and hungry people. Much like the Jews who had fled a few years earlier, the streams of refugees who inched slowly along fields and dirt roads often carried the remnants of their worldly possessions in a single suitcase. After several days it became clear to Gisela that they could not continue. Jutta and Barbara were suffering from night sweats, weight loss and chronic coughing. They had contracted tuberculosis and, like tens of thousands of German refugees, they were without medicine to treat the disease. In April 1945 the family's journey ended high in the Bavarian Alps in the village of Aschau im Chiemgau, close to the Austrian border, where a local family allowed them to take refuge in an attic.

The months Gisela spent in Aschau were the most difficult in her life. Most children in the area suffered from worms and lice and, without access to food or medicine, it looked likely that she was going to lose two starving children to hunger or tuberculosis.[8] On top of this, she was cut off from the rest of the world, unable to communicate with Robert in Prague, or with her parents in Liechtenstein. It was an upsetting and deeply frustrating time. 'We had plenty of money, but there was nothing to spend it on,' recalled Jutta.

Beginning on 18 April, Allied bombs pounded the nearby town of Rosenheim for three nights running, killing scores of people and making hundreds homeless. Then just a child, the film director Werner Herzog and his family had taken refuge in Sachrang, the neighbouring village to Aschau. His earliest memory is the bombing of Rosenheim causing the sky to turn orange and red.[9] Despite its distance from urban centres and other targets of Allied bombs, the Bavarian Alps were still a dangerous place in April 1945. Thousands of Nazi Werewolves (guerrilla fighters) took to the mountains that spring, intent on unleashing partisan warfare against the approaching Allied invaders. They terrorised the local population, carrying out sporadic acts of violence on those who showed defeatism. Even after parts of Germany were liberated, Gisela and the children needed to maintain the pretence that they were willing to die for the Nazi cause.

The American liberation of Aschau on 2 May 1945 drastically changed the family's sinking fortunes. Jutta remembers feeling jubilant when accepting chewing gum and bananas from American GIs. Like countless other European children, she also recalls her amazement at seeing a black person for the first time. Gisela's ability to speak English proved invaluable for her family's survival. In 1945 educated German women who spoke English were in high demand by the US army, which had a shortage of translators and secretaries. Within days of the Liberation, Gisela had managed to secure a position as an interpreter that gave her access to a world of special privileges. As one of the 25,000 German civilians employed by the US army in 1945, she received additional meals and a ration card.[10] Taking her meals at work ensured that she was able to exchange ration tickets for medicine for her children, soap, coffee, nylon stockings and cigarettes. She made sure always to have enough cigarettes to trade for food, and to give them to the children if she couldn't find enough sustenance. 'That's why I smoke,' said Jutta, slightly embarrassed. 'We didn't have enough to eat, so my mother gave us cigarettes.'

When news reached Aschau that the Soviets had entered Prague on 9 May, Gisela must have worried anxiously about Robert's fate. She would have weighed up in her mind the likely scenarios, to try and determine what had happened to her husband. He might have managed to go into hiding. He might even be en route to Liechtenstein or Stuttgart. Perhaps he had been taken prisoner and was languishing somewhere in Czechoslovakia. Perhaps there was another option, too terrible even to contemplate.

As spring turned to summer, Gisela left her children alone in the attic as she went every day to the American command post in Aschau. By that time the Americans needed translators to deal with a refugee crisis in Bavaria that was spiralling out of control, as tens of thousands of hungry and frightened displaced persons (DPs) arrived on foot, looking for sanctuary. In the months that followed the end of the war, when food and shelter were scarce, Bavarian officials took in 1.5 million people. Despite not having nearly enough trained linguists, the Americans, as the occupying power, were responsible for managing the DP problem. It was a colossal bureaucratic undertaking.[11]

On top of the refugee crisis, the Americans were still active in tracking down the bands of Werewolves, SS and army units who had gone into hiding in the mountains of Upper Bavaria. Some of these groups refused to surrender and continued their guerrilla warfare, while others gave up and attempted to blend in with the local civilian population. The US army took to the hills, seeking to rein in the last fighters of the Third Reich. Many fugitives took extreme measures to evade capture. Some *Waffen-SS* members are known to have broken into the homes of doctors and to have held them at gunpoint until they surgically removed their blood-group tattoos from their left underarm, which had been marked in case a blood transfusion was needed. In August 1945, three months after Germany surrendered, there were still somewhere between 10,000 and 15,000 SS men at large in Bavaria.[12] Once they were captured and brought in for questioning, the Americans required the assistance of people like Gisela, who could translate the questions posed by the Americans and the answers given by the Nazi renegades.

For a time, they also relied on the linguistic skills of SS Hauptsturmführer Lothar Schmidt who, like Gisela, found work as an interpreter for the US army. Like Gisela, Schmidt had arrived in Bavaria from Prague where, as a close confidant of Walter Bertsch, he had headed the personnel division at the Ministry of Economics and Labour. It was a position in which he gained a reputation for his heavy-handed methods towards the Czech population. As a leading figure of the SD in the city, Schmidt escaped at the Liberation and went into hiding. Shortly after placing him high on the list of their wanted war criminals, the Czechoslovak authorities arrested him in Altötting in August 1945.[13]

As I spoke with Jutta about the family's time in Aschau, I discovered that Gisela's spell as a translator in 1945 was her only experience of working life. Even though I knew from archival documents that she had not worked before the war, I thought that to support the family as a single mother she might have undertaken some form of paid employment in the years that followed. 'My mother was a difficult person,' said Jutta quietly. After so many hints and passing comments concerning Gisela's personality, it came as a relief to hear her say it at last.

Once communications were partially restored in early summer 1945, Gisela sent word of her circumstances to her parents in Vaduz. Her father immediately dispatched a car to Aschau to fetch Gisela and the children. Jutta's and Barbara's illnesses prevented this from happening. At this time Jutta was virtually blind, while Barbara was unable to move her arms. Even though Gisela had an ample supply of cigarettes and stockings, she had failed to find adequate medical care for her children. Considering them too weak to make the journey, Gisela arranged that thirteen-year-old Joachim should travel back with the chauffeur, while she would remain behind with the young girls. As Gisela continued her work with the Americans, her two daughters spent the summer recuperating in the small alpine village. Once they had regained some strength, they came down from the dark attic and spent summer 1945 playing on the streets of Aschau with other refugee children, waiting for the return of their grandfather's chauffeur.

In September 1945 the car arrived. When Gisela and the girls arrived in Vaduz a few days later, there was no sign of Robert, nor was there any news of his whereabouts.

In September 1944 the Nazis famously declared that Germany would never abandon the Protectorate and that any attempt to revolt 'would be drowned in blood'.[14] Prague was one of only a handful of European capital cities that remained occupied in the final days of the war. Even at this late stage, after the evacuation of families, the encirclement of the city by the Soviets and the suicide of Hitler, 4 May 1945 passed by as normal, with the Czech population remaining quiet. Accordingly, thousands of German officials obeyed the order to show up for work on 5 May. Within hours, their world was turned upside down. Many Germans later recalled that the events that followed came as a surprise.

Shortly after midday, resistance cells took over Prague radio and broadcast a call to arms to the city's residents to rise up against the Nazi occupiers. It marked the beginning of the Prague Uprising, which lasted three days. 'Kill Germans wherever you meet them!' cried out the Czech insurgents to the local population. In the hours and days that followed, this is precisely what some did. After six years of gruelling and humiliating foreign occupation, in which the Nazis were responsible for the deaths of between 36,000 and 55,000 Czechs – in addition to the 77,000 Jews and 7,000 Roma they murdered in the Holocaust – large swathes of the Czech population were eager for revenge.

Czech crowds formed and took to the streets in search of German soldiers, officials and civilians to round up and intern in cinemas, schools and other public spaces. Retribution varied from group to group, and ranged from harassment and jostling to outright killings. Such scenes were encouraged – and sometimes planned – by the Czechoslovak government-in-exile, which wanted to speed up the departure of German civilians from the territory.[15] Some Czechs wrecked German homes and properties, in some cases setting fire to the belongings of their former occupiers. In such instances German-owned furniture was not spared from the flames. The armchair that later contained Griesinger's papers, and that probably belonged to him, had suddenly become a target for destruction. It was fortunate to have made it through the Liberation unscathed.

In the lawless revenge of the Liberation, 6,000 Germans were killed, while a further 5,000 committed suicide and 50,000 Germans were wounded.[16] To shame their victims further, some Czech insurgents took to painting swastikas on the Germans' bodies and overcoats. Some Germans tried to lie low and pass themselves off as Czech. This was easier for Sudeten Germans, many of whom were bilingual. However, unfamiliar with the language, despite having lived in the Protectorate for some years, Germans from the Reich found it impossible to disguise themselves. Amid the violence, Czech paramilitaries formed the Revolutionary Guard, supposedly to oversee order. While the Revolutionary Guard interned Germans in barracks and other holding stations, they also, on occasion, masterminded some of the mass violence.[17] In 2010 a seven-minute video of one of the many massacres committed against Germans was discovered. Jiří Chmelnicek, an amateur film-maker, had recorded the Czechs and Soviets rounding up around forty German men, and at least one woman, from a cinema and lining them up against a wall before they were executed. After the war the Communist police threatened Chmelnicek to get him to turn over the film, but he refused and instead hid the reel. As I watched the video on YouTube, I paused the footage each time the camera focused on the face of an individual man digging his own grave. I held Griesinger's photograph against the screen to see whether I could identify him amongst the crowds. I could not.[18]

At the time of the insurgency, some Germans immediately tried to go into hiding or to look for places of sanctuary. A number of Czechs permitted German friends to stay for the odd night, but the dangers of sheltering a German were soon made clear to the population. By 6 May even the Red Cross in Prague no longer took in Germans.[19] Some German colleagues of Griesinger, such as Hanns-Martin Schleyer and Lothar Schmidt, were able to slip unnoticed out of Prague during the uprising. The planned escape of Griesinger's Corp brother Hans von Watter was less successful. He was killed shortly after fleeing the city. Overall, the number of those attempting to get away were few and far between. Most Germans remained behind, believing that being rounded up by the Czechs could not be a worse fate than falling into Soviet hands.[20]

Traces of Griesinger disappear, the moment the outbreak of violence begins. The Czechs were unable to find him, when they went to look for him at home on the first day of the uprising, and 'whereabouts unknown' was written on his police registration card for that day.[21] We know that Griesinger, unlike thousands of other Germans, did not destroy his identification papers in order to assume a new identity.[22] At the time of the uprising it is unlikely that Griesinger had any Czech friends willing to risk their lives to help him. He had not been in the Czech lands long enough to create any meaningful bonds, and he did not speak the language. During his spell at the ministry he had developed only poor working relations with Czech industrialists, who in May 1945 would have wanted nothing more than to see him punished for requisitioning their businesses and sending away their workers. Any Czechs with whom Griesinger worked at the ministry had problems of their own at the time and would have been unlikely to offer him assistance.[23] Known collaborators were being targeted for round-ups and attacks.

Griesinger might, as a last resort, have called for assistance from Anna, the maid, then six months pregnant, who continued to live at the Griesinger house on Zitekstrasse. At a time when Czechs were storming the homes of Germans living in Bubeneč, it seems unlikely that he would have contacted her there. In any event, Anna had other priorities that week, which probably ruled out her coming to the assistance of her former employer. Her fiancé, Josef, was active in the uprising against the Germans. He was away for three days, taking part in the fighting around the Old Town Hall. Anna did not know whether he would live to meet the couple's unborn child. Following Josef's safe return, she moved into his apartment the following week.[24]

By September Griesinger was in a Prague hospital, suggesting that he could not have strayed too far from the capital during the uprising. It is impossible to know whether he was captured alone or whether he surrendered while on service with his *Volkssturm* unit. Rather than go into hiding or fight to the last, he might have turned himself in voluntarily, in the hope that he might fall into American, rather than Soviet, hands. Amid the uncertain atmosphere, many Czechs wasted little time verifying whether the Germans they uncovered were staunch Nazis. Griesinger's significance as a state official and member of the SS was inconsequential. People who acted or looked German, not to mention those who sounded it, were targeted. Wherever Griesinger was during those fateful days, he knew the game was up.

★

Within five months of the uprising, Griesinger was dead. His death certificate, obtained by his mother after the war, gave dysentery as the cause. But what had happened during these five months? According to this document, Griesinger died on 27 September 1945 in an infirmary building on Salmovská, a small street in the heart of Prague, which housed a unit for Germans with infectious diseases. Thanks to a chance recollection from Jutta, there was no doubt Griesinger died (or was killed) inside a hospital. In one of my meetings with her, I paused momentarily as I went through my notes. We had been talking about Salmovská for some time. When I looked up, she seemed forlorn and was thinking intensely about something.

'I am starting to remember meeting someone who knew my father,' she said, after a couple of moments. 'It must have been ten or twelve years after the war.' Jutta spoke slowly, as she tried to recall details of the memory that was gradually coming back to her. 'I was probably about eighteen and was working as a secretary in Zurich, when I had a strange encounter with someone.'

She was on her lunch break and was looking at a shop window on the Bahnhofstrasse, when she suddenly noticed a short, bald, chubby man staring at her as though in a trance in the reflection. Jutta attempted to walk away, but as she turned, the man asked her if her last name was Griesinger. She had always resembled her father closely. In those days not only were they facially similar, but she had also inherited his tall slim build, dark eyes and hair and long face. Jutta had never seen the man before. She said he looked in his fifties, the same age Robert would have been, but in her eyes he seemed much older than her father. As shoppers went about their business on the busy Bahnhofstrasse, Jutta confirmed her last name with the stranger standing in front of her.

'He told me that he met my father in hospital in Prague before he died,' said Jutta. Attempting to cast her mind back to the chance meeting on the street sixty years earlier, she struggled to get the words out. She recalled her discomfort as she stood in his presence. It was an intense and unfamiliar situation for eighteen-year-old Jutta. Growing up far away from Stuttgart ensured that, apart from family members, she had never met anyone after the war who had once known her father.

'Do you know anything else about this man? His name perhaps?' I asked gently, pressing her for more information.

Jutta thought for a moment. 'He didn't say, and I'm sure I did not ask for it. It all happened so quickly,' she said, regretting the missed opportunity to discover more about her father's final days.

'Did you mention it to your mother?' I asked.

'At that time she did not want to speak about my father,' said Jutta. 'There was no point telling her.'

This chance encounter was proof enough that the hospital was not an invented detail made up by Czech authorities to cover up Griesinger's murder, which might have taken place somewhere else. It also ruled out that he was imprisoned. The city's prisons, such as Pankrác, which detained Frank, Bertsch and other leading officials from the Protectorate era, had their own internal hospital units. With medical facilities onsite, prisoners in Pankrác and elsewhere did not leave the grounds to receive treatment. Instead of a prison, Griesinger must, therefore, have been in an internment camp that lacked hospital facilities. In cases where Germans were transferred out of camps in Prague to receive treatment for dysentery, they were usually taken to Salmovská.[25]

Once the uprising ended, Germans held in public buildings were forcefully rounded up and made to march on foot to hundreds of makeshift internment camps that had sprung up across the country. Thirty-seven of these camps were situated in and around Prague. Others were further afield. Theresienstadt, the concentration camp that during the Occupation had been a transit camp as a prelude to deportation and murder for Jews, was among the largest.[26] If he still had them with him on his arrival at the camp, Griesinger would have handed over his watch, wallet and any other valuables. Interrogations soon followed. It was common to see Germans covered in blood after exiting the interrogation room.[27] For the Czech Revolutionary Guard and Soviet forces, it was important to weed out from among the civilian population any Germans who might have been in the *Wehrmacht*, the Protectorate administration and, most importantly, any former SS or Gestapo members. Unlike civilians and Sudeten Germans, who initially undertook forced labour and were later expelled from Czechoslovakia, Nazis faced even harsher punishments, ranging from criminal trials to summary executions.

Upon entering the camp, Griesinger managed somehow to distance himself from his past. In this climate, to be discovered to have been an ordinary Nazi amounted to a death sentence. Even before his interrogation began, Czech or Russian officials would have removed his shirt and looked for the blood-group tattoo that *Waffen-SS* members had on their left underarm. During his interrogation Griesinger somehow managed to convince the authorities that he had not been in the SS. Once inside the camp, it was by no means certain that his SS background would remain concealed, and SS members discovered there were beaten and sometimes killed.[28]

Nor did having passed himself off as a supposedly unimportant member of the Reich administration guarantee Griesinger's safety. Far from it. During the spring and summer of 1945 Czechs and Soviets did not distinguish between Germans. In their eyes, all Germans in the camps were potential targets for violent retribution. Months after the Liberation, attacks continued: German prisoners were beaten up daily. The level of cruelty depended on the person in charge of the camp. The commander of the camp at Kolín encouraged guards to knock out prisoners' teeth and stomp on their hands and heads. Women were singled out for specific types of maltreatment. The rape and sexual humiliation of women was pervasive. Sometimes the guards would take women and girls to their nightly alcohol-fuelled parties. Many would never be seen again.[29]

Throughout May and June 1945 Griesinger would have heard the cries and screams and witnessed the murders. Like many of the other 69,000 internees, he must have wondered when his turn would come.[30] If his strategy was to keep his head down and lie low for as long as possible, it seemed to work. The fact that ten years later on the Bahnhofstrasse a man who first met Griesinger in a Prague hospital, *after* his spell in an internment camp, was able to recognise Jutta as Griesinger's daughter suggests that his face could not have been badly disfigured.

Amid all the suffering, Griesinger might have spared a moment to reflect on his life. The strong new Germany that he and other members of the 'war-youth' generation had worked so hard to build had ended in failure. Ensuring that Germany would never have to endure the misery and disillusionment that came with the end of the First World War and its immediate aftermath had been his life's work. Yet as everything that he had worked for fell apart, it seemed history was repeating itself. In all likelihood, Griesinger would have thought also about Gisela and the children. In the absence of any news inside the camp, he did not know whether they had managed to reach Liechtenstein. It was possible they had not made it out of the country. He might have thought that perhaps they too were languishing in a camp in the Czech lands.

While it is impossible to know precise details of the abuse or punishment Griesinger suffered, the fact that he was severely ill during these months remains beyond doubt. He was not alone. In summer 1945 disease was rife in Czechoslovakia's 500 internment camps. Even though conditions inside the camps were in no way as deadly as those that Czech inmates at Buchenwald and Mauthausen, or Jewish deportees in Auschwitz, had experienced only a few months earlier, they were still abysmal. In some camps, such as the Strahov stadium, 10,000 prisoners slept outdoors without any blankets. Usually Germans had nothing to eat during their first days of incarceration. When food eventually arrived, it was insufficient. In summer 1945 Griesinger's diet will have consisted of a cup of ersatz coffee in the morning, a thin soup accompanied by 100 grams of bread at midday and a second coffee in the evening.[31] A damning report written by the illustrious foreign correspondent Eric Gedye on the front page of the *Daily Herald* on 9 October 1945, under the headline 'This is an Outrage to Humanity', drew international attention to the conditions of Germans interned in Czech 'horror' camps.[32] The conditions at the Salmovská infirmary were only marginally better than those in the camps, with prisoners living on 800 calories a day (instead of the 500–700 they were given in the camps). Nevertheless, the slight increase in the level of nutrition did little to improve their conditions. According to a report written by the Red Cross, most patients at Salmovská exhibited signs of cachexia, a wasting syndrome characterised by weight loss, weakness and fatigue.[33]

The final stone left to turn that might shed light on Griesinger's last days in Prague was the city's official register of deaths. Over a three-year period I had returned several times to Prague to search for details of Griesinger's life. When I arrived in spring 2017 to find out about his death, I knew it would be my last research visit to the city. The central Registry Office of Prague that records all births, marriages and deaths is in Vodičkova Street, in the city centre. I arrived at eight o'clock and took the 1920s Art Deco staircase to the first floor. The waiting area had the appearance of a hospital maternity unit. As I entered, I passed a mother rocking her newborn baby, who could not have been older than a week. To one side of the room, a baby-changing mat lay on top of a wooden table. I sat with the parents waiting to register their babies' births until my number was called. I was the only person holding a 'death' ticket.

When it was my turn, I went into a room where two women sat waiting to produce the first death certificate of the day. I felt fortunate that I was not there in grief to register a death, as neither seemed particularly sympathetic. I began to introduce myself, explaining that I was a historian working on a story and that I was in Prague for just a few days, when I was interrupted by Jitka, the more senior of the administrators, who put me in my place. 'I don't care about the story,' she said brusquely. 'We get historians in here all the time. Just tell me the name you're looking for, and their date of death.' She noted down Griesinger's details and left the room.

When she returned, she was carrying a large book under her arm. She placed it on the table in front of me. The year 1945 was written on the sticker on the front of the book. She told me that it was one of six tomes that contained the details of people who died in Prague that year. The book she handed me contained 2,200 names. Griesinger appeared as number 1,658. Just as on the death certificate prepared for Griesinger's family after the war, the cause of death was dysentery. However some of the information in the official registry differed. The document in his family's possession claimed that Griesinger was cremated and his ashes buried in a churchyard. Consulting the original document revealed that his body was buried in a mass grave in Ďáblice cemetery. There was no mention of a cremation or a churchyard. Something was amiss.

Still holding the registry of deaths, I wanted to record details of some of the people whose names appeared alongside Griesinger, but the enforcement of a rule that prevents public access to records for seventy-five years after their creation meant that I was only allowed to take down Griesinger's details.[34] Jitka typed Griesinger's details into a computer, to produce an official death certificate. Once it was printed, she asked me to pay the standard fee of 100 Czech crowns. Because I only had a bill of 2,000 crowns, Jitka left the book with me as she went to get change. This gave me some time to look more closely at it.

Griesinger's name appeared towards the end of a section of twenty people, each with German-sounding names. Next to each name was written, 'buried in a mass grave in Ďáblice, 1 October 1945'. Some had died as early as July. Among the twenty, Griesinger was the only person with the title of doctor. The men and women came from all walks of life and included a driver and a journalist. Even though they had not shared the same experience of war, their cause of death was similar. Most died of dysentery, tuberculosis, diphtheria and scarlet fever. There was also the odd case of measles and whooping cough. Nobody was recorded as having been shot. As soon as Jitka returned, she took the book away and directed me towards the door. By then, she had a queue of people outside waiting for her, who needed to obtain official proof of death for their relatives.

Was Griesinger the victim of an infectious disease, as the written evidence was guiding me towards, or was he murdered, as Jochen and Irmela believed and had told me? They seemed satisfied with the explanation of Mrs Helmichova, the Czech woman Wally Griesinger had sent to Prague immediately after the war to discover what became of her son and who returned to Stuttgart with earth from Griesinger's supposed grave. It was impossible to know. Haphazard attacks against Germans continued throughout Czechoslovakia, even after May's extra-judicial killings had ended. Details of these murders did not appear in the press or in official hospital records. Just as some prisoners shot in the chest had their deaths recorded as typhus, others who were beaten to death seemed suddenly to have contracted smallpox.[35] One of the worst killing sprees against Germans that summer occurred in Kolín, thirty-five miles east of Prague, on 23 and 24 September, the week Griesinger died.[36] The storming of hospitals to seek out German patients also continued to take place. In some instances Czech partisans or Red Army soldiers gleefully led a German patient to the top floor of the hospital, before throwing them off the roof. The soldiers would place bets to determine whether the bullets being shot from the ground would strike the falling body before it smashed onto the surface.[37]

Home to an assortment of unmarked mass graves stretching across several hectares, Ďáblice is a cemetery like no other. Some graves hold the bodies of Czech and British parachutists and their helpers, others those of ordinary Czechs whom the Nazis had dragged from their homes and savagely executed in acts of reprisal. It was only discovered in 2007 that a mass grave in Ďáblice contained the bodies of Ján Kubiš and Jozef Gabčík, Heydrich's assassins. Ďáblice also contains the mass graves of Germans tried and sentenced to death in 1946; among the most famous individuals are Karl Hermann Frank, Secretary of State for the Protectorate, and Kurt Daluege, Heydrich's replacement as Deputy Reich Protector. Nor are the mass graves confined solely to the war years; recently Ďáblice was found to contain the mass graves of 1950s victims of the Communist regime as well.[38]

The morning after locating Griesinger's name in Prague's official register of deaths for 1945 I set off early to try and find his final resting place. I was not hopeful. In the aftermath of the 1968 Prague Spring, the government opened an investigation into the state-led purges and atrocities of the 1950s. It was during this time that large parts of the cemetery's archive mysteriously caught fire.[39] As I waited for the gates to open, I watched as a middle-aged woman in a bright-pink jumper set up her flower stall at the entrance to the cemetery. At eight o'clock a groundsman unlocked the gate. I was the only visitor there that morning and I began to walk through the grounds, passing at the entrance a couple of gardeners and a workman repairing a wall. Three-quarters of those buried in Ďáblice do not have a tombstone. In the absence of plaques, shrines or other monuments, walking through the cemetery feels much like walking in a public park. I walked for about thirty minutes, following a cobbled path that cut through recently mown grass. As expected, there were no markers to any German graves.

As I came to the part of the cemetery that contains more recent rows of graves, I passed a couple of men. One appeared to be in his seventies and the other in his forties: a father and son perhaps. They each wore gloves and were crouching down next to a grave, clearing away the shrubbery and wiping the headstone. After I passed them, I made my way back to the entrance. The cemetery's office had just opened, and through a window I could see two women sitting at their desks, each speaking to a different couple. I went in. It was a small room; two chairs in front of each desk, and a couple of chairs for those waiting. Every word that was uttered could be heard by the rest of the room. In both cases the people speaking with the administrators were elderly and were accompanied by what looked like a middle-aged relative. The two women were taking down details and going through paperwork. They were arranging the funerals of someone recently deceased. I waited, feeling embarrassed at how trivial my query was going to seem in comparison. I got up to leave the office, but as I did so, I was stopped by one of the administrators, who beckoned me to her desk. I began by apologising for wasting her time. I felt very British.

I pulled out a copy of Griesinger's death record, which I had found the previous day in the registry office. I was surprised when the woman noted down word-for-word the details on a piece of paper, including the mention of a mass grave. Ďáblice must be one of only a handful of cemeteries where the staff don't flinch at the mention of a mass grave. After leaving the room for a few minutes to check some files at the back of the building, the woman returned, clutching an enormous book that contained handwritten lists of the marked graves from the 1940s. She thought having a look was worth a try. The book was too big to open on the table, so she put it on the floor and began turning the pages, looking for burials in October 1945. It came as no surprise when she said, sounding disappointed, that she could not find Robert Griesinger. I thanked her for going to the trouble, but just then an older woman, possibly wondering why her younger colleague was consulting such an old registry, approached us. As the first lady explained what I was looking for, Jarmila Malá, the second lady, stood nodding. At first I couldn't tell what the nod meant, but after a few seconds it became clear that she knew something.

Jarmila guided her young colleague to an enormous map of the cemetery that hung on one of the walls and began pointing at an area somewhere in the middle. 'The mass grave you're looking for is situated here,' the first lady said proudly. She was glowing; happy that they were able to help.

'But surely she's mistaken?' I asked. 'She must think I'm looking for the graves of the more famous Nazis from the Protectorate – Frank or Daluege, perhaps.'

Jarmila began to shake her head as this information was relayed to her by the younger woman.

'She knows the grave you're looking for,' said the first lady.

'But how can she be so sure? It's impossible. You yourself just confirmed that there aren't any records.'

'Jarmila has worked here for over forty years,' she continued. 'She heard all the war stories from cemetery workers who were here when she started, and who are long dead. She knows the tens of thousands of graves in this cemetery better than anyone.'

Moments later, Jarmila had donned a black leather jacket and we hurriedly returned to the cemetery. This time I was looking for something specific. I followed Jarmila back along the cobbled path and soon came across an area that most closely resembled a park. There were no tombstones or other monuments to be seen. Twenty metres from the cemetery wall, we approached a large wooden cross that emerged out of the ground. I had not noticed it earlier. Jarmila stopped and pointed at the cross. 'This is the spot you're looking for,' she said. She then swiftly turned round and left me alone at the cross.

Because no written evidence can prove it, I will never know for certain whether this cross was Griesinger's final resting place. I wanted to believe that Jarmila's version was true, but was also aware how easily stories can become tangled and events misremembered over time. Even so, I spent a few minutes walking around the small purple flowers that grew next to the cross, trying to absorb every detail of the terrain. I tried to picture that October day in 1945 when a truck arrived from the Salmovská hospital morgue, carrying twenty-two bodies, one of which was thirty-eight-year-old Dr Robert Arnold Griesinger. When his corpse arrived here, Griesinger had only been dead for four days. While he would certainly have been very thin, his body would also have been in a far better condition than those Germans being buried with him, who had died more than two months earlier and at the height of summer.

On the morning of the burial the Czech workers who unloaded the corpses from the truck would have passed by the mass graves containing executed Czech resisters and other Czechs who had fallen victim to Nazi terror over the preceding years. They must have known that the grave they were preparing was for German corpses. Some workers might even have taken delight in hurling the bodies into the ground. Just as Griesinger might have disclosed to someone what he had done with his private papers, which at the time of his burial were probably already inside the armchair, so the workers at Ďáblice might have revealed the location of the mass grave to a person making enquiries. Seventy years earlier, Mrs Helmichova might also have stood in this exact spot, before she leaned down to gather up some of the earth from the grave, which she placed in a jar and took back to Stuttgart to give to Griesinger's mother.

It appeared that I was not the only person with the knowledge of what was buried below the wooden cross. Somebody else had recently visited this remote corner of the cemetery and had left two small candle jars lying at the foot of the cross. The memory of what lay beneath had not been forgotten.

Chapter XI

Gisela Went Out to Dance

The Second World War devastated Europe. In addition to the near-destruction of European Jewry, the Soviet Union lost twenty million people, and the Nazis were responsible for the murder of hundreds of thousands of Roma, homosexual and disabled people. Millions of Europeans had lost their homes, livelihoods and were displaced. In 1945 they sought desperately to rebuild the continent from the ashes of war. German families were no exception. By the war's end, more than five million German soldiers had been killed or were missing, and it is estimated that between 500,000 and 2.1 million German civilians lay dead. Allied bombs had razed most German towns and cities to the ground, creating fourteen million refugees. For months, cold and starving civilians were dispersed among the ruins without adequate shelter or news of loved ones. At the end of the war, as three million soldiers languished in Soviet POW camps, Red Army soldiers raped hundreds of thousands of German girls and women.[1] Unlike elsewhere in Europe, children of Nazis experienced the end of the war not as liberation, but as a catastrophe. Their whole world, and all the certainties they knew, had collapsed around them. As a public and private narrative of victimhood came to define how Germans processed the war years, most did not dwell on their earlier support for the Nazis.

The Second World War took its toll on Gisela. It had fractured her life and thrown it into the air. She didn't know where the pieces would fall. Not yet thirty-five at the war's end, she was a widow

Barbara, Gisela, Jutta and Joachim, *c.* 1946

set to raise three children, two of whom suffered from tuberculosis. In early 1946 Gisela's father, Hermann Nottebohm, arranged for his daughter and her children to move to a health resort in Arosa, Switzerland, to recuperate for a few months. One night, when the children were in bed, Gisela went out to dance. In our interviews, both Jutta and Barbara spoke of their mother's passion for and skill at dancing. It was a hobby that took up a lot of her time. Since fleeing Prague and losing her husband, Gisela must have yearned for moments alone to escape and forget her predicament. While at the dance Gisela met Walter Jehli, a Swiss ski instructor who, at twenty-three, was twelve years her junior. With so many millions of soldiers killed in the war, meeting single men was rare. It was a luxury not afforded to most of Hitler's two million war widows who had remained in Germany after 1945.[2]

Walter was tall and blond, with an athletic build and light chis-elled features. The pair entered into a relationship. Walter swiftly adopted the role of a father figure, taking Gisela and the three children onto the pistes and teaching them to ski. After just a few months Gisela and Walter were married. Still in mourning, Gisela wore a long black dress to the ceremony. When I discussed the wedding with Jutta, she omitted to mention the reason for the couple's swift decision to marry. It was only when looking at photographs of Gisela and Walter's wedding with Barbara that I found out Gisela was pregnant. The bouquet, which she made sure to hold below her chest, was so unusually large it seemed almost as though she was trying to hide behind it.

Gisela and Walter on their wedding day, 1946

Gisela's decision to remarry was another life-changing moment for the family. It paved the way for a period of feuding, separation and financial problems. Gisela's parents were livid at their daughter's decision to marry a ski instructor – a position they thought was beneath her. Hermann Nottebohm promptly disinherited her. Once again, external factors forced the Griesinger children to move residence. Like so many European children in the 1940s, they were becoming accustomed to upping sticks and creating new homes, sometimes hundreds of miles away. Gisela moved to Zurich, where her new husband hoped to launch a career as a furniture upholsterer. Money was a constant worry, exacerbated by the arrival of the newest mouth to feed: Jürgen, born in 1947.

In the years 1947–50 the family switched apartments regularly. In each new area of Zurich, the Griesinger girls started at a different school. Jutta recalled the difficulties that came with changing schools: the comments she received from the other pupils who made fun of her accent when she spoke, and the way they mocked her dark, 'non-Swiss' facial features. The misery that accompanied the final phase of Jutta's war did not end suddenly in 1945. She struggled to adjust and settle into post-war life. Her turbulent relationship with Walter added to her sense of isolation. Whereas Joachim and Barbara reacted favourably to the arrival into their family unit of the entertaining and exciting ski instructor, Jutta had difficulty accepting her mother's choice of husband. Family life was not a happy place as she entered her teenage years.

Jutta found relaxing her visits to Hermann and Harriet Nottebohm – her maternal grandparents – where another relative also resided. From the late 1940s Gisela's uncle Friedrich Nottebohm, lived in Liechtenstein with his brother and sister-in-law while he was waiting for his nationality case to appear before the International Court of Justice in The Hague.[3] Jutta and Barbara remembered their Uncle Friedrich as a charming man, who was quite the joker. During the time they spent with him as teenagers they did not know that he was involved in a seminal legal case with important consequences for international law.[4]

A further respite came in 1950 when Gisela's father intervened, agreeing to pay for Jutta and Barbara to attend boarding school in Arosa. There followed a period of happiness and stability for the sisters. They attended Belri, an international boarding school for girls. Overnight, Jutta and Barbara suddenly found themselves mixing and forging friendships with the daughters of diplomats and leading businessmen from all over the world. In summer the school decamped to the French Riviera, where it occupied a hostel in Menton. It was a world away from the difficult life that the Griesinger girls left behind in suburban Zurich, yet it was one into which Jutta still struggled to fit. She greatly missed her mother and wanted to be closer to her. Jutta returned to Zurich, where she finished her high-school education. When she was nineteen she began courting Herbert Mangold, whom she later married.

By the time Barbara had finished school, family life had broken down almost completely and there was nothing for her to return to in Zurich, except disagreement and shortages. While the sisters were studying in Arosa, various changes had taken place at home. Joachim was no longer living with the family, having moved out when he married the younger sister of Walter, his step-father. Overnight, Gisela's sister-in-law became her daughter-in-law.

Momentous events in her life ensured that Gisela did not dwell for long on this unusual betrothal. In 1952 she gave birth to Peter, her fifth child. The prospect of a new mouth to feed took its toll on the family finances. Gisela and Walter were constantly arguing and their marriage was on its last legs. Gisela's erratic behaviour did little to ease tensions. Jutta recalled that while Walter was out at work, Gisela often disappeared for hours on end, leaving the teenage girl alone to look after her half-brothers. She was not too young to realise her mother's dependency on alcohol and heroin, supplied by a local doctor. It is possible that Gisela had encountered stimulants earlier in her life. During the war it was not uncommon for German housewives to become addicted to drugs, especially methamphetamine ('crystal meth'), then available over-the-counter as Pervitin, to combat depression.[5] Living with an addict mother who ignored her daughter's needs deeply affected Jutta, who often had to cancel social activities with friends as she took on the role of carer, doing the shopping and preparing the family's meals. She stood by Gisela during this time, offering her support as she tried to hide her mother's drug abuse from friends and neighbours. While this was going on, the teenage Jutta lived in fear of one of Gisela's intense outbursts. Her school work suffered and she was plagued constantly by low self-esteem.

By the late 1950s Gisela and Walter had separated. After she divorced Walter, Gisela was able to get by on the small allowance she received from her father.

Within this context the ability for Barbara to lead a normal happy existence in Zurich after the completion of her studies was also impossible. Given the events in their daughter's life, Gisela's parents acted as the intermediaries in convincing Wally Griesinger to take in the granddaughter she barely knew. In 1957 Wally invited seventeen-year-old Barbara to live with her in Stuttgart, which, twelve years after the end of the war, was experiencing colossal change and economic prosperity under Konrad Adenauer's leadership. Barbara relocated to the same house once inhabited by her father. In stark contrast to her life with Gisela in Zurich, which did not contain anything belonging to Robert, Barbara suddenly detected her father's presence in every room of the Griesinger family house.

At the time of her arrival, Wally's existence was defined by a desire to preserve her lost son's memory. She had been unable to mourn him immediately, not only because she was without news of the whereabouts of Robert's final resting place, but because other events were going on in her life that required immediate attention. In the final months of the war the Allies continued to drop bombs on Stuttgart. Even after the war's end, officials made Wally share the inhabitable parts of her home with refugees whose houses and apartments had been completely decimated. Several families were packed into every room. It was a difficult time, which was set to become worse.

Barbara, Wally and Jutta Griesinger in Stuttgart

Within months of the French liberators' arrival in Stuttgart, Wally found herself under investigation for her support of the Nazi party. Measures were put in place to bring her to trial, as part of a wider denazification programme. Even though it was quickly established that Wally had never joined the Nazi party, in the eyes of the authorities, her membership of the *NS-Frauenschaft*, the Nazi party's women's league, implied her support for Nazi ideology. Wally denied the charges. She maintained that she joined the league in the mid-1930s when the conservative women's association in which she had been active fell under the umbrella of the *NS-Frauenschaft*. Wally defended herself half-heartedly. In autumn 1947, at the height of the investigation, she was not in a position to dedicate time to clearing her name.[6] Two years after losing her son, her husband became critically ill and, on 6 November 1947, Adolf Griesinger died at the age of seventy-five.

In the weeks after his death, Wally placed an obituary for her husband in the *Stuttgarter Nachrichten*. The piece doubled to include details of Robert's passing two years earlier in Prague. It marked the first occasion for her to grieve publicly for her son. Wally ended the entry by listing herself as their sole survivor.[7] Albert, her youngest son, was not mentioned in the obituary. According to all her grandchildren, Robert had been Wally's favourite son. Jochen believed that Adolf preferred Albert, Jochen's father, who before the war had moved hundreds of miles away to the Ruhr, to work as a horse trainer. It was there that Albert married Gertraut and had two sons, Jochen and Rolf. Albert had lived in Robert's shadow all his life, a situation that worsened after his brother failed to return from Prague.

Like other grieving widows and mothers, a new-found faith helped Wally cope with mourning her lost son. Shortly after the war she found solace in the regular company of Father Rauber, a local priest, who encouraged her to convert to Catholicism. Wally forbade anyone from being in the house when the pastor called. Her grandchildren spoke of her vulnerability at this time, and of Father Rauber's resourcefulness at extorting large sums of money from her in exchange for the promise that she would one day be reunited with Robert. Wally could never again bring herself to look to the future. Finding ways to memorialise Robert preoccupied the way she navigated the difficult post-war years. Shortly after meeting Father Rauber, Wally constructed a memorial shrine to Robert in the corner of her living room, even commissioning an immense bronze bust of his face to serve as its centrepiece. Candles and photographs of Robert surrounded the effigy, over which a black shroud hung.

Barbara came to live in a house of mourning for a father she had not known, but whose spirit flickered in and out of her life. Despite Wally's determination to safeguard her son's memory, she refused to discuss him. Barbara remembered trying to bring up the subject of her father, probing Wally with questions about Robert's earliest years, but getting absolutely nowhere. Barbara even tried to speak to Anna, Wally's lady's maid, who had been with the family for decades. Under Wally's instruction, Anna declined to respond to her questioning.

Robert's passing soured Wally and Gisela's delicate mother-in-law / daughter-in-law relationship. Wally did not hide from Barbara her contempt for Gisela, whom she blamed for her son's death, and refused all contact with her former daughter-in-law. The situation was so dire that Wally did not allow Gisela to attend the reception to mark Barbara's confirmation in Stuttgart in 1958. Barbara recalled that her mother stayed in a nearby hotel. After attending the church service, Gisela hoped to be invited back to the same house where, twenty years earlier, the then Frau Griesinger had been a regular visitor. Even though it was a relatively grand affair and included all of Barbara's friends and relatives, an invitation did not arrive. Barbara recalled that in between the ceremony and the party she snuck out to be with her mother at her hotel, where they sat and talked on Gisela's bed.

In the late 1950s Wally was not the same person who, forty years earlier, had revelled in motherhood and had written touching, loving messages in Robert's Child Book. The devastation that had accompanied national defeat in two world wars had toughened her and given way to a stoic bitterness. Barbara's relations with Wally during the five years she spent living with her were cordial. She often felt more of a lodger than a family member. Much of the difficulty stemmed from having spent so much of her childhood with the allegedly corruptible Gisela, whom Barbara so closely resembled. Not only did Wally withhold grandmotherly affection, but she went to some length to create a distance from Barbara. When meeting a new person, Wally deliberately avoided referring to Barbara as her granddaughter, or even introducing her by her name. She was always, simply, 'Robert's daughter'. Barbara recalled feeling upset and embarrassed each time this occurred. Stuttgart was a lonely existence, made bearable thanks to Jutta's occasional visits, accompanied by her husband and son, Michael, Robert's first grandchild, who was born in 1961.

In one of our meetings Barbara told me she had not returned to the Griesinger house in Stuttgart since Wally died in 1976. Like Jutta, she had also lost contact with her cousin, Jochen. When Barbara asked if Jochen was still alive, I told her he was and that

Wally Griesinger with Jutta's son, Michael. The bust of
Robert's head is on the mantelpiece c. 1963

I had visited the house. She did not ask any questions about him
or Irmela, getting up instead to prepare tea in the kitchen. While
his wife was away, Fritz told me that Barbara had little to do with
anyone in her family, including her half-brothers. 'They write once
or twice a year,' he said, 'but we barely have any contact with Jutta.
She has only been to our house twice in the past thirty years,' he
added.

'Once,' said Barbara, who had been listening from the kitchen
and now stepped out to correct her husband. 'She's only been here
once.' She wanted to stress the point. Barbara told me that after

the Griesinger sisters were married there was some contact, but it was sparing.

'Perhaps she told you?' Barbara looked at me probingly.

Jutta hadn't said anything explicitly, but I had guessed that something had made the sisters, who had been so close as children, drift apart. The first time I met Jutta in Switzerland, she still had not told her sister about the discovery of their father's documents, even though she had known the story of the armchair for several months. 'I plan to tell her everything in my Christmas card,' she said. When I first broached the possibility of arranging a meeting with Barbara, Jutta gave me her sister's phone number and left me to call. She didn't offer to make the introduction. It was clear something was amiss between Griesinger's daughters. I wondered at the time what was preventing Jutta from picking up the phone or writing to her sister. She noticed my confusion. 'We're not in regular contact,' she said, as a way of explaining herself. 'They have their lives and I have mine.'

In a family that was prone to closing doors on the past, perhaps the weight of maintaining strong relations in a difficult post-war climate, where each was attempting to carve out a new life, proved too much. Gisela's temperament, or the strain of the inheritance battle against Jochen and Irmela that followed Wally's death, might also have played its part. Whatever the reason, it is difficult to imagine that the weakening of sisterly bonds was not in some way connected to the trauma that Robert had introduced into the family.

The more I visited Jutta at her home north of Zurich, the more she opened up about her life since the war ended. She became more relaxed, even excited at the prospect of having the opportunity to talk openly about her past. As she did so, I became increasingly aware of how the long shadow of the past affected Jutta's present. Over the course of our meetings Jutta revealed how the loss of her father made a significant impact on her life, affecting her identity and her interactions with others. Growing up, she was devoted to her father, a real 'daddy's girl'. Their special bond was strengthened by Jutta's striking physical resemblance to Griesinger

– something friends and relatives would comment on at every opportunity. As a girl, Jutta remembered constantly wanting to try to catch Robert's attention, and gave as an example her decision to emulate her father's love of horse riding, taking it up at an early age.

Unlike her older sister or her father, Barbara never took up the sport. She had not known her father in the same way as Jutta. She did not feel the pressure to want to please him.

'I've spent my whole life wishing my father was alive,' said Jutta at one point, looking dejected. 'Of course it got easier as I got older, but when I was younger, I couldn't get over losing him.' She explained that Robert's sudden death, and her loyalty to his memory, made her incapable of forging a good relationship with her stepfather.

On the rare occasions when Jutta had to explain at school, either to friends or teachers, what had happened to her father, she always replied that he died while working as a lawyer in the war.

'Were you ever embarrassed to say your father worked for the Third Reich?'

'It was never an issue,' responded Jutta without reserve. 'People simply weren't interested. Nobody ever asked questions about it.'

Jutta was far from alone. School friends draped their parents' wartime lives in silence and generally did not ask one another what their parents had done during the war. This was not always a conscious decision; rather, it was impossible to talk about a subject that had never been spoken of.[8]

'What about your children?' I asked. 'What did they know?'

'That's a good question,' said Jutta. 'They knew about him from when they were small,' she said reclining in her seat. She did not recall her son or daughter ever asking probing questions, wanting to learn more about their grandfather. Preserving Robert's memory for her children was not a priority for Jutta. Unlike her sister, Barbara, she did not display pictures of her father in prominent positions in the family home. In fact the only photograph of her father not in a drawer or an album was a small head-shot of Robert smiling directly at the camera, which Jutta kept in a gold frame on her bedside table. She explained that because her husband had also lost his father before they married, it was normal for the children not to have a grandfather figure in their lives. In this regard, Griesinger's absence from family life was not as striking as it might otherwise have been.

During one of our interviews, somebody knocked at the door and a woman in her early fifties let herself into the room. Jutta introduced me to Astrid, her daughter, who lives in the apartment next door. With dark eyes and a long face, Astrid had the Griesinger look about her. I asked her to tell me how the grandfather she had never met was spoken of in her childhood. She responded that Griesinger's presence in their lives was insignificant. Other than the small photograph of Robert that Jutta kept by her bed, Astrid could not recall any signs of, or discussions about, Robert in her youth. 'She must have told me bits and pieces, but to be honest I wasn't curious,' she told me. 'I didn't ask any questions. Grandpa was dead, it was just a fact.'

Even though she was looking at me, Astrid glanced at Jutta every so often, the play of emotions moving over her face as she thought back. Jutta watched her daughter closely as we spoke. She was curious to hear for the first time the role Robert had played in her daughter's life.

I wanted to know whether having a German grandfather who did not return from the war had made a difference to Astrid as she grew up in Switzerland. I wondered whether she ever tried to conceal her German heritage, or if it was something that came up in conversation at school or with her friends. Astrid told me that it did, but not in the way I expected.

'When I was young I was proud of it,' she said. 'I found it fascinating that my mother had been a refugee and had to escape Prague.' Astrid remembered feeling special at school that she was not 100 per cent Swiss. There was a certain glamour attached to being slightly different from the other children. Only as a teenager in the mid-1970s did Astrid begin to think about the Second World War in a thoughtful way. But even then she had difficulty distinguishing 1939–45 from other historical events that she learned about at school, such as the foundation of the old Swiss confederation in 1291 and the occupation of Switzerland by Napoleon's forces.

'Because my grandfather was a lawyer in Prague, and therefore not in Germany, I thought he was not involved in any of the atrocities,' said Astrid. 'Until you got in touch with my mother, I didn't even realise that he was a part of the Nazi system.'

I saw that Jutta's mode of turning a blind eye, and not seeking to probe with any vigour Griesinger's contribution to the Third Reich, had trickled down a generation. My interest in her grandfather was a wake-up call for Astrid. She said she was shocked when she saw copies of documents that I had left Jutta, on which Griesinger had ended some of his letters with 'Heil Hitler'. Since my first visit to her mother, she had begun to think further about her grandfather and was eager to discover more about him.

Astrid, like Jutta, maintained a degree of sympathy towards Griesinger. When I asked her what she felt towards her grandfather, she told me she did not reproach him for his Nazi past. 'He did not want to be part of it,' she said, possibly not realising the extent to which these words misrepresented Griesinger's actions. The seemingly relaxed and indifferent attitude that she expressed towards her grandfather's position under National Socialism is understood by historians to be a common response among grandchildren of party members, who did not believe their grandparents were Nazis.[9] Even faced with the evidence that I had presented, Astrid's first loyalty lay ostensibly with family.

Epilogue

Hanging on a wall in my childhood house in 1980s London was a photograph of two people whom I knew had been affected by the Holocaust. I had never learned their names. Despite my great interest in the Second World War, I had never asked about their story. In the black-and-white photograph a blond toddler, wearing nothing but his underwear and an enormous smile, was perched on his proud mother's lap. The pair were seated beneath a tree on a sunny day.

In the weeks after receiving Griesinger's papers from Jana, I visited my paternal grandmother, then in her mid-eighties, at her home in Golders Green and brought along the photograph. For some time I had wanted to know more about the mother and child in the picture: delving into Griesinger's past had unexpectedly made me curious about my own family's wartime experience.

'The lady, Nunia, is my aunt – my mother's sister – and Ryszard, the little boy, is my cousin,' said my grandmother as soon as I pulled out the photograph. 'I suppose the picture was taken in the Polish countryside in the mid-1930s. My mother tried desperately to get them out of Poland.'

In 1937, then just a nine-year-old girl, my grandmother vividly remembered sitting in the lobby of the Polish embassy at Portland Place in London watching her mother, who had left Warsaw in the 1920s, filling in form after form, hoping to secure visas for Nunia, her other sisters and their families to join her in Britain.

Nunia and Ryszard Seidenros *c.* 1933

'Trips to the embassy were always something of a treat,' she said, as she stood by the kitchen sink to warm the pot while she prepared the tea. At Portland Place my grandmother always found something new to discover and marvel at. She recalled her amazement at feeling warm each time she entered any room, thanks to the building's fitted carpets, a furnishing she had never seen before.

My great-grandmother's perseverance was eventually rewarded: she successfully obtained visas for her relatives to join her in London. But they didn't leave Poland. With the benefit of hindsight, it is alarming that her family did not take advantage of the opportunity to flee. 'They were so stupid,' said my grandmother, angry with her relatives for not knowing then what we know now. 'They had a good life in Poland. They were convinced they would be okay.'

But neither my grandmother's family, nor the rest of Europe's Jews, had crystal balls. In 1937 German forces had not yet marched across the country's borders to occupy neighbouring states. Her family could not have realised that turning down the opportunity to leave Warsaw would seal their fate. The photograph of Nunia and Ryszard enjoying the outdoors is the only photograph left of them in the world. They perished in the Warsaw Ghetto in 1942, shortly before other relatives were rounded up and put on trains to Treblinka.

'It didn't have to turn out this way,' said my grandmother as we sat looking at Nunia and Ryszard's photograph. 'I still get nightmares thinking about just how close they were to surviving.'

The conversation soon turned to Griesinger and the discovery of his documents. I took out Griesinger's passport and placed it on the kitchen table.

My grandmother began to sift through it. She was irate at the sight of the swastika on every page. 'I know you're a historian of the Second World War,' she said suddenly, 'but it never occurred to me that you touched these sorts of papers, or that you brought your work home with you. Please get this out of my house.'

After 1945, as the Stuttgart cityscape was rebuilt from the ashes of the Third Reich, the significance of buildings that had played a role during the Nazi years was gradually lost on a new generation of Germans, seeking to move on. After the war, the regular police were reinstalled in the offices of the Hotel Silber, where they remained until the mid-1980s, when the building was ceded to the Ministry of the Interior. The building on the Dorotheenstrasse remained relatively inconspicuous until 2008, when it lay at the centre of a series of demonstrations. After a petition by local action and citizens' groups, hundreds of protesters took to the streets of Stuttgart, brandishing huge banners that aimed to draw public attention to plans to demolish the building and turn it into an upmarket Breuninger department store. In an attempt to preserve the building, protesters invoked the Hotel Silber's shadowy past. Overnight, the building in which Griesinger went to work each day between 1935 and 1937 came to symbolise the darkest period of the city's history.

In mid-1930s Stuttgart, scores of Socialist, Communist and Jewish Germans who ended up in the torture cells of the Hotel Silber, or in a Württemberg concentration camp, did not know the name of the bureaucrat whose instructions led to their incarceration. Even though Robert Griesinger was known to dozens of Czech business leaders whose livelihoods he ruined, his identity was concealed from the tens of thousands of Czech workers forced to go to Germany as a result of his decisions. The impact of his professional choices on the lives of those targeted outlived the Third Reich. Many who survived Gestapo incarceration and forced labour in German factories and mines were haunted by their experiences of National Socialism. Others were plagued for the rest of their lives by ill-health. Griesinger's actions also took their toll on these people's families, creating an impact felt for decades afterwards. His lowly position ensured that relatives and orphaned children of those who did not return from the camps or forced labour never learned the identity of the person who was responsible for their grief.

After the war the Allies and most Germans held the Nazi state and its leaders, together with the Gestapo and the SS, responsible for the atrocities carried out between 1933 and 1945. Despite his significance in the lives of a number of the regime's victims, Griesinger remained, simply, a nameless and faceless bureaucrat. This book shows that it is possible to trace the life of one of those ordinary Nazis whose role in war and genocide seems to have vanished from the historical record. Returning texture and agency to one such perpetrator affords Griesinger the opportunity to stand in for the thousands of anonymous ordinary Nazis whose widespread culpability wreaked havoc on so many lives and whose biographies have, until now, never seen the light of day. Given the scarcity of people still able to remember personal elements of these individual lives that were never confined to paper, one wonders whether they are ever likely to be written.

The papers hidden in Jana's chair – which gave no indication of Griesinger's involvement in the SS, the Gestapo or the occupation authorities in the Protectorate – and the absence of any incriminating reference to him in books or online had at first led me to believe that Griesinger was detached from the horrors of war and the Holocaust. Unravelling his trail revealed that this was not the case. Even if the distress Griesinger inflicted never reached the heights of more prominent desk murderers such as Adolf Eichmann, he and thousands of low-ranking officials like him were active participants in Nazi terror. Post-war claims of not having known about the fate of the Jews disappear, when confronted with the evidence. Far from being a 'small cog' in a larger machine, who never left his office, as so many desk murderers later claimed, Griesinger's extreme-nationalist background, the close positioning of his desk at the Hotel Silber to the torture chambers in the cellar, his membership of the SS, his drafting of forced labour in Prague, his travel to forced-labour sites in the Protectorate and his proximity to the murder of Jews and Communists in Ukraine in summer 1941 by members of his *Wehrmacht* unit rendered him culpable. Robert Griesinger knew what was going on.

Contrary to being 'anodyne', as the historical record would attest, ordinary Nazis such as Robert Griesinger entered into loving personal relationships and made professional decisions to better themselves and their families. Many had doting mothers and complex personal lives. Men like Griesinger effortlessly switched from being kind, gentle and funny to displaying their cold-blooded cunning and indifference. For prisoners at the Hotel Silber, Jews in villages in western Ukraine, soldiers in the Red Army and Czech workers, Griesinger's role embodied terror and mistrust, while in the eyes of his colleagues and superiors he was a dedicated and ambitious, though ultimately uninspiring, administrator. During his lifetime, his friends would have been struck by his loyalty and dedication to fraternity life, and most extended members of his family upheld his positive virtues. After his death, Griesinger was quickly either turned into a black sheep or exonerated by a process of selective forgetting.

Over the course of my search, a combination of oral and written sources enabled me to confront silences in the official archives. While we will never know how Griesinger's documents came to be concealed in a Czech armchair, or whether he ever murdered a civilian while serving with the *Wehrmacht* in the east, interviews with Griesinger's relatives, coupled with the discovery of his mother's diary, revealed intricate details of how he was able to navigate a period of the past that we think we know so well. Relying less on the images of the SS from popular culture, which generally portray individual members as sadistic psychopaths, and more on local records to probe Griesinger's involvement in the *Allgemeine SS*, exposed the intimate spaces of low-ranking SS men, revealing the SS to have been a much more multifaceted organisation than is commonly recognised. Griesinger was able to dip in and out of SS participation as it suited him. The SS impacted on family life only as much as he wanted it to. He did not wear the notorious black uniform every day, nor did his SS membership later lead to the *Waffen-SS* or the SS Security Police, a route taken by Stahlecker and other former colleagues. The ambition, drive and antisemitism of the SS became just another strand of Griesinger's professional life. SS membership did not damage a man's social standing. On the contrary, both Jutta and Barbara spoke of the enduring affection Gisela's parents felt for their son-in-law. It was the Swiss ski instructor, and not the SS officer, who was considered an improper match for their daughter.

Griesinger's story takes in slavery, migration, war and genocide: some of the most seismic events and themes in modern world history. Researching his past led me to the role of women in the slave trade in pre-abolition New Orleans, Fritz Rothschild's exemption from having to wear the yellow star in occupied Paris, and the appearance of Gisela's uncle Friedrich Nottebohm before the International Court of Justice in The Hague. While most Nazis didn't need enslaver ancestors to hate Jews, the fact that Griesinger could find so many in his family tree takes us away from seeing Nazism as an inherently local or solely German phenomenon, to show us instead international influences on ordinary Nazis. Those migrating from the New to the Old World brought with them ideas on race and racial thinking from beyond the boundaries of the German nation state. Exploring events in Prague in spring 1945 through the prism of a single German figure casts a shadow over the euphoria of the local Czech population that accompanied the city's liberation.

The picture of Griesinger that I have unfolded here incorporates many hours of conversation with surviving family members, and years spent searching for written documents trying to substantiate memories that might have been suppressed and reshaped with the passage of time. Even so, some notable voices are absent. In 2018 several people were still alive who knew Robert or Gisela intimately. Joachim, Gisela's son, was twelve when his stepfather died. According to Jutta, Joachim had vivid memories of Robert, but she urged me not to contact him. He had made it clear to her that he wanted nothing to do with my enquiries. Similarly, Gisela's third husband, Walter, was also still alive. Barbara and Jutta had seen him fairly recently, at the funeral of his sister, whom Joachim had married in the 1950s. Meeting Walter involved upsetting tenuous family dynamics, so I decided against it – a decision that I still regret.

Marion Venzmer, Gisela's niece, was the little girl looking side-long into the camera at Robert and Gisela's wedding banquet in February 1936. When I reached her on the telephone, she absolutely refused to accept my reason for contacting her. 'No one would be interested in him,' she exclaimed, before demanding to be told why I was really calling. There was also Griesinger's illegitimate child, of whose existence Irmela seemed so sure, but whose identity proved impossible to uncover. With the sources at my disposal I did the best I could to re-create the life of an SS officer, but at times I felt the frustration of not having access to more precious witnesses, whose memories might have unlocked more insights into Griesinger's identity.

Griesinger left a weighty mark on his family who, years after his death, continued to suffer from the choices he made. In an act to humiliate her former daughter-in-law, Wally took in Barbara to live with her – the daughter always accused of not having enough Griesinger in her. But it was perhaps in the aftermath of his mother's passing that Griesinger's significance and earlier actions were called into question. The long inheritance battle that ensued after Wally's death in 1976, resulting from a change that she had made to her will shortly before she died, soured family relations for ever. Griesinger's daughters, by then in their late thirties, were pitted on one side of a Stuttgart courtroom against Albert, Robert's brother, and his two sons. When Barbara and Jutta came to the Griesinger house midway through the proceedings, to try and claim as a memento some of their grandmother's possessions, they recall being met with derision and bitterness.

Forty years later, Jochen was not proud of his behaviour. He had been angry with his cousins for making him endure years of legal wrangling at great expense. On the occasion of one of their visits, he let his temper get the better of him. As the sisters scoured the property for relics of their father and grandmother that they intended to remove, Jochen recalled picking up the colossal bronze bust of Robert's head that Wally had commissioned shortly after his death and, without telling Barbara, carrying it down to her car, where he placed it on the passenger seat. He fastened the seatbelt around Robert's bust before returning inside.

In the same way that Griesinger was denied a proper final resting place, so the large bust of his head – which for decades sat surrounded by candles in a prominent position in the living room of his mourning mother – also endured a humiliating afterlife. Today the bust of Robert Griesinger lies wrapped in newspapers in a cardboard box in Jutta's attic.

Notes

Abbreviations

ABS	Archiv bezpečnostních složek (Security Services Archive, Prague)
AG	Adolf Griesinger
AUoH	Archives of the University of Hohenheim
BAB	Bundesarchiv, Berlin-Lichterfelde (German Federal Archive)
BfZ	Bibliothek für Zeitgeschichte, Stuttgart (Library of Contemporary History)
CDJC	Centre de Documentation Juive Contemporaine, Mémorial de la Shoah, Paris
DAKO	Derzhavnyi arkhiv Kyivs'koi oblasti (The State Archives of the Kiev Oblast)
DSK	Das Schwarze Korps
GFA	The Griesinger Family Archive
HStAS	Hauptstaatsarchiv Stuttgart (Main State Archive, Stuttgart)
MHP	Archives of the Ministry of Economics and Labour
MLA	Marriage Licence Applications of the Main Office for Race and Settlement
NAP	Národní archiv v Praze (National Archive, Prague)
NARC	The Notarial Archives Research Center, Civil District Court Building, New Orleans
RG	Robert Griesinger
RSHA	Reich Main Security Office
RuSHA	SS Main Office for Race and Settlement
SD	The Sicherheitsdienst (the security and intelligence service of the SS)
SK	Sammlung Knoch
SS	Schutzstaffel (Protection Squads)
SSt	Sammlung Sterz
StAL	Staatsarchiv Ludwigsburg (State Archive, Ludwigsburg, Baden-Württemberg)
StASt	Stadtarchiv Stuttgart (City Archives of Stuttgart)
StAT	Stadtarchiv Tübingen (City Archives of Tübingen)
SZ	Süddeutsche Zeitung
WG	Wally Griesinger
WGCB	Wally Griesinger's 'Child Book'
WGD	Wally Griesinger's diary

Epigraph

1 Quoted in Gitta Sereny, 'Children of the Reich', in Elaine Halleck (ed.), *Living in Nazi Germany* (Farmington Hills, 2004), 75.

Introduction

1 The national press covered the Winter Olympics on the front cover of every edition during the ten days of the competition. See the front covers of *Der Angriff* and *Völkischer Beobachter*, especially 7, 8 and 9 February 1936.

2 Hauptstaatsarchiv Stuttgart (hereafter HStAS), E151 / 01 / Bü 284, List of people and roles of those working in section IIIc of the Political Police, 1 March 1936. As a result of the destruction of documents at the end of the war, no definitive list survives that sheds light on the exact number of employees at the Political Police. I am grateful to Sigrid Brüggemann and Roland Maier for providing me with the figure of 200 and for so much information on the Hotel Silber, much of which appears in their publication: Ingrid Bauz, Sigrid Brüggemann and Roland Maier (eds), *Die Geheime Staatspolizei in Württemberg und Hohenzollern* (Stuttgart, 2012). Brüggemann and Maier's figure of 200 appears in line with cities of a comparable size, such as Düsseldorf, where the Political Police employed 291 workers, forty-nine in administrative roles and 242 who carried out police work. See Robert Gellately, *The Gestapo and German Society: Enforcing Racial Policy, 1933–1945* (Oxford, 1990), 45.

3 Horst Junginger, *The Scientification of the 'Jewish Question' in Nazi Germany* (Leiden, 2017), 320.

4 For more on how people were affected in the longer term by their experience under Nazism, see Mary Fulbrook, *Reckonings: Legacies of Nazi Persecution and the Quest for Justice* (Oxford, 2018), 6.

5 Biographies of low-ranking officials who were not direct killers do not exist. Except for the rare occasion that a descendant, or someone with an intimate connection to an 'ordinary German', researches the Nazi past of a particular individual, their names, identities and trajectories are generally lost from history. Alex J. Kay points to a recent trend of biographical sketches of mid- and lower-level perpetrators and reveals that the average length of an entry is around a dozen pages. See Alex J. Kay, *The Making of an SS Killer: The Life of Colonel Alfred Filbert, 1905–1990* (Cambridge, 2016), 128, n. 11. According to him, there exists only a small handful of individual biographical accounts of mid-level SS and police functionaries involved in genocide; Kay, *The Making of an SS Killer*, 1.

6 Two categories of Germans under Nazism generally emerge, when employing party or administrative rank, or participation in the Final Solution, as a benchmark from which to judge an individual's significance to the period. Hitler, Himmler, Heydrich and all those at the very top of the regime make up the first. But this category also includes Stahlecker, Harster, Bilfinger and other less high-ranking characters, whose zeal towards policy implementation or Nazi ideology renders their actions worthy of scrutiny, and their names worthy of being remembered. Hitler's millions of nameless and faceless followers make up the second category, placed together to construct a single grouping referred to commonly as 'ordinary Germans'. It is a broad term that encompasses a variety of individuals, ranging from standard school teachers and factory workers who were not party members,

to 'real Nazis' – Germans who took part in violent collective projects, such as concentration-camp staff or mobile killing units. For a discussion of 'Real Nazis', see Michael Mann, 'Were Perpetrators of Genocide "Ordinary Men" or "Real Nazis?" Results From Fifteen Hundred Biographies', *Holocaust and Genocide Studies*, vol. 14, 2000, 332–3.

7 This should not suggest that 'ordinary Germans' were somehow immune from contributing to mass murder. As Raul Hilberg, Christopher R. Browning and others have shown, most perpetrators and killers were 'ordinary Germans' who were drawn from a wide spectrum of German society. See Raul Hilberg, *The Destruction of the European Jews* (3rd edn, New Haven, CT, 2003), 1084; Christopher R. Browning, *Ordinary Men: Reserve Police Battalion 101 and the Final Solution in Poland* (London, 2001), 192.

8 Veronika was not her real name.

9 Jana was not her real name.

10 I am grateful to Ben Frommer at Northwestern University for providing this information. On the trials lasting just a few minutes, see Benjamin Frommer, *National Cleansing: Retribution against Nazi Collaborators in Postwar Czechoslovakia* (Cambridge, 2005), 249.

I: A 'Real' Nazi

1 I am grateful to Elizabeth St George, Jeremy Morrison and Eugenio Donadoni for alerting me to Thonet's bentwood furniture.

2 In December 1941 Hitler gave permission for the launch of 'Operation Furniture' (*Möbel Aktion*), which saw the furniture of Jews who had been deported from France, Belgium, Luxembourg and the Netherlands becoming the property of the Reich. From January 1942 until the Liberation, the Germans confiscated tables, chairs, wardrobes, beds and hundreds of other objects from Jewish homes, which were transported east, where they were intended to furnish the newly acquired homes and offices of German administrators working in Nazi territory. Later, items were also delivered to German families who had been victims of Allied bombing raids. By late 1943, 24,000 freight cars had shipped east almost one million cubic metres of furniture. In Paris alone, the Nazis removed items from 38,000 'abandoned properties'. In the Protectorate of Bohemia and Moravia, Jewish furniture and possessions were confiscated the moment their owners left for Theresienstadt. Before they were made available to German civil servants in the Czech lands, Jewish workmen removed all visible signs of an object's previous owner, taking off monograms from silver and cutting out bookplates and other identifiable marks. In January 1944 fifty-four large warehouses contained the furniture and other household goods of Jews who had either been killed in the east or who were languishing in Theresienstadt. See Götz Aly, *Hitler's Beneficiaries: Plunder, Racial War, and the Nazi Welfare State* (New York, 2006), 119–23; Shannon L. Fogg, *Stealing Home: Looting, Restitution, and Reconstructing Jewish Lives in France, 1942–1947* (Oxford, 2017); Livia Rothkirchen, *The Jews of Bohemia and Moravia: Facing the Holocaust* (Lincoln, NE, 2005), 116, 129.

3 I am grateful to Eva Škvárová for her insight.

4 Ibid.

5 I also visited several antique-furniture warehouses further afield, in the vicinity of Olšany cemetery.

6 On the number of personnel and informants at the StB, see: https://zpravy.
aktualne.cz/small-but-effective-communist-secret-police-dissected/r~i:article:6126
86/?redirected=1505699944

7 Národní archiv v Praze (National Archive, Prague; hereafter NAP), PR II-EO
1420/5. Griesinger registered with the Prague city police on 8 March 1943.

8 Archiv bezpečnostních složek (Security Services Archive, Prague, hereafter ABS),
Study Institute of the Ministry of the Interior (Ministerstvo Vnitra – MV), 107-8-
30, Directory of German public servants in Prague. The document also confirmed
Griesinger was in the SD.

9 Bundesarchiv, Berlin-Lichterfelde (hereafter BAB), VBS 286 SS Officers' Service
Records (SSO/ SS-Führerpersonalakten) 031A File of RG. See also R 1501,
Reichsministerium des Innern (Ministry of the Interior) no. 206781. RG's hand-
written CV from 19 March 1937 (hereafter CV, March 1937).

10 BAB, Marriage Licence Applications of the Main Office for Race and Settlement
(hereafter MLA), R 9361 III/58950, RG's handwritten family tree. Undated. Probably
autumn 1935.

11 Wolf-Dieter Obst, 'Nachts, als das alte Stuttgart unterging', Stuttgarter Nachrichten,
25 July 2014.

12 Rebecca L. Boehling, A Question of Priorities: Democratic Reforms and Economic
Recovery in Postwar Germany: Frankfurt, Munich, and Stuttgart under US Occupation,
1945–1949 (Providence, RI, 1996), 90.

13 For more on Klett's background and appointment as mayor in April 1945, see ibid.,
94–104; 'Wie Stuttgart sein Gesicht verlor', Die Welt, 16 October 1999.

14 Staatsarchiv Ludwigsburg (hereafter StAL), EL 902/20 Bü 91743. Denazification
Records. File on WG.

15 For this information I am grateful to Dr Roland Müller, Chief Archivist at the
Stadtarchiv Stuttgart (City Archives of Stuttgart), who has dedicated his profes-
sional life to the study of Stuttgart during the Third Reich. On the destruction
of SS papers, see H. G. Adler, Theresienstadt 1941–1945: The Face of a Coerced
Community (2nd edn, Cambridge, 2017), 160–1; Christopher Dillon, Dachau and the
SS: A Schooling in Violence (Oxford, 2015), 12, 109.

16 We notice a similar phenomenon in autobiographical accounts. See the recent case
of 'uncle Franz-Karl' in Nora Krug, Heimat: A German Family Album (London, 2018).

II: Inheriting Ideas from the New World

1 United States Passenger and Crew Lists: Robert Griesinger Snr set sail from
Liverpool aboard The China in 1867. Full details available at ancestry.com.

2 Andrea Mehrländer, The Germans of Charleston, Richmond and New Orleans during the
Civil War Period, 1850–1870 (Berlin, 2011), 49, 286–8; William Robinson Konrad, 'The
Diminishing Influences of German Culture in New Orleans Life Since 1865', The Louisiana
Historical Quarterly, vol. 24, no. 1, January 1941, 127–67. For an excellent recent discussion
on German-Americans, see Thomas Lekan, 'German Landscape: Local Promotion
of the Heimat Abroad', in Krista O'Donnell, Renate Bridenthal and Nancy Reagin
(eds), The Heimat Abroad: The Boundaries of Germanness (Ann Arbor, MI, 2005), 141–66.

3 Williams Research Center, The Historic New Orleans Collection, New Orleans,
1868 City Directory (reel 2), Griesinger is listed as an agent for Clason & Co.,
commission merchants.

4 Blake Touchstone, 'Slavery in Louisiana', in Randall M. Miller and John David
Smith (eds), Dictionary of Afro-American Slavery (Westport, 1997), 415; Robert C.
Reinders, End of an Era: New Orleans, 1850–1860 (New Orleans, 1964), 28.

5 '"Purchased Lives" Exhibit Helps New Orleans Come to Terms with Domestic Slave Trade', 3 June 2015, http://wwno.org/post/purchased-lives-exhibit-helps-new-orleans-come-terms-domestic-slave-trade.

6 Lina's father arranged for August Reichard to be Lina's tutor after his death. During the Civil War, Reichard, who owned five enslaved workers, established a German battalion to fight for the Confederacy. It is impossible to know how far Reichard's political views influenced Lina, and whether she fell prey to her tutor's views on slavery, freedom and race. See Mehrländer, *The Germans of Charleston, Richmond and New Orleans*, 139, 204. Brian Purnell and Jeanne Theoharis, 'Introduction', in Brian Purnell, Jeanne Theoharis and Komozi Woodard (eds), *The Strange Careers of the Jim Crow North: Segregation and Struggle outside of the South* (New York, 2019), 3.

7 I am indebted to Mary Lou Eichhorn for her encyclopaedic knowledge of Paul Emile Johns. The cultural historian of Louisiana Alfred E. Lemmon has written various pieces on Johns. See Lemmon's entry on Johns in David Johnson (ed.), *Encyclopaedia of Louisiana* (Louisiana Endowment for the Humanities, 2010–present). Available at https://64parishes.org/entry/paul-emile-johns. Article published 30 January 2013.

8 The Notarial Archives Research Center, New Orleans (hereafter NARC), Notarial Acts of Felix De Armas, Act 314, the sale of an enslaved person from George Manouvrier to Paul Emile Johns, May 1833. No legal transactions existed to suggest that Johns ever resold Reuben.

9 Ibid., Notarial Acts of Felix De Armas, Act 346, the sale of an enslaved person from Manuela Perez Favre D'Aunoy to J. V. Delassize, 1826.

10 Ibid., Notarial Acts of Jean-Baptiste Garic, succession papers of Jean Baptiste Honoré Destrehan de Beaupré, 26 February 1765, 28; Jean Baptiste Honoré Destrehan de Beaupré, son of one of Louis XIV's councillors, was France's powerful royal treasurer of the colony of Louisiana. See also William D. Reeves, *History of Destrehan Plantation in St Charles Parish, for the River Road Historical Society* (unpublished manuscript), 57.

11 See Reiner Pommerin, *Sterilisierung der Rheinlandbastarde: Das Schicksal einer farbigen deutschen Minderheit 1918–1937* (Düsseldorf: Droste, 1979); Katharina Oguntoye, *Eine afro-deutsche Geschichte: Zur Lebenssituation von Afrikanern und Afro-Deutschen in Deutschland von 1884 bis 1950* (Berlin, 1997), 110–40. See also the documentary *Hitler's Forgotten Victims* (dir. David Okuefuna and Moise Shewa, 1997), available at: https://www.youtube.com/watch?v=xlvC4QjwNbs&feature=youtu.be

12 On the Destrehan family, see Reeves, *History of Destrehan Plantation in St Charles Parish*. I am grateful to Melissa Monica of the Destrehan Plantation for providing me with so much information on Catalina. I am also grateful to Lauren Hooks, a descendant of Catalina, who kindly shared details of the Honoré family history.

13 Alecia P. Long, 'Woman Order (General Order No. 28)', in Lisa Tendrich Frank (ed.), *Women in the American Civil War*, vol. 1 (Santa Barbara, CA, 2008), 593–4.

14 Emily Toth, *Kate Chopin* (Austin, TX, 1993), 105.

15 Emily Toth and Per Seyersted (eds), *Kate Chopin's Private Papers* (Bloomington, IN, 1998), 103–10; Per Seyersted, *Kate Chopin: A Critical Biography* (Oslo, 1969), 31–9.

16 During this time Robert Griesinger Snr was appointed to the Board of Trustees for Louisiana Mutual Insurance Company and was made a director for the Germania Insurance Company of New Orleans. In March 1874 Clason and Co. announced Robert's promotion to director. See *The Daily Picayune*, 21 February 1871 and 24 March 1872; *New Orleans Times*, 14 August 1872; *New Orleans Republican*, 24 March 1874.

17 James Q. Whitman, *Hitler's American Model: The United States and the Making of Nazi Race Law* (Princeton, NJ, 2017), 5, 80, 127–8.
18 Robert Griesinger Snr tried desperately to revive the family's sinking finances. To keep his American Dream alive, he left Lina and five-year-old Adolf in New Orleans in 1876 and headed to San Francisco, which, twenty years earlier at the height of the Gold Rush, had offered opportunities to thrive professionally. Robert set himself up as a stockbroker and became a member of the recently created Pacific Stock Exchange. Nevertheless, by the time Griesinger Snr arrived out west, the gold had dried up and he struggled to find his way professionally in San Francisco. See San Francisco City Directory, 1877–80. Griesinger Snr was even taken to court by an investor. See *Sacramento Daily Union*, 23 November 1878.
19 On return migration, see Ran Abramitzky, Leah Boustan and Katherine Eriksson, 'To the New World and Back Again: Return Migrants in the Age of Mass Migration', *ILR Review*, vol. 72, issue 2, 300–22; Tara Zahra, *The Great Departure: Mass Migration from Eastern Europe and the Making of the Free World* (New York, 2016), 114–16.
20 It would be wrong, however, to consider German antisemitism in purely racial terms. Historians have recently shown the incoherence of Nazi racial thinking, especially when it came to Jews. While Hitler's venomous attacks on Jews were without doubt couched in racial language, Jews' purported lack of national allegiance and the alleged menace of global Jewry proved more of a threat to the security of the nation than Jews' blood and racial make-up. Griesinger's antisemitism was more influenced by the First World War and its immediate aftermath than it was by his ancestry in the American South. See Mark Roseman, 'Racial Discourse, Nazi Violence, and the Limits of the Racial State Model', in Devin O. Pendas, Mark Roseman and Richard F. Wetzell (eds), *Beyond the Racial State: Rethinking Nazi Germany* (Cambridge, 2017), 31–57.

III: 'Zero Hour'

1 See Paul Connerton, *How Societies Remember* (Cambridge, 1989), 7; Claudia Koonz, 'Between Memory and Oblivion: Concentration Camps in German Memory', in John R. Gillis (ed.), *Commemorations: The Politics of National Identity* (Princeton, 1994), 262–3. See also Nicholas Stargardt, *Witnesses of War: Children's Lives under the Nazis* (London, 2005), 330–1, 334, 341.
2 Robert G. Moeller, *War Stories: The Search for a Usable Past in the Federal Republic of Germany* (Berkeley, CA, 2001), 13.
3 Barbara Rogers, 'Facing a Wall of Silence', in Alan L. Berger and Naomi Berger (eds), *Second Generation Voices: Reflections by Children of Holocaust Survivors and Perpetrators* (Syracuse, NY, 2001), 293.
4 Alf Lüdtke, '"Coming to Terms with the Past": Illusions of Remembering, Ways of Forgetting Nazism in West Germany', *Journal of Modern History*, 65 (September 1993), 554; Gabriele Rosenthal, 'National Socialism and antisemitism in intergenerational dialogue', in Gabriele Rosenthal (ed.), *The Holocaust in Three Generations: Families of Victims and Perpetrators of the Nazi Regime* (London, 1998), 241.
5 I am grateful to Dirk Moses for introducing me to this term.
6 Stargardt, *Witnesses of War*, 378; Wolfgang Benz, 'Postwar Society and National Socialism: Remembrance, Amnesia, Rejection', *Tel Aviver Jahrbuch für deutsche Geschichte*, XIX, 1990, 9.
7 Dieter Hahn, quoted in Wolfgang W. E. Samuel, *The War of our Childhood: Memories of World War II* (Jackson, MS, 2002), 247.

8 Telephone interview and email correspondence with Peter Ströbel, 28 August and 3 September 2015.

9 Sibylle Hübner-Funk, 'Hitler's Grandchildren in the Shadow of the Past: The Burden of a Difficult Heritage', *Tel Aviver Jahrbuch für deutsche Geschichte*, XIX, 1990, 106.

10 Fulbrook, *Reckonings*, 7–10, 424. On how grandchildren glossed over and misunderstood their grandparents, see Harald Welzer, Sabine Moller, Karoline Tschuggnall (eds), '*Opa war kein Nazi*': *Nationalsozialismus und Holocaust im Familiengedächtnis* (Frankfurt am Main, 2002).

11 Andreas Eichmüller, 'Die Strafverfolgung von NS-Verbrechen durch westdeutsche Justizbehörden seit 1945: Eine Zahlenbilanz', *Vierteljahrshefte für Zeitgeschichte* 56.4 (2008), 621–40. See also Caroline Sharples, *Postwar Germany and the Holocaust* (London, 2016), 71; and Fulbrook, *Reckonings*, 231–65.

12 Norbert Frei, *Adenauer's Germany and the Nazi Past: The Politics of Amnesty and Integration* (New York, 2002), 23–4.

13 *Jewish Telegraphic Agency*, 1 February 1967, and Carol Ann Lee, *The Hidden Life of Otto Frank* (London, 2002), 272–3; Caroline Sharples, *West Germans and the Nazi Legacy* (Oxford, 2012), 1. For coverage of the Harster trial in the Swiss press, see Neue Zürcher Zeitung, 23, 24 and 25 January 1967, 24 and 26 February 1967. On the 'desk murderer', see Anne C. Heller, *Hannah Arendt: A Life in Dark Times* (Boston, 2015), 10.

14 Dan Bar-On, *Legacies of Shame: Encounters with Children of the Third Reich* (Cambridge, MA, 1989), 11–12.

15 Fulbrook, *Reckonings*, 445, 451.

16 Gerald L. Posner, *Hitler's Children: Sons and Daughters of Leaders of the Third Reich Talk about Their Fathers and Themselves* (New York, 1991), 6–7.

17 Private Archives of Jochen and Irmela Griesinger (hereafter the Griesinger Family Archive, GFA), Letter from WG and AG to RG, 29 March 1945.

18 Ibid., Wally Griesinger's diary (hereafter WGD), 7 March 1917.

19 Ibid., Article from November/December 1918.

20 Marion A. Kaplan, *The Making of the Jewish Middle Class: Women, Family, and Identity in Imperial Germany* (New York, 1991), 148–9. I am grateful to Marion Kaplan for alerting me to Mumm's political trajectory.

21 The newspaper should not be confused with the *Süddeutsche Zeitung* that was founded in Munich in 1945, one of Germany's most liberal newspapers. On the *Süddeutsche Zeitung* (hereafter, SZ), after the First World War, see Martin Ulmer, 'The Stereotype of the Jewish Modernizer as Illustrated by Antisemitic Criticism of the Big City', in Hubert Cancik and Uwe Puschner (eds), *Antisemitismus, Paganismus, Völkische Religion* (Munich, 2004), 34–5.

22 GFA, Wally Griesinger's 'Child Book' (hereafter WGCB), 6 March 1911.

IV: The 'War-Youth' Generation

1 See Merith Niehuss, 'Party configurations in state and municipal elections in Southern Germany, 1871–1914', in Karl Rohe (ed.), *Elections, parties and political traditions: Social foundations of German parties and party systems, 1867–1987* (New York, 1990), 83–105.

2 On Daimler and Bosch, see Johannes Bähr and Paul Erker, *Bosch: History of a Global Enterprise* (Munich, 2015); on the urbanisation of the city, see Jill Stephenson, *Hitler's Home Front: Württemberg under the Nazis* (London, 2006), 7.

3 Fred Uhlman, *Reunion* (new edn, London, 2015), 32–3.

4 GFA, WGCB.

5 Ibid., 6 March 1911, 27 January 1918.
6 See Keith Cartwright, *Reading Africa into American Literature: Epics, Fables, and Gothic Tales* (Lexington, KY, 2002), 137.
7 Lillian, Dunbar and Anna Christ were the grandchildren of Lina's sister Mathilde Christ (née Johns). Lillian was born in 1896, Dunbar in 1899 and Anna in 1905. I am grateful to Kiki Ulrich, Dunbar Christ's daughter, and to Charlotte Ulrich Schillaci, Dunbar Christ's granddaughter, for providing information on the Christ family.
8 I am grateful to the designer Tom Carey for providing the details of Lina's chair.
9 In the flat above the Griesingers lived the septuagenarian General Hermann Freiherr von Bilfinger, one of Württemberg's most revered soldiers, who had won the Iron Cross 1st Class during the Franco-Prussian War of 1870–71. Major Eugen Klotz and his family occupied the ground floor of the Griesingers' apartment block. See the reference for Alexanderstrasse 35 in Stadtarchiv Stuttgart (StASt), *Amtliches Stuttgarter Adreßbuch* for 1916.
10 GFA, WGCB, 25 August, 9 September 1914.
11 Ibid., 2 December 1915, undated entry from January 1916, undated entry from April 1916.
12 George Bernard Shaw's preface to Lina Richter, *Family Life in Germany under the Blockade* (London, 1919), 4.
13 For a similar situation in Berlin, see Belinda Davis, *Home Fires Burning: Food, Politics and Everyday Life in World War I Berlin* (Chapel Hill, NC, 2000).
14 GFA, WGCB, 30 August, 29 December 1917.
15 Alan Cramer, 'Blockade and Economic Warfare', in Jay Winter (ed.), *The Cambridge History of the First World War*, vol. 2 (Cambridge, 2014), 460–1.
16 The Reformrealgymnasium concentrated less on the study of ancient antiquity and more on modern European civilisation: French and English took precedence over Greek and Latin. On the Reformrealgymnasium at this time, see Brigitte Ankersdorfer's contribution to the pamphlet designed to mark the school's seventy-fifth anniversary, '75 Jahre Zeppelin-Gymnasium Stuttgart, 1912–1987', 38–9. I am grateful to the current headmaster, Holger zur Hausen, for giving me a copy.
17 Wally's references to shortages begin in early March 1917. GFA, WGD, see especially entries from March and June 1917. See also Davis, *Home Fires Burning*, 190–218.
18 Mary E. Cox, 'Hunger Games: Or How the Allied Blockade in the First World War deprived German children of nutrition, and Allied food aid subsequently saved them', *Economic History Review*, vol. 68, no. 2, 2015, 605–6.
19 GFA, WGCB, 4 February 1918, undated entry from June 1918, 25 June 1918.
20 Ibid., WGD, 25 October, 9 November 1918; Peter Hoffmann, *Stauffenberg: A Family History, 1905–1944* (3rd edn, Montreal and Kingston, 2008), 14.
21 GFA, WGD, 8, 9, 13, 20 November 1918.
22 Hoffmann, *Stauffenberg*, 14–5; Annegret Kotzurek and Rainer Redies, *Stuttgart von Tag zu Tag, 1900–1949: eine Chronik* (Tübingen, 2009), 52; Lieutenant Paul Hahn describes how his troops suppressed the insurrection in Paul Hahn, *Erinnerungen aus der Revolution in Württemberg* (Stuttgart, 1922); See also ibid., diary entries from January 1919.
23 Avner Offer, *The First World War: An Agrarian Interpretation* (Oxford, 1989), 34.
24 Emily Balch, 'Some Data on Conditions of Milk Supply in Central Europe', in *The Famine in Europe: The Facts and Suggested Remedies* (London, 1920), 72–3.
25 Letter in *The Nation*, 10 August 1920.
26 Robert W. Whalen, *Bitter Wounds: German Victims of the Great War* (Ithaca, NY, 1984), 95.

27 Testimony of Robert Uhland, a former pupil, in the pamphlet designed to mark the school's seventy-fifth anniversary, '75 Jahre Zeppelin-Gymnasium Stuttgart, 1912–1987', 14.

28 The great German writer Hermann Lenz was also a pupil at the school. Lenz made repeated references to life at the Gymnasium in many of his autobiographical works, most notably in *Andere Tage* (*Other Days*), which he published in 1968. See the interview with Hermann Lenz in the pamphlet '75 Jahre Zeppelin-Gymnasium Stuttgart, 1912–1987', 111. See also the testimony of Dr Max Löffler, a former pupil, in the same pamphlet, 10; and the testimony of Prof. Dr Robert Uhland, a former pupil, 14.

29 On these characteristics, see Mann, 'Were Perpetrators of Genocide "Ordinary Men" or "Real Nazis"?', 339.

30 On Robert's results at school, see StAL, E309 II, 2012/122 Bü 32, RG's Abitur certificate, 7 May 1925; On sport at the Reformrealgymnasium see the testimony of Prof. Dr Robert Uhland, a former pupil, in the pamphlet '75 Jahre Zeppelin-Gymnasium Stuttgart, 1912–1987', 14.

31 GFA, WGCB, 19 August 1920, 31 January, 21 May 1921.

32 Ibid., undated entries from February and Easter 1922, Easter 1923, 30 November 1924.

33 Ibid., undated entries from Easter and November 1923 and from April 1924.

34 Karla Poewe, *New Religions and the Nazis* (New York, 2006), 113–15. See also Ulrich Herbert, *Best: Biographische Studien über Radikalismus. Weltanschauung und Vernunft, 1903–1989* (Bonn, 1996), 43–4; Michael Wildt, *An Uncompromising Generation: The Nazi Leadership of the Reich Security Main Office* (Madison, WI, 2009), 36.

35 GFA, tracts, details of meetings and other party material of the *Württembergische Bürgerpartei* belonging to Wally and Adolf Griesinger; Testimony of Prof. Dr Robert Uhland, a former pupil, in the pamphlet '75 Jahre Zeppelin-Gymnasium Stuttgart, 1912–1987', 15.

36 Hermann Beck, *The Fateful Alliance: German Conservatives and Nazis in 1933: The Machtergreifung in a New Light* (New York, 2008), 35. The *Freikorps* comprised paramilitary units of First World War veterans who had fought against the Communists.

37 GFA, WGCB, undated entry from November 1923.

38 Benjamin Ziemann, *Contested Commemorations: Republican War Veterans and Weimar Political Culture* (Cambridge, 2013), 58.

39 GFA, WGCB, undated entry from Easter and November 1923.

40 BAB, R 1501, no. 206781. Copy of RG's personnel file, 29 May 1936. See also the report on RG by Wegerle, summing up his achievements at the Ministry, 18 June 1936.

41 Robert Gerwarth, *The Bismarck Myth: Weimar Germany and the Legacy of the Iron Chancellor* (Oxford, 2005), 108. See also Wolfgang R. Krabbe, 'Die Bismarckjugend der Deutschnationalen Volkspartei', *German Studies Review*, vol. 17, no. 1, February 1994, 21.

42 GFA, WGCB, undated entry from November 1923; William Mulligan, *The Creation of the Modern German Army: General Walther Reinhardt and the Weimar Republic, 1914–1930* (New York, 2005), 222.

43 Ulmer, 'The Stereotype of the Jewish Modernizer', 34–5.

44 Larry Eugene Jones, 'Conservative Antisemitism in the Weimar Republic: A Case of the German National People's Party', in Larry Eugene Jones (ed.), *The German Right in the Weimar Republic: Studies in the History of German Conservatism,*

Nationalism, and Antisemitism (New York, 2014), 85–8; Ernest Hamburger and Peter Pulzer, 'Jews as Voters in the Weimar Republic', *Leo Baeck Institute Year Book*, vol. 30, no. 1, 1985, 24. On the antisemitism of the Württembergische Bürgerpartei at this time, see Junginger, *The Scientification of the 'Jewish Question' in Nazi Germany*, 299–300.

45 On the Jewish population of Stuttgart, see Maria Zelzer, *Weg und Schicksal der Stuttgarter Juden. Ein Gedenkbuch* (Stuttgart, 1964), 32. See the Stolpersteine map of the Jews of Stuttgart at: https://www.stolpersteine-stuttgart.de/index.php?docid=965&mid=76. It was something of a novelty for Wally to spend time with Jews. When she encountered a Jewish family while on a walking holiday in summer 1918, she felt the need to mention their Jewishness to distinguish them from other guests. See GFA, WGCB, 14 August 1918.

46 StASt, Fond 358 Archives of the Zeppelin Gymnasium, Schülerzeugnislisten and Zeugnislisten, 1924–5.

47 I am grateful to Judit Vamosi for telling me about the project during a meeting in Stuttgart. While it was impossible to determine the fates of all seventeen boys, we know that at least five managed to emigrate to Britain, Palestine and South America.

48 StASt, Fond 358 Archives of the Zeppelin Gymnasium, Zeugnislisten for class 9a and 9b, 1924–5. On Edgar Fleischer, see: http://www.stolpersteine-gp.de/en/fleischer-rosa/. On Walther Hummel, see: https://www.jewishgen.org/yizkor/nuremberg/nur006.html

49 StASt, Fond 358 Archives of the Zeppelin Gymnasium, Zeugnislisten for class 9b, 1924–5; Susanne Rueß, *Stuttgarter Jüdischer Ärzte Während Des Nationalsozialismus* (Würzburg, 2009), 283–5.

50 Interview with Judy Kaplan, 22 May 2017.

51 StASt, Fond 358 Archives of the Zeppelin Gymnasium, Zeugnislisten for class 9b, 1924–5; GFA, WGCB, 30 November 1924, 24 February, 7 March 1925.

52 GFA, WGCB, 22 April 1925.

V: Hollow Talk

1 Stadtarchiv Tübingen (hereafter StAT), A573, the *Einwohnermeldekarte* (resident registration card) of RG.

2 Uwe-Dietrich Adam, *Hochschule und Nationalsozialismus: Die Universität Tübingen in Dritten Reich* (Tübingen, 1977), 29–30.

3 Oleg Morozov, 'The Historical Past of Tübingen University within the 1927 Jubilee Context', *History of Education and Children's Literature*, vol. 9, no. 1, 301–20.

4 Christian Ingrao, *Believe and Destroy: Intellectuals in the SS War Machine* (Cambridge, 2013), 25.

5 Dirk Walter, 'German Racial League for Defense and Defiance', in Richard S. Levy (ed.), *Antisemitism: A Historical Encyclopedia of Prejudice and Persecution*, vol. 1 (Santa Barbara, CA, 2005), 266.

6 Susannah Heschel, *The Aryan Jesus: Christian Theologians and the Bible in Nazi Germany* (Princeton, NJ, 2008), 180–5.

7 Wildt, *An Uncompromising Generation*, 48.

8 In 1924 the German Society for Racial Hygiene set up a branch in Tübingen. Otmar Freiherr von Verschuer, who conducted research on twins and later organised the funding for his friend, Dr Josef Mengele, to conduct his experiments on Jewish, Roma and Sinti twins at Auschwitz, served as its secretary. During his

time in Tübingen, von Verschuer captivated students with his passionate lectures on race hygiene, and even held adult evening classes on eugenics. Hans-Walter Schmuhl, *The Kaiser Wilhelm Institute for Anthropology, Human Heredity, and Eugenics, 1927–45* (Dordrecht, 2008), 52. See also Henry Friedlander, *The Origins of Nazi Genocide: From Euthanasia to the Final Solution* (Chapel Hill, NC, 1995), 135; Robert Jay Lifton, *The Nazi Doctors: Medical Killing and the Psychology of Genocide* (London, 1986), 358, 362.

9 Heinz Howaldt, *Suevia Tübingen, 1831–1931*, vol. 2 (Tübingen, 1931), 321. Griesinger's grandfather, Robert Senior, had an older brother, Julius, who was the first Griesinger to join Suevia Tübingen in 1855. Julius later became a prominent judge in Württemberg, rising to the position of state councillor in the court of his Corps brother, King Wilhelm II, who had joined Suevia Tübingen in the 1860s.

10 Sonja Levsen, 'Constructing Elite Identities: University Students, Military Masculinity and the Consequences of the Great War in Britain and Germany', *Past and Present*, no. 198 (February 2008), 171.

11 Edward B. Westermann, 'Drinking Rituals, Masculinity, and Mass Murder in Nazi Germany', *Central European History*, vol. 51, 2018, 371; Howaldt, *Suevia Tübingen*, vol. 1, 256.

12 Howaldt, *Suevia Tübingen*, vol. 2, 321.

13 In a letter from 1934, long after their university days, Gustav Albrecht affectionately addressed Griesinger as 'Robi' and made mention of Adolf and Wally. Letter from Gustav Albrecht Sayn-Wittgenstein-Berleburg to RG, 23 March 1934, in the possession of Barbara Schlegel.

14 Archives of the University of Hohenheim (hereafter AUoH), the Stammliste of RG.

15 In October 1943 Griesinger's shares were worth 112,000 Reichsmark. To put this amount into perspective, Albert Speer, Reich Minister of Armaments and War Production, earned 18,000 Reichsmark in 1943 as his annual salary as a secretary of state in Hitler's cabinet. See Martin Kitchen, *Speer: Hitler's Architect* (New Haven, CT, 2015), 75.

16 On Griesinger's courses away from Tübingen see AUoH, the Stammliste of RG. On his perceptions on life in Berlin see, for example, articles by Reinhard Mumm and others in the *SZ*.

17 StAL, E309 II, 2012/122 Bü 32, Studienbuch of RG and separate lists of classes that he took. Report on RG's exam script after taking the first set of state law exams (*Referendarexamen*), spring 1930. He was taught by Philipp von Heck, a pioneer in the Jurisprudence of Interest; and by Carl Sartorius, a renowned expert in Public Law.

18 Sibylle Kästner, Viola Maier and Almut Schülke, 'From Pictures to Stories: Traces of female PhD graduates from the Department of Prehistoric Archaeology, University of Tübingen, Germany', in Margarita Diaz-Andreu and Marie Louise Stig Sørensen (eds), *Excavating Women: A History of Women in European Archaeology* (London and New York, 1998), 267.

19 StAT, A573, the *Einwohnermeldekarte* (resident registration card) of RG. In 1934 the Wacker sisters received money from the state to renovate their house. See StAT, A150/7178. For this information I am grateful to archivist Udo Rauch. On evening meals at the house see Edith Glaser, *Hindernisse, Umwege, Sackgassen: Die Anfänge des Frauenstudiums in Tübingen, 1904–34* (Weinheim, 1992), 199.

20 A small SA march in Tübingen by students in 1929 received scant attention. Adam, *Hochschule und Nationalsozialismus*, 22–3; Rudy Koshar, 'Two "Nazisms": The Social Context of Nazi Mobilization in Marburg and Tübingen', *Social History*, vol. 7, no. 1, 34–5.

21 Detlef Mühlberger, *Hitler's Followers: Studies in the Sociology of the Nazi Movement* (London, 1991), 75.

22 Wildt, *An Uncompromising Generation*, 47–55.

23 The Nazis won all the seats in Graz, while at Breslau and at Heidelberg they gained 70 per cent and 60 per cent respectively. See Adam, *Hochschule und Nationalsozialismus*, 24. See also Geoffrey J. Giles, 'National Socialism and the Educated Elite in the Weimar Republic', in Peter D. Sachura (ed.), *The Nazi Machtergreifung* (London, 1983), 58–9.

24 Ingrao, *Believe and Destroy*, 17.

25 StAL, E309 II, 2012/122 Bü 32, RG's certificate from the first set of state law exams, spring 1930. His grade is noted as: *Gesamtzeugnis IIIa unten (befriedigend)*.

26 BAB, R 1501, no. 206781. Report on RG by Wegerle, summing up his achievements since joining the ministry, 18 June 1936.

27 See Richard F. Wetzell, *Inventing the Criminal: A History of German Criminology, 1880–1945* (Chapel Hill, NC, 2000), 236; and Nikolaus Wachsmann, *Hitler's Prisons: Legal Terror in Nazi Germany* (New Haven, CT, 2004), 82.

28 His analysis contained a single reference to Jews, which occurred during Griesinger's historical overview, when he described the emergence of the modern form of usury in northern Italy in the thirteenth and fourteenth centuries. Robert Griesinger, 'Der Wucher nach geltendem deutschen Strafrecht und in den Entwürfen zu einem Allgemeinen Deutschen Strafgesetzbuch', Inaugural-Dissertation, University of Tübingen, August 1931, 15, a copy of which is held at Columbia University Law Library, New York. I am indebted to legal historian and criminal defence attorney Douglas G. Morris for this information. It is worth noting that the doctoral theses of other young lawyers from this era, who later joined the SS and committed some of the most heinous atrocities against Jews, do not reveal anything of their authors' politics. Their *völkisch* or antisemitic impulses are entirely absent. See Ingrao, *Believe and Destroy*, 38–9.

29 The first article in the *SZ* appeared on 22 February 1931, 5.

30 Atina Grossmann, *Reforming Sex: The German Movement for Birth Control and Abortion Reform, 1920–1950* (New York, 1995), 79.

31 Ibid., 84–6. See also *SZ*, 25 February 1931, 2.

32 In the second half of 1931 alone, unemployment in Germany rose by 2.1 million. In 1932, 43.7 per cent of the German workforce was out of work, compared to 13.1 per cent in 1929. The situation worsened as Brüning's deflationary policies spiralled out of control. See Patricia Clavin, *The Great Depression in Europe, 1929–1939* (Basingstoke, 2000), 112.

33 In the elections of May 1928 the Nazis polled only 2.6 per cent of the vote and gained twelve Reichstag seats. Two years later they accumulated 18.3 per cent of the vote and 107 seats. Even though the Nazi share of the vote in Württemberg increased from 1.9 per cent in 1928 to 9.4 per cent in 1930, this only represented half of what the party achieved nationally.

34 Mühlberger, *Hitler's Followers*, 51, 54.

35 Stephenson, *Hitler's Home Front*, 32.

36 The Nazi party founded a branch in Stuttgart in May 1920. Officials in Württemberg were so convinced that the party would not take off locally that – unlike in most German regions – it was not initially outlawed. The Nazi party was only banned nationally in November 1923 following the Beer Hall Putsch. Nevertheless, the lifting of the ban in February 1925 did little to drum up local support. The state's liberal parliamentary tradition, dating back to the nineteenth century, also ensured that extremist parties fared poorly in elections.

37 Stephenson, *Hitler's Home Front*, 40–1.
38 In autumn 1930 only 4,000 people in the whole of Württemberg were members of the Nazi party. Less than two years later, however, Nazi membership in Württemberg reached 21,000. Much of the party's advance was down to the Nazi Regional Leader (*Gauleiter*) of Württemberg-Hohenzollern, Wilhelm Murr. A brutish former factory worker known for his vehement antisemitism, Murr led a campaign of targeted propaganda throughout Württemberg, making breakthroughs for the party in formerly unwinnable areas. Mühlberger, *Hitler's Followers*, 59; Stephenson, *Hitler's Home Front*, 41.
39 Nevertheless, the figure there still fell short of the national toll of 37 per cent of Germans who voted for Hitler.
40 GFA, WGD, 11 February and 28 December 1918.
41 Beck, *The Fateful Alliance*, 110–12.
42 Bruce Campbell, *The SA Generals and the Rise of Nazism* (Lexington, KY, 1998), 120.
43 Douglas G. Morris, 'Discrimination, Degradation, Defiance: Jewish Lawyers under Nazism', in Alan E. Steinweis and Robert D. Rachlin (eds), *The Law in Nazi Germany: Ideology, Opportunism, and the Perversion of Justice* (New York, 2013), 109–10.
44 On Ella Kessler-Reis see https://www.stolpersteine-stuttgart.de/index.php?docid=721&mid=30. On Jewish women lawyers see Harriet Freidenreich and Marion Rowekamp, 'Lawyers in Germany and Austria', *Jewish Women: A Comprehensive Encyclopedia*, Jewish Women's Archive – https://jwa.org/encyclopedia/article/lawyers-in-germany-and-austria
45 StAL, E309 II, 2012/122 Bü 32, Letter from Hedinger, Lenckner & Drescher, 23 March 1933.
46 Robert Gellately, *Backing Hitler: Consent and Coercion in Nazi Germany* (Oxford, 2001), 53–4.
47 Detlef Mühlberger, *The Social Bases of Nazism, 1919–1933* (Cambridge, 2003), 4, 46.
48 StAL, E309 II, 2012/122 Bü 32, Transcript from RG's final law exams, 20 June 1933.
49 Ian Kershaw, 'Hitler and the Germans', in Richard Bessel (ed.), *Life in the Third Reich* (Oxford, 2001), 45.
50 BAB, R 1501, no. 206781. RG's CV, March 1937. Given that Himmler had enacted a moratorium on SS recruitment between April and November 1933, it is unclear how Griesinger was able to join at this time.
51 See Richard J. Evans' review of Adrian Weale, *The SS: A New History* (London, 2010), *New Statesman*, 23 August 2010. For a brief historiographical discussion, see Peter Longerich, *Heinrich Himmler* (Oxford, 2012), xii.
52 I refer here to enquiries about low-ranking SS officers by professional historians. Investigations that do exist have not been written by historians. Rather, they are usually written by descendants of the individual SS officer in question. For two excellent recent accounts, see Martin Davidson, *The Perfect Nazi: Uncovering my Grandfather's Secret Past* (London, 2010), and Derek Niemann, *A Nazi in the Family: The Hidden Story of an SS Family in Wartime Germany* (London, 2015). On historians' lack of attention to individual SS officers, see Herbert F. Ziegler, *Nazi Germany's New Aristocracy: The SS Leadership, 1925–1939* (Princeton, NJ, 1989), 10–11. To date, the closest academic study is Mary Fulbrook, *A Small Town Near Auschwitz: Ordinary Nazis and the Holocaust* (Oxford, 2012). In her groundbreaking study Fulbrook follows the career of one man, Udo Klausa, her godmother's husband, who was not in the SS. Rather, during the war he was the *Landrat* (civil administrator) of Będzin County in Poland, at a time when 15,000 Jews were deported to their deaths. It is chiefly through the prism of Będzin that Fulbrook constructs her narrative.

53 Dillon, *Dachau and the SS*, 26.

54 Frederic C. Tubach, *German Voices: Memories of Life during Hitler's Third Reich* (Berkeley and Los Angeles, CA, 2011), 107–8.

55 See *Das Schwarze Korps* (hereafter, *DSK*), 5 December 1935, 3.

56 Remarks from Himmler in June 1931, quoted in Longerich, *Heinrich Himmler*, 122.

57 Robert Lewis Koehl, *The Black Corps: The Structure and Power Struggles of the Nazi SS* (Madison, WI, 1983), 30.

58 Only a handful of studies exist on the *Allgemeine SS*. The finest example is by Bastian Hein, *Elite für Volk und Führer: Die Allgemeine SS und ihre Mitglieder, 1925–1945* (Munich, 2012).

59 Koehl, *The Black Corps*, 53–5, 79, 311, n. 19.

60 Ziegler, *Nazi Germany's New Aristocracy*, 125–6.

61 Ibid., 128, n. 8.

62 StAL, PL 506 Bü 128, SS-Oberabschnitt Südwest. To offer some examples, Fridolin Schwab was expelled after missing a session, as was another member who could no longer afford to pay his fees.

63 In 1983 the town's name was changed to Bad Urach.

64 I am grateful to local historian Stefanie Leisentritt for providing this information.

65 William Teeling, *Crisis for Christianity* (London, 1939), 151.

66 BAB, R 1501, no. 206781. RG's CV, March 1937. On the events of the day, see 'Herr Hitler at Munich', *The Times*, 10 November 1933, 13.

67 BAB, R 1501, no. 206781. RG's CV, March 1937.

68 Ibid.; Stadtarchiv Tettnang UA218, 1890-1938, Address card of RG.

69 BAB, R 1501, no. 206781. Report on RG's progress at Urach, 3 January 1934.

70 See diary entry on 7 February 1934 in Victor Klemperer, *I Shall Bear Witness: The Diaries of Victor Klemperer, 1933–41* (London, 1998), 51.

71 See information from a 1933 population listing at: https://treemagic.org/rademacher/www.verwaltungsgeschichte.de/friedrichshafen.html

72 See Koehl, *The Black Corps*, 100–1.

73 BAB, R 1501, no. 206781. RG's CV, March 1937. On the new uniform, see Chris McNab (ed.), *Hitler's Elite: The SS, 1939–1945* (Oxford, 2013), 90–1.

74 Amy Carney, *Marriage and Fatherhood in the Nazi SS* (Toronto, 2018), 42.

75 StAL, PL 506 Bü 18, SS-Oberabschnitt Südwest, Collection of Circulars, Letter from Prützmann, 10 July 1934.

76 Ibid., SS-Oberabschnitt Südwest, SS Training Schedules.

77 See *DSK*, 12 December 1935, 3.

78 Hein, *Elite für Volk und Führer*, 183.

79 BAB, R 1501, no. 206781. RG's CV, March 1937.

80 Frank-Rutger Hausmann, 'English and Romance Studies in Germany's Third Reich', in Wolfgang Bialas and Anson Rabinbach (eds), *Nazi Germany and the Humanities* (Oxford, 2007), 341, 345.

81 BAB, R 1501, no. 206781. See RG's completed questionnaire on 4 May 1937 and his CV from December 1941.

82 StASt, Fond 358 Archives of the Zeppelin Gymnasium Schülerzeugnislisten and Zeugnislisten, 1924–5.

83 Anon, *The Brown Network: The Activities of the Nazis in Foreign Countries* (New York, 1936), 106.

84 Barbara Lambauer, *Otto Abetz et les Français ou l'envers de la Collaboration* (Paris, 2001), 78. See also Hans Manfred Bock, *Topographie deutscher Kulturvertretung im Paris des 20. Jahrhunderts* (Tübingen, 2010), 34–5.

85 Just as in France official records on Griesinger in Britain have not survived. The Home Office archives, for example, preserve as public records only the visa applications of foreigners who later applied for naturalisation; Griesinger did not seek British citizenship. Nor did he need to register with the German embassy. My search for him in the archives of language schools in Brighton and Eastbourne did not yield any results.

86 'How German boys live in London', *European Herald*, 23 February 1934, 8.

87 For more on Germans in Britain at this time, see James J. Barnes and Patience P. Barnes, *Nazis in Pre-War London, 1930–1939: The Fate and Role of German Party Members and British Sympathizers* (Brighton, 2005).

88 Paul B. Jaskot, 'Das Schwarze Korps', in Levy (ed.), *Antisemitism*, 645.

89 Details of Oberer Kuhberg are found in Silvester Lechner, 'Ulm-Oberer Kuhberg', in Geoffrey P. Megargee (ed.), *The United States Holocaust Memorial Museum Encyclopedia of Camps and Ghettos, 1933–1945*, vol. I, Part A (Bloomington, IN, 2009), 168–170.

90 Similarly, Ulm's local newspapers *Ulmer Tagblatt* and *Ulmer Sturm* do not shed any light. I am grateful to Ulm archivist and local historian Josef Naßl for this information.

91 George C. Browder, *Foundations of the Nazi Police State: The Formation of Sipo and SD* (Lexington, KY, 1990), 108.

92 Gellately, *The Gestapo and German Society*, 50–7.

93 Wildt, *An Uncompromising Generation*, 11, 40–1.

VI: The SS Family

1 The Nottebohms made up part of a significant German population who had settled in the Central American country in the late nineteenth century, when the Guatemalan government actively encouraged German immigration as a means to improve the country's infrastructure. By the early 1930s four of the six largest coffee operations in Guatemala were German-led. At this time Nottebohm Hermanos was the second-largest producer, with eleven *fincas* (farms) and four million trees. See Regina Wagner, *The History of Coffee in Guatemala* (Bogotá, 2001); David McCreery, *Rural Guatemala, 1760–1940* (Stanford, CA, 1994), 234.

2 BAB, MLA, R 9361 III/58950, A signed report by Gisela Grosser on the circumstances of her divorce, 26 January 1936. I discovered during an interview with Barbara Schlegel that Gisela's marriage to Otto had been arranged.

3 Hermann and Harriet Nottebohm had relocated from Hamburg to Vaduz in 1931.

4 I am grateful to Jutta Mangold and Irmela Griesinger for these details.

5 In reality, the average age of marriage for an SS man was thirty-two. See Carney, *Marriage and Fatherhood in the Nazi SS*, 41, 72.

6 See Michelle Mouton, *From Nurturing the Nation to Purifying the Volk: Weimar and Nazi Family Policy, 1918–1945* (Cambridge, 2007), 69–106.

7 BAB, MLA, R 9361 III/58950, A signed report by Gisela Grosser on the circumstances of her divorce, 26 January 1936.

8 Monitoring such a vast operation proved almost impossible in practice. See Peter Longerich, *Heinrich Himmler* (Oxford, 2012), 355.

9 BAB, MLA, R 9361 III/58950, RG requesting an engagement licence from the authorities in Berlin, 18 October 1935.

10 Fulbrook, *Reckonings*, 36.

11 BAB, MLA, R 9361 III/58950, Chef des Sippenamtes to RG, 17 January 1936.

12 StAL, Denazification Records, Egloff file, EL 902/20 Bü 80725.

13 BAB, MLA, R 9361 III/58950, Dr Egloff's completed medical report on Gisela Grosser, 7 November 1935. Egloff recorded Gisela's height as 164 cm and her weight as 57 kg.

14 Ibid., Griesinger named Stahlecker and Ströbel in a letter to Berlin on 25 November 1935. Their completed questionnaires were dated 16 and 18 December 1935.

15 See Heinz Höhne, *The Order of the Death's Head: The Story of the SS* (2nd edn, London, 1980), 156; Koehl, *The Black Corps*, 82.

16 As Goebbels noted in his diary in August 1935, 'Bad mood in the country. We must get a tighter grip on it.' Quoted in Ian Kershaw, 'Social Unrest and the Response of the Nazi Regime, 1934–1936', in Francis R. Nicosia and Lawrence D. Stokes (eds), *Germans Against Nazism: Nonconformity, Opposition and Resistance in the Third Reich, Essays in Honour of Peter Hoffmann* (New York, 1990), 166. This chapter is the best account of the deterioration of living standards during these years.

17 Radio broadcast from Stuttgart reported in *The Times*, 17 October 1935, 13.

18 Kershaw, 'Social Unrest and the Response of the Nazi Regime', 161.

19 BAB, MLA, R 9361 III/58950, RG telegram to Berlin, 16 January 1936.

20 Ibid., telegram from the RuSHA to RG, 16 January 1936; Longerich, *Heinrich Himmler*, 354.

21 BAB, MLA, R 9361 III/58950, see RG's telegrams and responses of the RuSHA on 18, 21, 22 and 27 January 1936.

22 Longerich, *Heinrich Himmler*, 354.

23 An irregularity on one of Gisela's forms was causing the delay. Gisela had an ear infection on the day she completed a questionnaire on her medical health and accidentally filled in the column reserved for people who were mute or deaf. BAB, MLA, R 9361 III/58950, see RG's telegrams and responses of the RuSHA on 21, 22 and 27 January 1936. See also BAB, R 1501, no. 206781. Letter from the Württemberg Political Police to the Ministry of the Interior asking for RG to be made a permanent civil servant, 28 December 1935. A line added later shows this was approved on 17 January 1936.

24 The couple's *Familienstammbuch* is in the possession of their youngest daughter, Barbara Schlegel.

25 Hilary Earl, *The Nuremberg SS-Einsatzgruppen Trial, 1945–1958: Atrocity, Law and History* (Cambridge, 2009), 115.

26 David Cesarani, *Eichmann: His Life and Crimes* (London, 2004), 44.

27 Their wedding was not even listed in the newspaper's announcement section for the south-west. Among Griesinger's associates in the SS, the SD and later at Hohenheim we find published notices of births and marriages of Erhard Jung, Martin Sandberger and Wilhelm Ströbel. See *DSK* 26 September 1935, 4 March and 1 July 1937.

28 See, for example, the case in William Combs, *The Voice of the SS: A History of the SS Journal 'Das Schwarze Korps'* (New York, 1986), 30.

29 See Ian Kershaw, *Popular Opinion and Political Dissent in the Third Reich: Bavaria, 1933–1945* (new edn, Oxford, 2002), 239; and Ian Kershaw, *Hitler, 1889–1936: Hubris* (London, 1998), 573.

30 See 'Snow Comes to Garmisch', *The Daily Telegraph*, 6 February 1936, 16.

31 See 'Anti-Jew Campaign in Bavaria: Truce for Olympic Games', *The Times*, 29 January 1936, 9; David Clay Large, *Nazi Games and the Olympics of 1936* (New York, 2007), 114, 120.

32 William Shirer, *Berlin Diary* (New York, 1941), 46-7.
33 The introduction of the Four-Year Plan later in 1936 aimed to revitalise the German economy, rendering it self-sufficient and ultimately prosperous.
34 Cornell University Law Library, Donovan Nuremberg Trials Collection, APO 403, US Army Interrogation Division, Interrogation of Rudolf Bilfinger by S. W. Brookhart, 27 October 1945. On 18 April 1946 Bilfinger appeared as a witness at Hans Frank's trial at Nuremberg. On Brookhart, see Robert Conot, *Justice at Nuremberg* (New York, 1983), 233.
35 George C. Browder, *Hitler's Enforcers: The Gestapo and the SS Security Service in the Nazi Revolution* (Oxford, 1996), 19. Even though the records of the Stuttgart Gestapo were destroyed, it is possible to find fragments of correspondence that it sent out to other ministries and organisations.
36 Gellately, *The Gestapo and German Society*, 14, 130.
37 Edward Timms, *Anna Haag and her Secret Diary of the Second World War: A Democratic German Feminist's Response to the Catastrophe of National Socialism* (Bern, 2016), 74-5.
38 Griesinger sent a report only weeks before their arrest underlining the need to monitor released prisoners. Josef Steidle, one of the leaders of the Communist Party in Württemberg, who had earlier been arrested and was later released, was a key player in the plot to steal armaments plans. StAL, F 202 II Bü 773, Circular written by RG, 19 November 1935.
39 Stephenson, *Hitler's Home Front*, 42.
40 Gellately, *Backing Hitler*, 58.
41 I am grateful to Sigrid Brüggemann and Roland Maier for providing me with information on denunciations, much of which appears in their publication: Bauz, Brüggemann and Maier (eds), *Die Geheime Staatspolizei in Württemberg und Hohenzollern*.
42 Browder, *Hitler's Enforcers*, 50.
43 Junginger, *The Scientification of the 'Jewish Question' in Nazi Germany*, 318.
44 Stahlecker and Harster had been members of right-wing nationalist and antisemitic movements. On the SD in Stuttgart who had studied in Tübingen, including Gustav Adolf Scheel, Eugen Steimle and Martin Sandberger, see Wildt, *An Uncompromising Generation*, 47-55, 97-100; and Junginger, *The Scientification of the 'Jewish Question'*, 283-358.
45 See StAL, F 199 II Bü 548, Circular written by RG, 21 November 1935; and F 209 II Bü 478, Circular written by RG, 19 November 1935. I am grateful to Sigri Brüggemann and Roland Maier for their help in deciphering the 'No. 5' reports.
46 StAL, F 209 II Bü 478, Circulars written by RG, 8 May 1937 and 4 October 1937.
47 See Paul Sauer, *Dokumente über die Verfolgung der jüdischen Bürger in Baden-Württemberg durch das nationalsozialistische Regime 1933-1945*, vol. 1 (Stuttgart, 1966), 42.
48 Thomas H. Etzold, 'An American Jew in Germany: The Death of Helmut Hirsch', *Jewish Social Studies*, vol. 35, no. 2, 1973, 125. See also http://virtuell.geschichtsort-hotel-silber.de/fragen-sie-die-historiker/antwort/thema/haben-sie-informationen-ueber-helmut-hirsch-der-1936-in-stuttgart-verhaftet-und-1937-in-berlin-hing/1/
49 BAB, R 1501, no. 206781, Report on RG sent to the Ministry of the Interior, 28 December 1935; Statement on RG and the appointments of *Regierungsratstellen*, 29 May 1936.
50 Longerich, *Heinrich Himmler*, 168; Robin Lumsden, *Himmler's SS: Loyal to the Death's Head* (Stroud, 2009), 48.
51 BAB, MLA, R 9361 III/58950, telegram from RG to the RuSHA, 25 November 1935; StAL, PL 506 Bü 17, SS-Oberabschnitt Südwest, Schedules and materials for sched-

ules; Dr Wilhelm Egloff, the SS doctor in charge of Griesinger's SS *Sturm*, who carried out Gisela's medical examination, also lived on Wörthstrasse (today Rieckestrasse). On Julius L. Wernick's chocolate factory, A. G. Kakao- und Schokoladenfabrik, on the premises, see: http://www.wirtemberg.de/schokolade6. htm

52 StAL, PL 506 Bü 6, SS-Oberabschnitt Südwest, Reports on SS 'Evening Events and Morning Celebrations, 1936–1939', Report from Karlsruhe, 20 October 1936.

53 See *DSK*, 4 June 1936, 4.

54 See *DSK*, 22 May 1935, 4.

55 StAL, PL 506 Bü 95, SS-Oberabschnitt Südwest, Matters of the SS, 1935–44, Report on visit to Stuttgart of Frick and Hess, 24 August 1938. On Alvensleben, see Mark C. Yerger, *Allgemeine-SS: The Commands, Units and Leaders of the General SS* (Atglen, PA, 1997), 45, n. 54.

56 Carney, *Marriage and Fatherhood in the Nazi SS*, 143, 146.

57 BAB, MLA, R 9361 III/58950, A signed report by Gisela Grosser on the circumstances of her divorce, 26 January 1936. On the recital, see *DSK*, 13 February 1936, 3.

58 See Carney, *Marriage and Fatherhood in the Nazi SS*, 45–57, 147.

59 See *DSK*, 19 December 1935, 3.

60 See Ibid., 6 March 1935, 3; 27 March 1935, 4.

61 Kay, *The Making of an SS Killer*, 37.

62 Griesinger also entered the SD when he joined the Gestapo in 1935. Gustav Adolf Scheel was the man responsible for recruiting Tübingen graduates to join the SD as full-time employees. See Junginger, *The Scientification of the 'Jewish Question'*, 283–9.

63 In May, Stahlecker moved to Breslau and was replaced as head of the Political Police by Joachim Boës, who moved to Stuttgart from the north of Germany. At around the same time, Wilhelm Harster and Rudolf Bilfinger both left for Berlin – Harster, Stahlecker's deputy, to take up a position at the Political Police in Berlin, and Bilfinger to join the Reich Main Security Office (RSHA). Harster was replaced by Heinrich Fehlis, who had come from the Gestapo in Berlin.

64 HStAS, E151 / 21 / 292, Personnel files of the Ministry of the Interior, On 18 July 1938 Griesinger listed by hand all the addresses he had lived at since July 1933, including the dates he moved in and out.

65 NAP, ÚŘP, Kart. 92, sign. Z Pers. I, Dossier on RG's removal costs from Hohenheim to Prague in March 1943. Includes details of his move from Stuttgart to Hohenheim on 30 September 1938.

66 See Jane Caplan, *Government Without Administration: State and Civil Service in Weimar and Nazi Germany* (Oxford, 1988), 230–9. Even though by 1936 the economy had managed to recover and wages in some sectors had increased, civil servants did not benefit. On the contrary, the rise in living costs substantially lowered the real value of their incomes. A married *Regierungsrat* with two children suffered from a monthly deficit of 44.43 RM.

67 Tim Mason, *Nazism, Fascism and the Working Class*, ed. Jane Caplan (Cambridge, 1995), 162–3.

68 See adverts in *Berliner Illustrirte Zeitung*, no. 6, 6 February 1936, 189; no. 7, 13 February 1936, 227; no. 14, 1 April 1936. 100 RM in 1936 was the equivalent in 2016 of £1,760 ($2,345). See Carney, *Marriage and Fatherhood in the Nazi SS*, 60. On the *Regierungsrat*'s salary, see David Schoenbaum, *Hitler's Social Revolution: Class and Status in Nazi Germany, 1933–1939* (London, 1967), 231. In May 1936 Griesinger's job was advertised at an annual starting salary of 4,800 RM. In April 1940 he was

earning 5,200 RM. In 1938 he was earning something in between these two figures. See BAB, R 1501, no. 206781. Copy of RG's personnel file, 29 May 1936; HStAS, E151 21 292, Details on RG's salary, 22 April 1940.

69 Marion A. Kaplan, *Between Dignity and Despair: Jewish Life in Nazi Germany* (Oxford, 1998), 71–2. Griesinger was more aware than most of the scale of Jewish emigration and its financial implications. In November 1935 he had written a report detailing measures to prevent the illegal transfer of property abroad, which he sent to all police departments in Württemberg. See StAL, F 199 II Bü 548, Circular written by RG, 21 November 1935.

70 See Roland Müller, *Stuttgart zur Zeit des Nationalsozialismus* (Stuttgart, 1988), 291–6.

71 See the reference for Griesinger's house on Schottstrasse in StASt, *Amtliches Stuttgarter Adreßbuch*, 1936 and 1937.

72 Schulz was not the couple's real name.

73 The *Stolpersteine* map offers just one way of determining the parts of the city in which Jews resided: https://www.stolpersteine-stuttgart.de/index.php?docid=965& mid=76

74 On multi-family houses at this time see Michael Harloe, *The People's Home? Social Rented Housing in Europe & America* (Oxford, 1995), 174.

75 Carney, *Marriage and Fatherhood in the Nazi SS*, 146.

76 BAB, R 1501, no. 206781, RG's CV, March 1937.

77 See Robert M. Kennedy, *The German Campaign in Poland (1939)* (2nd edn, Bennington, VT, 2015), 19; Albert Seaton, *The German Army, 1933–45* (London, 1983), 70.

78 BAB, R 1501, no. 206781, RG's CV, March 1937.

79 Richard J. Evans, *The Third Reich in Power, 1933–1939* (London, 2005), 108.

80 Carney, *Marriage and Fatherhood in the Nazi SS*, 51.

81 According to the plans in the possession of Herr Schulz and the *Amtliches Stuttgarter Adreßbuch* for 1935 and 1936, two other Jewish familes – the Weils and the Flegenheimers – lived within twenty metres. A couple of doors along on Schottstrasse, lived Josef Flegenheimer and his wife Irme. Like Griesinger, Flegenheimer, a sugar producer, also had a father who had moved from the United States to Germany after the US Civil War. In 1937 the Flegenheimer family left Germany and eventually settled in the United States. For more information on the Flegenheimer family see *The Des Moines Register*, 12 September 1943, 1. Dr Hermann Weil, a lawyer and director of the Salamander shoe factory, owned the house on Robert Bosch Strasse that overlooked the Griesinger's garden. See http://www.alemannia-judaica.de/images/Images%20159/WEIL-1-AUF.pdf

82 In the mid-nineteenth century Fritz Rothschild's grandfather, Elias, moved the family from Rust (Baden) to Stuttgart. See genealogical information at: https://www.geni.com/people/Fritz-Rothschild/6000000020291662049. According to the Rothschild's granddaughter, Helga Rothschild, Fritz was known to friends and family by his middle name, Jakob.

83 StASt, 177/1 Standesamt, Familien-Register Band 57, 977.

84 Interview with Helga Rothschild.

85 On the emigration figures and on 'mixed messages', see Kaplan, *Between Dignity and Despair*, 67, 72–73; interview with Helga Rothschild.

86 On the antisemitic laws in Stuttgart, see Müller, *Stuttgart*, 282–309.

87 StAL, EL 350I, Bü 21904, Compensation claim from Helene Rothschild.

88 Ibid.

89 Jacques Delarue, *Trafics et Crimes sous l'Occupation* (Paris, 1968), 56.

90 Ben Wubs, *International Business and National War Interests: Unilever between Reich and Empire, 1939–45* (London, 2008), 124.

91 Nicholas Stargardt, *The German War: A Nation Under Arms, 1939–1945* (London, 2015), 193.

92 Mémorial de la Shoah, CDJC, Paris, XXVa-164, Report from Röthke on exemptions to the Yellow Star, 25 August 1942.

93 Ibid., XXVa-200, Certificate of Exemption to the Yellow Star for Fritz and Helene Rothschild, 9 September and 23 September 1942. See also Renée Poznanski, *Jews in France during World War II* (Hanover, NH, 2001), 440–6.

94 The forms Helene Rothschild filled in on her return to Paris are available at: Mémorial de la Shoah/Archives Nationales de France, F9 5725, Fichier adultes du Camp de Drancy. On the numbers of survivors, see Alexandre Doulut, Serge Klarsfeld and Sandrine Labeau (eds), *1945: Les rescapés juifs d'Auschwitz témoignent* (Paris, 2015), 305.

95 After the war some Jewish women who had been deported on Convoy 74 wrote memoirs or gave testimonies about their incarceration in Auschwitz. See Denise Toros-Marter, *J'avais Seize ans à Pitchipoï* (Paris, 2008); USC Shoah Foundation Oral History Interviews with Esther Alicigüzel, Dora Aziza, Fanny Bialka, Maud Bloch and Simone Polak. Odette Abadi/Rosenstock's account is in Fred Coleman, *The Marcel Network: How One French Couple Saved 527 Children from the Holocaust* (Washington, DC, 2013), 123–32.

96 StAL, EL 350I, Bü 21904, Compensation claim from Helene Rothschild.

97 Interview with Helga Rothschild.

VII: Lebensraum

1 See the case of Alfred Filbert, in Kay, *The Making of an SS Killer*, 24–6.

2 King Wilhelm I of Württemberg founded the college in 1818, as a response to the famine that followed 1816, the year without a summer. The king planned to encourage a new system of agricultural education. Agricultural colleges were traditionally more practically orientated than universities. Hohenheim began to award doctorates in 1918, and in 1922 it obtained a rectorial constitution. Nevertheless, the difference in status between an agricultural college and an agricultural university was significant and is well explained in Jonathan Harwood, *Technology's Dilemma: Agricultural Colleges between Science and Practice in Germany, 1860–1934* (Bern, 2005), 92–100; and Peter M. Jones, *Agricultural Enlightenment: Knowledge, Technology and Nature, 1750–1840* (Oxford, 2016), 179. On 1816, see William K. Klingaman and Nicholas P. Klingaman, *The Year Without Summer: 1816 and the Volcano that Darkened the World and Changed History* (New York, 2016).

3 NAP, ÚŘP, Kart. 92, sign. Z Pers. I, Dossier on RG's removal costs from Hohenheim to Prague in March 1943. Includes details of his move from Stuttgart to Hohenheim on 30 September 1938.

4 See the interview with Dr Anja Waller at: https://www.uni-hohenheim. de/117993?&L=0&tx_ttnews%5Btt_news%5D=31101&cHash=b75b960ecc9ae27e1c 30d9d7141ed944

5 AUoH, Personnel file of RG.

6 Ibid., Landwirtschaftliche Hochschule Hohenheim, Vorlesungsverzeichnis für das Winterhalbjahr 1943/44, 11.

7 I am grateful to Dr Ulrich Fellmeth for this information.

8 AUoH, Landwirtschaftliche Hochschule Hohenheim, Vorlesungs-Derzeichnis summer and winter lecture courses, 1938–45.

9 HStAS, E151 / 21 / 292, Personnel files of the Ministry of the Interior, Letter from RG to the Württemberg Minister of the Interior (Dr Schmid), 19 September 1938.

10 Harwood, *Technology's Dilemma*, 105–6.

11 For more on German universities at this time, see Steven P. Remy, *The Heidelberg Myth: The Nazification and Denazification of a German University* (Cambridge, MA, 2002).

12 I am grateful to Dr Anja Waller for sharing her evidence with me.

13 StAL, EL 902/20 Bü 90414. Denazification Records, File of Erhard Jung; AUoH, Reden und Abhandlungen, Investiture speech of Dr Erhard Jung, 26 April 1938.

14 I am grateful to Dr Ulrich Fellmeth for this information.

15 On Griesinger's SS promotions, see BAB, VBS 286 SS Officers' Service Records (SSO/ SS-Führerpersonalakten) 031A File of RG.

16 Honacker's report is reproduced in full in Sauer, *Dokumente über die Verfolgung der jüdischen Bürger*, 33–7. See also 'Die Nacht als die Synagogen brannten'. Texte und Materialien zum Novemberpogrom 1938. Landeszentrale für politische Bildung Baden-Württemberg 1998, S.4; https://www.lpb-bw.de/publikationen/pogrom/pogrom10.htm

17 Stephenson, *Hitler's Home Front*, 143; Longerich, *Heinrich Himmler*, 409.

18 Robert P. Ericksen, *Complicity in the Holocaust: Churches and Universities in Nazi Germany* (New York, 2012), 169; Remy, *The Heidelberg Myth*, 177–217; Frank Stern, *The Whitewashing of the Yellow Badge: Antisemitism and Philosemitism in West Germany, 1945–1952* (Oxford, 1992), 158–212.

19 StAL, EL 902/20 Bü 90414. Denazification Records, File of Erhard Jung. See especially the depositions by Dr R. Seeman, Otto Lander, Karl Beißwenger and Maria Kühnle.

20 It took German historians until the late 1990s to begin research on their predecessors. For many, to have to investigate the earlier behaviour of their mentors and colleagues was a subject too close to home. For an overview of historiographical changes, see Remy, *The Heidelberg Myth*, 234–45. See also Ericksen, *Complicity in the Holocaust*, 183–4.

21 Günther Franz, *Der deutsche Bauernkrieg* (Munich, 1933; 12th edn, Darmstadt, 1984); and *Der Dreißigjärige Krieg und das deutsche Volk* (1st edn, Jena, 1940). On the importance of Franz's work, see John Theibault, 'The Demography of the Thirty Years War Re-visited: Günther Franz and his Critics', *German History*, vol. 15. no. 1, 1997, 5; Joachim Whaley, *Germany and the Holy Roman Empire*, vol. 1: *Maximilian I to the Peace of Westphalia, 1493–1648* (Oxford, 2012), 234; Thomas A. Brady Jr, '1525 And All That: The German Peasants' War in Modern Memory', in Melissa Etzler and Priscilla Layne (eds), *Rebellion and Revolution: Defiance in German Language, History and Art* (Newcastle, 2010), 5–6. On the dedication, see Peter Burke, *A Social History of Knowledge*, vol. 2: *From the Encyclopedia to Wikipedia* (Cambridge, 2012), 227.

22 AUoH Eduard Springer's memoirs.

23 Karl Baedeker, *Southern Germany (Baden, Black Forest, Wurtemberg, and Bavaria), Handbook for Travellers* (13th edn, Leipzig, 1929), 181.

24 See *Stuttgarter Neues Tagblatt*, 11 October 1938, 6. On the Palast-Lichtspiele, see Judith Breuer, 'Der ehemalige Metropol-Palast in Stuttgart, eines der letzten deutschen Lichtspieltheater von großstädtischem format', *Denkmalpflege in Baden-Württemberg*, Jahrgang 19, Heft 3, 1990, 97–107.

25 As an over-age SS reservist in the class of 1896–1909, Griesinger was scheduled for demobilisation after the fall of France. At this time recruitment for the *Waffen-SS* was aimed at the classes 1910–18. See George H. Stein, *The Waffen SS: Hitler's Elite Guard at War, 1939–1945* (New York, 1966), 46, n. 51, 96.

VIII: Stavyshche

1 Erwin Boehm, *Geschichte der 25. Division* (Stuttgart, 1983), 24; HStAS, E151 / 21 / 292, Personnel files of the Ministry of the Interior, Letter from RG to Wilderer, 15 March 1940.
2 Boehm, *Geschichte der 25. Division*, 28–9.
3 Bibliothek für Zeitgeschichte (hereafter BfZ), Sammlung Sterz (hereafter SSt), Letter from Erich N., 25th Inf. Div., 27 June 1940. At the end of the campaign the 25th Infantry had lost 676 men, with hundreds more wounded. See Boehm, *Geschichte der 25. Division*, 74. On front-line plunder, see Julia S. Torrie, *German Soldiers and the Occupation of France, 1940–1944* (Cambridge, 2018), 27–30.
4 BfZ, SSt, Letter from Erich N., 25th Inf. Div., 27 June 1940.
5 Boehm, *Geschichte der 25. Division*, 75.
6 Torrie, *German Soldiers*, 67–9. On the possibility of a famine, see Daniel Lee, *Pétain's Jewish Children: French Jewish Youth and the Vichy Regime, 1940–1942* (Oxford, 2014), 46–7.
7 I have taken descriptions of summer 1940 in Bourges from BfZ, SSt, Letters from Erich N., 25th Inf. Div., 27 June, 21 July; Hans S., 25th Inf. Div., 27 July, 12 August; Sammlung Knoch (hereafter SK), Letters from Willy F., 25th Inf. Div., 6 July, 10 July, 17 July, 19 July, 27 July, 3 August, 8 August. On shopping as a 'female' activity, see Torrie, *German Soldiers*, 70.
8 Alain Rafesthain, *Le Cher sous Vichy, La Vie Quotidienne, 1940–1944* (2006), 24–5.
9 Stargardt, *The German War*, 53–9. Jews were only allowed to shop at designated times, using different ration cards from 'Aryans'. They were entitled to considerably less than Aryans. See Kaplan, *Between Dignity and Despair*, 151.
10 BfZ, SSt, Letter from Erich N., 25th Inf. Div., 24 October 1940.
11 Dr Otterbach covered Griesinger's teaching in 1939–40; Oberregierungsrat Dallinger covered it between 1941 and 1944. See AUoH, Landwirtschaftliche Hochschule Hohenheim, Vorlesungs-Derzeichnis summer and winter lecture courses, 1938–45.
12 Tubach, *German Voices*, 175. I am grateful to Fritz Tubach for introducing me to Bertsch's descendants. I am especially grateful to Bertsch's grandson Matthias Bertsch for responding to my questions about his family.
13 HStAS, E151 / 21 / 292, Personnel files of the Ministry of the Interior, Note on RG's application for a transfer to Prague, 18 October 1940.
14 Barbora Štolleová, 'Between Autonomy and the Reich Administration Economic Department of the Reich Protector's Office (1939–1942)', *Prague Economic and Social History Papers*, vol. 24, no. 2, 2016, 55–6; Drahomir Jancik, 'Les "Activités d'Aryanisation" de la Bömische Escompte-Bank dans le Protectorat de Bohême et de Moravie entre 1939 et 1945', *Revue d'Histoire de la Shoah*, 2007 / 1 no. 186, 166. For more on Bertsch and his office's contribution to the Holocaust, see Wolf Gruner, *The Holocaust in Bohemia and Moravia: Czech Initiatives, German Policies, Jewish Responses* (Oxford and New York, 2019), 304, 323–4, 338. I am grateful to Wolf Gruner for providing me with a copy of his book before it was released officially.

15 HStAS, E151 / 21 / 292, Personnel files of the Ministry of the Interior, Note on RG's application for a transfer to Prague, 18 October 1940.

16 Ibid., 26 November 1940.

17 AUoH, Landwirtschaftliche Hochschule Hohenheim, Vorlesungs-Derzeichnis summer and winter lecture courses, 1938–45.

18 Ibid.; BAB, VBS 286 SS Officers' Service Records (SSO/ SS-Führerpersonalakten) 031A File of RG.

19 Boehm, *Geschichte der 25. Division*, 76–7.

20 Ibid., 77.

21 BfZ, SSt, Letters from Hans S., 25th Inf. Div., 14 June and 22 June 1941; Gerd R., 25th Inf. Div., 22 June 1941; Walter K., 25th Inf. Div., 24 June 1941; SK, Letter from Willy F., 25th Inf. Div., 26 June 1941.

22 In June 1941 the ghetto was not yet surrounded by a fence, with guarded gates to control entry and exit. Rather it was an open ghetto, and Jews were still permitted to access other parts of the city before the night-time curfew set in. Martin Dean, 'Lublin', in Geoffrey P. Megargee (ed.), *The United States Holocaust Memorial Museum Encyclopedia of Camps and Ghettos, 1933–1945*, vol. II: *Ghettos in German Occupied Eastern Europe*, Part A (Bloomington, IN, 2012), 675–6.

23 On the German press, see David Bankier, 'Signaling the Final Solution to the German People', in David Bankier and Israel Gutman (eds), *Nazi Europe and the Final Solution* (Jerusalem, 2009), 24–5.

24 BfZ, SSt, Letters from Walter K., 25th Inf. Div., 24 June 1941; and Hans S., 25th Inf. Div., 14 June and 22 June 1941. On German soldiers' letters home in which Jews are mentioned, see Walter Manoschek (ed.), *'Es gibt nur eines für das Judentum: Vernichtung': Das Judenbild in deutschen Soldatenbriefen 1939–1944* (Hamburg, 1995).

25 Omer Bartov, *Hitler's Army: Soldiers, Nazis, and the War in the Third Reich* (Oxford, 1991), 83, 89–93.

26 Ibid., 65.

27 Stargardt, *The German War*, 161.

28 Rolf-Dieter Müller, *Enemy in the East: Hitler's Secret Plans to Invade the Soviet Union* (London, 2015), 248.

29 Nigel Askey, *Operation Barbarossa: The Complete Organisational and Statistical Analysis, and Military Simulation*, vol. IIa (2013), 461.

30 Timothy Snyder, *Bloodlands: Europe Between Hitler and Stalin* (London, 2010), 166; Bartov, *Hitler's Army*, 83.

31 Bundesarchiv-Militärarchiv (Military Archives, Freiburg) RH 26–25 / 68, S. 6. War Diary or after-action reports (*Kriegstagebuch*, KTB) of the 25th Motorised Infantry Division, 25 May–22 December 1941. The details of the violence come from an entry in late June 1941. I am grateful to Felix Römer for sharing this source with me.

32 Ibid. Details of the murder of 150 Jews appear in TB IC, 'Battle of Rivne', 6. I am grateful to Alexander Kruglov for informing me of the murders carried out by the 25th Motorised Infantry Division in Lutsk on the way to Rivne. See also Ben H. Shepherd, *Hitler's Soldiers: The German Army in the Third Reich* (New Haven, CT, 2016), 173.

33 Jeffrey Burds, *Holocaust in Rovno: The Massacre at Sosenki Forest, November 1941* (New York, 2013), 36.

34 Christopher R. Browning, *The Origins of the Final Solution: The Evolution of Nazi Jewish Policy, September 1939–March 1942* (Lincoln, NE, 2004), 222–3.

35 BfZ, SSt, Letters from Helmut D., 25th Inf. Div., 1 July 1941; Hans S., 25th Inf. Div., 12 August 1941.

36 David Stahel, *Kiev 1941: Hitler's Battle for Supremacy in the East* (Cambridge, 2013), 6–7. Rarely did a *Wehrmacht* division's war diary ever mention mass killings carried out by the German armed forces. In East and West Germany in the 1950s it was not considered to be in anyone's interest to draw attention to the crimes of the young soldiers, who ten years later were striving to create a new society. See Omer Bartov, *The Eastern Front, 1941–45, German Troops and the Barbarisation of Warfare* (2nd edn, Basingstoke, 2001), xxi.

37 It took until the 1990s for pioneering historians such as Omer Bartov and Walter Manoschek, together with specialists at the Institute for Social Research in Hamburg, to break the silence about *Wehrmacht* atrocities. In spring 1995 a travelling exhibit entitled 'War of Extermination: The Crimes of the Wehrmacht, 1941–1944' generated controversy when it attempted to bring to public attention the role of Hitler's army in the Holocaust.

38 Operational Situation Report USSR, no. 58, in Yitzhak Arad, Shmuel Krakowski and Shmuel Spector (eds), *The Einsatzgruppen Reports: Selections from the Dispatches of the Nazi Death Squads' Campaign against the Jews in Occupied Territories of the Soviet Union, July 1941–January 1943* (New York, 1989), 94.

39 Report by Walter Stahlecker, 'Initially Difficult to Set a Pogrom in Motion', in Ernst Klee, Willi Dressen and Volker Riess (eds), *'The Good Old Days': The Holocaust as Seen by Its Perpetrators and Bystanders* (New York, 1991), 24.

40 Bartov, *The Eastern Front, 1941–45*, xxii.

41 Derzhavnyi arkhiv Kyivs'koi oblasti (The State Archives of the Kiev Oblast, DAKO), Fond 1 opis (index) 129, case (file) 705. Recipients of Poor Relief in Stavyshche, 1893.

42 Boehm, *Geschichte der 25. Division*, 102; BfZ, SK, Letter from Willy F., 25th Inf. Div., 19 July 1941.

43 I am grateful to Martha Weinman Lear for sharing with me this detail and others, many of which appeared in her article 'The Roots People', *The New York Times Magazine*, 31 July 1994, 32–3.

44 Boehm, *Geschichte der 25. Division*, 102; BfZ, SK, Letter from Willy F., 25th Inf. Div., 19 July 1941.

45 See Janina Struk, *Photographing the Holocaust: Interpretations of the Evidence* (London, 2004), 57–73; Wendy Lower, *Nazi Empire-Building and the Holocaust in Ukraine* (Chapel Hill, NC, 2005), 79; Stargardt, *The German War*, 42.

46 The details that follow on the *Aktions* in the district of Tarashcha are from Alexander Kruglov, 'Tarashcha', in Geoffrey P. Megargee (ed.), *The United States Holocaust Memorial Museum Encyclopedia of Camps and Ghettos, 1933–1945*, vol. II, Part B (Bloomington, IN, 2012), 1605–6.

47 Witness and police reports on the murder of the Jews of Stavyshche are available on the website of the Execution Sites of Jewish Victims investigated by Yahad-in Unum: http://yahadmap.org/#village/rozkishna-kyiv-ukraine.743

48 BfZ, SSt, Letter from Helmut D., 25th Inf. Div., 11 July 1941. See also Lower, *Nazi Empire-Building and the Holocaust in Ukraine*, 37; Boehm, *Geschichte der 25. Division*, 108.

49 BfZ, SSt, Letter from Hans S., 25th Inf. Div., 17 July 1941. The statistic on the *Volksdeutsche* in Ukraine is from Yitzhak Arad, *The Holocaust in the Soviet Union* (Lincoln, NE, 2009), 569, n. 98.

50 BfZ, SK, Letters from Willy F., 25th Inf. Div., 5 July, 22 July and undated letters from August 1941.

51 BfZ, SSt, Letters from Hans S., 25th Inf. Div., 17 July, 12 August 1941.

52 Ibid., 12 August 1941; SK, Letter from Willy F., 25th Inf. Div., 22 July 1941; Boehm, *Geschichte der 25. Division*, 106–10. On the social dynamics of comradeship in the *Wehrmacht* see Thomas Kühne, *Hitler's Soldiers, Male Bonding and Mass Violence in the Twentieth Century* (Cambridge, 2017).

53 Gisela's driving licence – valid from August 1941 until August 1946 – is in the possession of her son, Peter Jehli.

54 Known as Stahlecker's Memorandum, the document was discovered more than forty years after the war in the Latvian Historical State Archive and at the time was hailed as a real find by historians researching the origins of the Final Solution. See Christopher R. Browning, *The Path to Genocide: Essays on Launching the Final Solution* (Cambridge, 1992), 109; Peter Longerich, 'From Mass Murder to the "Final Solution": The Shooting of Jewish Civilians during the First Months of the Eastern Campaign within the Context of Nazi Jewish Genocide', in Bernd Wegner (ed.), *From Peace to War: Germany, Soviet Russia and the World, 1939–1941* (Providence, RI, 1997), 267.

55 Information from Griesinger's *Wehrmacht* file, available at the Deutsche Dienststelle (WASt), Berlin. Uncoded file. On German losses at Kiev see Stahel, *Kiev 1941*, 310.

56 An *Einsatzgruppen* report written a day before Babi Yar included details of the planned execution, which was welcomed by the German army. See Arad, *The Holocaust in the Soviet Union*, 173–5; Karel C. Berkhoff, *Harvest of Despair: Life and Death in Ukraine under Nazi Rule* (Cambridge, MA, 2004), 65–9, 75–6; Operational Situation Report USSR, no. 97, in Arad, Krakowski and Spector (eds), *The Einsatzgruppen Reports*, 164–5. On the speed with which knowledge of Babi Yar spread, see Victor Klemperer's diary entry for 19 April 1942, in Victor Klemperer, *To The Bitter End: The Diaries of Victor Klemperer, 1942–1945* (London, 1999), 39; Peter Fritzsche, *Life and Death in the Third Reich* (London, 2008), 152.

57 BAB, R 1501, no. 206781. RG's CV from December 1941.

58 Minister Speidel, the permanent Württemberg representative (*Vertretung*) in Berlin, believed that Griesinger's experience afforded him two options. The first was to take on the position of district commissioner (*Gebietskommissar*), similar to the role of a *Landrat* (head of the district administration), with which Griesinger was already familiar from his pre-war days. Hundreds of civil servants were appointed to this function, tasked with overseeing the administration within a newly occupied town or territory, which on average spread over 2,300 square kilometres and contained 108,000 inhabitants. Griesinger's second option, which according to Speidel had far greater possibilities for promotion, was to head a department within one of the General Regions (*Generalbezirke*). The General Regions were considerably larger than the district commissions. The Bielorussian *Generalbezirk*, for example, encompassed 225,000 square kilometres, with a population of some 9,850,000. For his dossier to be sent to Alfred Rosenberg, Reich Minister for the Occupied Eastern Territories, Griesinger had to choose one of Speidel's options. He chose the second. BAB, R 1501, no. 206781, Report on RG from the Ministry of the Interior, Berlin, 9 December 1941; Letter from RG to Speidel in Berlin, 21 December 1941. On the appointment of the *Gebietskommissar* in the east, see Lower, *Nazi Empire-Building and the Holocaust in Ukraine*, 101. On the General Regions, see Shalom Cholawski, *The Jews of Bielorussia During World War II* (Amsterdam, 1998), 47.

59 Stargardt, *The German War*, 272, 281–3.

60 GFA, WGD. Entry from 18 January 1942, which begins, 'I have come across this book quite by chance.' Ostensibly this entry was the only record Wally made

during the war; it appeared on the final page of her diary, and no other pages followed. On closer examination of the volume, I noticed tear marks and trimmings of paper that stuck out from the side of the page. When I turned to examine the leaves at the very front of the diary, I saw that the first nine sheets were not properly attached to the book; their return side, which would have formed the final nine pages of the book, were missing. They had been carefully removed, using either scissors or a knife. Multiple reasons might explain the absence of these final pages. Wally might simply have been in need of some paper and may have taken them from the back of her diary to serve another purpose. On the other hand, her motivation for wanting to remove these pages might not have been as innocent. She may have regretted some of her later entries and decided to destroy the evidence.

61 Lots of promotions were awarded on 20 April 1942, the date of Hitler's birthday. AUoH, Landwirtschaftliche Hochschule Hohenheim, Vorlesungs-Derzeichnis summer and winter lecture courses, 1938–1945. Erhard Jung and Gustav Rösch were the highest-profile SS members at Hohenheim to volunteer to fight in the east. Richard Vogel, Rösch's replacement, was neither a party nor an SS member. I am grateful to Dr Anja Waller and Dr Ulrich Fellmeth for this information.

IX: Beer Bottles

1 NAP, ÚŘP, Kart. 92, sign. Z Pers. I, Dossier on RG's removal costs, Letter from RG to Schenker & Co., 1 April and 9 July 1943; Discussion of removal costs allocated to RG, 13 October 1943.

2 Before 1939 the street was known as Kotkova, but as with so many streets in Prague, officials later changed the Czech name to sound more German.

3 After the war Schleyer became one of West Germany's most powerful industrialists. In September 1977 he was kidnapped by the left-wing terrorist organisation, the Red Army Faction, which sought the release of eleven of its members from prison. When the German government refused the demands, the Faction executed Schleyer. His body was discovered in the boot of a car in France a month later.

4 Stargardt, *The German War*, 347. Malte Klein, 'Die Nacht vor 70 Jahren bleibt in Erinnerung', *Stuttgarter Zeitung*, 12 March 2013.

5 Eagle Glassheim, *Cleansing the Czechoslovak Borderlands: Migration, Environment, and Health in the Former Sudetenland* (Pittsburgh, PA, 2016), 38.

6 See testimony of Josef Dvořák at http://pametnaroda.cz/en/dvorak-josef-1919

7 Chad Bryant, *Prague in Black: Nazi Rule and Czech Nationalism* (Cambridge, MA, 2007), 88–9.

8 Robert Gerwarth, *Hitler's Hangman: The Life of Heydrich* (New Haven, CT, 2011), 221.

9 Ibid., 227.

10 News Flashes from Czechoslovakia under Nazi Domination, Release no. 114 (Chicago) 5 January 1942.

11 Gerwarth, *Hitler's Hangman*, 227.

12 Charles R. Shrader, 'Lidice Massacre', in Alexander Mikaberidze, *Atrocities, Massacres and War Crimes: An Encyclopedia* (Santa Barbara, CA, 2013), 413.

13 Jaroslav Čvančara, 'Z jeviště na popraviště: Příběh herečky Anny Čalounové-Letenské', *Paměť a dějiny*, vol. 3, issue 2, 2009, 101–15. For a similar account of the execution, see Rothkirchen, *The Jews of Bohemia and Moravia*, 155.

14 Neil Short, *Kill Hitler: Operation Valkyrie 1944* (Oxford, 2013), 50. In summer 1943 the *Waffen-SS* had 19,389 members in the Protectorate. Petr Kaňák and Jan Vajskebr, 'Waffen-SS v Protektoráty Čechy a Morava', *Historie a vojenství*, c. 3, 2005, 72–81.

15 Dr Erwin Weinmann graduated with a PhD in medicine in 1935. Weinmann gave up his position as a resident at the University Hospital in Tübingen to become a full-time employee of the SD in Stuttgart in 1936. He remained in Prague until May 1945, when he disappeared. In 1968 West German officials believed he was working as an advisor to the Egyptian police in Alexandria. See Callum MacDonald and Jan Kaplan, *Prague: In the Shadow of the Swastika, A History of the German Occupation, 1939–1945* (Vienna, 2001), 88; Wildt, *An Uncompromising Generation*, 363.

16 ABS, 2M: 11034, Documents of the Ministry of the Interior, File on Dr Anne-Marie Dietlová, August 1945.

17 NAP, Archives of the German State Ministry, 110–7–55 (69 and 85), List of German civil servants in the SS, 22 March 1945. Some of Griesinger's colleagues were also high up in the SA. Wilhelm Dennler another senior figure at the ministry was one of only 336 men who became an *SA-Brigadeführer*.

18 In 1967 Von Schmoller's Nazi past was revealed by *Tidsignal*, a Swedish magazine. ABS, 107-8-30. Directory of German public servants belonging to the SS in Prague, 22 March 1945. The post-war industrial leader, Hanns-Martin Schleyer, offers another example.

19 See *Der Neue Tag* and *Prager Abend*, 8 March and 9 April 1943. Many meetings, especially lectures by leading party figures, were held at the Deutsche Haus, a historical cultural centre in Prague.

20 Bryant, *Prague in Black*, 179.

21 Gerwarth, *Hitler's Hangman*, 263–70.

22 ABS, Archives of the Ministry of Economics and Labour (hereafter, MHP), File 305-701-4, Walter Bertsch's post-war interrogation; NAP, ÚŘP, Kart. 67, Organigram of the Ministry of Economics and Labour from 1943. In 1943 the Ministry of Economics and Labour employed a staff of 1,741, a number that included ninety-three Reich Germans, officials who, like Griesinger, came directly from Germany; and thirty-two Protectorate Germans, men and women born and raised in what until recently had been Czechoslovakia. Most of the ministry's lower-ranking bureaucrats, planners and researchers were Czech.

23 Bryant, *Prague in Black*, 182.

24 As miners, the men fell under Griesinger's area of responsibility. See 'Forerunners of Herbert Kappler', *Czechoslovak Life*, issue 1, 1978, 29; MacDonald and Kaplan, *Prague*, 88.

25 NAP, ÚŘP, Kart. 66 and 67, List of personnel, including an organigram of the Ministry of Economics and Labour from 1943. The ministry was located on the corner of the Beim St Franziskus (today the Dvořák Embankment) and Berlinerstrasse (*Revoluční*).

26 The length of time he was away from Prague is obvious from stamps in his passport, discovered inside the chair.

27 NAP, MHP, 782/0/1, Box 197, see letters and reports addressed to RG, sent from colleagues at the ministry and various economics groups dated 3, 4, 16, 19 and 29 February 1944. Beer bottles were only one of a number of items at the forefront of Griesinger's mind. During his time at the ministry he was involved in a number of cases concurrently. At the same time as the beer-bottle debacle, Griesinger examined regulatory proposals and drafted legislation in a range of areas to facilitate production and resolve shortages. In mid-February 1944 acquiring new construction parts, especially grinding wheels, was high on his agenda. See NAP, MHP, 782/0/1, Box 197, see newspaper clipping of the *Deutscher Reichsanzeiger und Preußischer Staatsanzeiger* from 7 February 1944, and letter from RG to a colleague at the ministry on 21 February.

28 Patrick Crowhurst, *Hitler and Czechoslovakia: Domination and Retaliation* (London, 2013), 152–4; Šárka Jarská, 'Czechs as Forced and Slave Labourers during the Second World War', in Alexander von Plato, Almut Leh and Christoph Thonfeld (eds), *Hitler's Slaves: Life Stories of Forced Labourers in Nazi-Occupied Europe* (New York, 2010), 48.

29 Bryant, *Prague in Black*, 182.

30 Jarská, 'Czechs as Forced and Slave Labourers during the Second World War' in von Plato, Leh and Thonfeld (eds), *Hitler's Slaves*, 49.

31 Crowhurst, *Hitler and Czechoslovakia*, 165–6.

32 Oliver Rathkolb, 'Forced Labour in Industry', in Jörg Echternkamp (ed.), *Germany and the Second World War*, vol. IX/II (Oxford, 2014), 709.

33 Christian Goeschel, *Suicide in Nazi Germany* (Oxford, 2009), 135.

34 Jarská, 'Czechs as Forced and Slave Labourers during the Second World War', in von Plato, Leh and Thonfeld (eds), *Hitler's Slaves*, 50.

35 Bryant, *Prague in Black*, 195.

36 NAP, MHP, 782/0/1, Box 197, Report on meeting 8 September 1944.

37 Ibid., 782 Dodatky II, Box 57, Letter from Anton Beran to RG 8 May 1944; Letter from Anton Beran to Karl Hermann Frank, 8 May 1944; Notes and reports written by RG on Beran's business, July 1944, 7 and 29 March 1945.

38 Letter from Walter Bertsch to the Ministry for Social and Health Administration in Prague, 17 April 1941, quoted in Gruner, *The Holocaust in Bohemia and Moravia*, 217.

39 Gruner, *The Holocaust in Bohemia and Moravia*, 304.

40 See Rothkirchen, *The Jews of Bohemia and Moravia*, 242; See also https://encyclopedia.ushmm.org/content/en/article/theresienstadt-concentrationtransit-camp-for-german-and-austrian-jews?series=18010

41 Rothkirchen, *The Jews of Bohemia and Moravia*, 116, 133; Jan Láníček, *Czechs, Slovaks and the Jews, 1938–48: Beyond Idealisation and Condemnation* (London, 2013), 81.

42 Wolf Gruner, *Jewish Forced Labor under the Nazis: Economic Needs and Racial Aims, 1938–1944* (Cambridge, 2006), 169–73. See also Gruner, *The Holocaust in Bohemia and Moravia*, 361.

43 Gruner, *The Holocaust in Bohemia and Moravia*, 359.

44 NAP, MHP, 782/0/1, Box 197, Letter from the Production Committee of Ceramics, Stone and Earth to RG, 20 September 1944. As the Red Army made rapid advances towards Prague, German officials ordered the deportation of thousands of Protectorate Jews to Theresienstadt. Their number included a large proportion of Jewish forced labourers. See Rothkirchen, *The Jews of Bohemia and Moravia*, 133.

45 Bryant, *Prague in Black*, 184.

46 Státní oblastní archiv v Litoměřicicích (State Regional Archives Litoměřicicích), Collection of Nazi Occupational Materials, Box 7, Inventory 27, signature 112-474-2/62–63, List of names put forward by Bertsch, 18 December 1944; HStAS, EA3/150/719, Files of the Ministry of Culture, see telegram from Bertsch to Dr Bauer, 20 February 1945; Letter from the Ministry of Culture to the Government Bureau of North Württemberg, 22 May 1956.

47 NAP, ÚŘP, Kart. 92, sign. Z Pers. I, Dossier on RG's removal costs from Hohenheim to Prague, 1943.

48 Hans von Watter, Walther Fuchs and Gustav von Schmoller were three notable appointments. See Frank Raberg, 'Das Aushängeschild der Hitler-Regierung: Konstantin Freiherr von Neurath, Außenminister des Deutschen Reiches (1932–1938)', in Michael Kißener and Joachim Scholtyseck (eds), *Die Führer der Provinz: NS-Biographien aus Baden und Württemberg* (1997), 507.

49 Even before the Occupation, more German than Czech films were screened in Prague. The dwindling status of Czech cinema continued during the war, with only a dozen films released each year in Czech. Peter Demetz, *Prague in Danger: The Years of German Occupation, 1939–1945: Memories and History, Terror and Resistance, Theater and Jazz, Film and Poetry, Politics and War* (New York, 2008), 193.

50 Stargardt, *The German War*, 13.

51 In his ambitious plans that he was going to leave until after the German victory, Heydrich intended to Germanise parts of the Czech population. Some Czechs, whom he deemed racially worthy, would be allowed to stay after the war, whereas those considered undesirable would be expelled or even killed. Fifty per cent of Czechs were expected to be Germanised, a figure far higher than elsewhere in central and eastern Europe. Only 3 per cent of Poles and Russians were set to receive the privilege. In reality, Heydrich found ways to implement Germanisation long before the end of the war. In spring 1942 he duped Czech parents and teachers into believing he was attempting to avert an outbreak of tuberculosis, by sending five mobile X-ray machines, replete with teams of racial experts, to examine children in Czech schools. See Tara Zahra, *Kidnapped Souls: National Indifference and the Battle for Children in the Bohemian Lands, 1900–1948* (Ithaca, NY, 2008), 176–81, 231–52. I was unable to determine which school the Griesingers sent their children to, as the archives and class lists of the primary schools close to their house in Bubeneč have not been preserved. It is likely they went to a school on Bílá Ulice (Weissstrasse). I am grateful to archivist Petra Krátká for carrying out a full search of German primary schools in the Prague City Archives.

52 Even as late as March 1945 Griesinger continued to send precious items to his parents in Stuttgart. His last package home contained electric batteries. There was a reference to this in GFA, AG's letter to his son, 29 March 1945.

53 MacDonald and Kaplan, *Prague*, 137–8; Bryant, *Prague in Black*, 73.

54 NAP, Domovni arch PR II-EO 1420/5, Prague VI Bubeneč, Zítkova no. 749.

55 *Der Neue Tag*, 20 June 1943, 8.

56 NAP, Domovni arch PR II-EO 1420/5, Prague VI Bubeneč, Zítkova no. 749.

57 Statni oblastni' archive v Plzni (State Archives Regional of Pilsen), Anna K.'s application to register with the Pilsen police, 10 September 1945; NAP, Index card registered with the local authorities detailing the Prague residences of Anna K. and Josef K., Applications to register with the Prague police, 11 February 1950.

58 NAP, Anna K. and Josef K., Applications to register with the Prague police, 11 February 1950. They were still listed in the Prague phone book in 1983, a copy of which is held at the Archiv hlavního města Prahy (Prague City Archives). For information on Dlouhá Street in the 1950s I am grateful to Jakub Beneš.

59 As part of Operation Valkyrie, Ferdinand Schaal, Wehrmacht commander in Bohemia and Moravia, was set to carry out the arrests of Nazi officials. See Peter Hoffmann, *The History of the German Resistance, 1933–1945* (3rd edn, Montreal and Kingston, 1996), 461–5. See also Peter Hoffmann, *Stauffenberg*, 272–3, 280–1.

60 Florian Huber, *Promise Me You'll Shoot Yourself: The Downfall of Ordinary Germans, 1945* (London, 2019), 47, 82, 92, 119, 226, 229.

X: The Man on the Bahnhofstrasse

1 MacDonald and Kaplan, *Prague*, 140, 148. Adolf Griesinger mentions Jutta's letter in his own letter to RG on 29 March 1945.

2 Christian Falvey, 'The Bombing of Prague from a New Perspective', *Radio Prague International in English*, 13 December 2011, available at https://www.radio.cz/en/ section/czech-history/the-bombing-of-prague-from-a-new-perspective

3 AG mentions Robert's participation in the *Volkssturm* in his letter to RG on 29 March 1945.

4 ABS, MHP, File 305-701-4, Walter Bertsch's post-war interrogation.

5 Tubach, *German Voices*, 177. Details that follow on Gisela and the children's flight from Prague is based on my conversations with Jutta Mangold and Barbara Schlegel.

6 See Richard Bessel, 'The Shadow of Death in Germany at the End of the Second World War', in Alon Confino, Paul Betts and Dirk Schumann (eds), *Between Mass Death and Individual Loss: The Place of the Dead in Twentieth-Century Germany* (New York, 2008), 52. For the most recent figure of 82,000 in the final three months, see Richard Overy, *The Bombing War: Europe 1939–1945* (London, 2013), 476.

7 Overy, *The Bombing War*, 396–7.

8 Roderick Stackelberg was a refugee child from late 1944 in nearby Rohrdorf and in chapter two of his autobiography recalls the lice and worm endemic. See Roderick Stackelberg, *Out of Hitler's Shadow: Childhood and Youth in Germany and the United States, 1935–67* (Bloomington, IN, 2010).

9 Interview with Werner Herzog in Paul Cronin (ed.), *Herzog on Herzog* (London, 2002), 5.

10 Petra Goedde, *GIs and Germans: Culture, Gender, and Foreign Relations, 1945–1949* (New Haven, CT, 2003), 88–9.

11 Peter H. Merkl, *Small Town and Village in Bavaria: The Passing of a Way of Life* (New York, 2012), 27; Adam R. Seipp, *Strangers in the Wild Place: Refugees, Americans, and a German Town, 1945–1952* (Bloomington, IN, 2013), 48.

12 Perry Biddiscombe, *Werwolf! The History of the National Socialist Guerrilla Movement, 1944–1946* (Cardiff, 1998), 187–8.

13 ABS, MHP, File 305-311-2, Lothar Schmidt's post-war file. See another of Schmidt's files in MHP 315-49-35, which contains details of his role in the SD.

14 Frederick L. Schuman, 'Czechoslovakia', in Charles Earle Funk (ed.), *The New International Year Book 1944* (New York, 1945), 164.

15 Frommer, *National Cleansing*, 25, 35, 42.

16 Bryant, *Prague in Black*, 239.

17 Eagle Glassheim, 'The Mechanics of Ethnic Cleansing: The Expulsion of Germans from Czechoslovakia, 1945–1947', in Philipp Ther and Ana Siljak (eds), *Redrawing Nations: Ethnic Cleansing in East-Central Europe, 1944–1948* (Oxford, 2001), 206; R. M. Douglas, *Orderly and Humane: The Expulsion of the Germans after the Second World War* (New Haven, CT, 2012), 96–7.

18 Jan Puhl article in *Der Spiegel*, 2 June 2010; http://www.spiegel.de/international/ europe/massacre-in-czechoslovakia-newly-discovered-film-shows-post-war-execu- tions-a-698060.html

19 Emil Franzel, *Die Vertreibung Sudetenland, 1945–1946* (Munich, 1980), 395. This refer- ence refers to the closure of the Red Cross for Germans. Nevertheless, Franzel's account must be used with considerable caution, for he was known to have exag- gerated details of the levels of violence meted out to Germans in spring 1945.

20 Wolfram Angerbauer, *Die Amtsvorsteher der Oberämter, Bezirksämter und Landratsämter in Baden-Württemberg 1810 bis 1972* (Stuttgart, 1996), 571.

21 NAP, PR II-EO 1420/5. This information is listed on RG's registration form with the Prague city police.

22 To give only one example from this time: on 26 April 1945 Hans Schneider, who worked for the *SS Ahnenerbe* (Ancesteral Heritage Division) in Berlin, destroyed

his documents and changed his name to Hans Schwerte. He enjoyed a glittering post-war career until his past was discovered in 1995.

23 ABS, 2M: 11034, Documents of the Ministry of the Interior, File on Dr Anne-Marie Dietlová, August 1945. Dr Anne-Marie Dietlová had daily dealings with the Ministry of Economics and Labour thanks to her position as a senior employee at the Central Association of Industry in the Protectorate. Dietlová knew Griesinger; his name appeared on a list of ministry employees in a file that she prepared for Czech prosecutors after the war, when, as a suspected collaborator, she was detained with her eighteen-month-old daughter in the Bystřice internment camp.

24 NAP, Domovni arch PR II-EO 1420/5, Prague VI Bubeneč, Zítkova no. 749; NAP Police Directorate Prague, General Registry, File of Anna K.; Interview with Magdalena K., the daughter of Anna K.

25 I am grateful to Ivana Dejmková for this information.

26 Frommer, *National Cleansing*, 53. It is impossible to know the precise camp in which Griesinger spent the summer months of 1945 prior to his entry to Salmovská hospital, as comprehensive lists of detained Germans from these months do not exist. It was only in the autumn of 1945, when the police replaced the army as overseers of the camps, that lists of internees were first compiled. When Griesinger died in September 1945, only a handful of camps were administered by the police. In the case of Strahov, one of the largest camps, which held 10,000 Germans in a football stadium, there is not a single list of detainees' names. I am grateful to Ivana Dejmková for this information.

27 Frommer, *National Cleansing*, 55.

28 Douglas, *Orderly and Humane*, 132.

29 Frommer, *National Cleansing*, 54–7; Glassheim, *Cleansing the Czechoslovak Borderlands*, 47–8; Douglas, *Orderly and Humane*, 141–2.

30 See Frommer, *National Cleansing*, 53–4.

31 Douglas, *Orderly and Humane*, 144.

32 Matthew Frank, *Expelling the Germans: British Opinion and Post-1945 Population Transfer in Context* (Oxford, 2007), 184.

33 Douglas, *Orderly and Humane*, 145.

34 I visited in 2017. Only after 2020 will these books be available to consult freely.

35 I am grateful to Ivana Dejmková for this information.

36 Frommer, *National Cleansing*, 56, 116–17.

37 I am grateful to the many archivists and local historians in Prague who told me about this and other similar forms of killings that befell hospitalised Germans in Bohemia and Moravia in spring and summer 1945. See also Tomáš Staněk, *Verfolgung 1945: Die Stellung der Deutschen in Böhmen, Mähren und Schlesien (außerhalb der Lager und Gefängnisse)* (Cologne, 2002), 95; Igor Lukes, *On the Edge of the Cold War: American Diplomats and Spies in Postwar Prague* (Oxford, 2012), 50.

38 A present campaign seeks to uncover the graves in Ďáblice of forty Czech babies born in Pankrác Prison to female prisoners, who died a couple of days after birth through lack of proper care. Drawing attention to the persecution of Czechoslovak citizens by the country's post-war government – and not investigating German mass graves – is the priority among researchers and activists interested in the history of Ďáblice. None of the cemetery's experts, including Jaroslav Čvančara, Jiří Línek and Jiří Padevět, knew anything about German mass graves when I consulted them.

39 I am grateful to Jiří Línek for this information.

XI: Gisela Went Out to Dance

1 Norman M. Naimark, *The Russians in Germany: A History of the Soviet Zone of Occupation, 1945–1949* (Cambridge, MA, 1995), 132–3.
2 For the statistic on German war widows, see Katharina Tumpek-Kjellmark, 'From Hitler's Widows to Adenauer's Brides: Towards a Construction of Gender and Memory in Postwar West Germany, 1938–1963', PhD thesis (Cornell University, 1994), i. The details that follow on Gisela and the children's post-war lives are based on my interviews with Jutta Mangold and Barbara Schlegel.
3 To this day, law professors all over the world continue to debate and teach their students about the Nottebohm Case and the Nottebohm Principle, named after Friedrich Nottebohm, whose case was held before the International Court of Justice in The Hague in 1955. It is regarded as among the most important citizenship cases in international law. The case hinged on the concept of nationality. In 1905 twenty-four-year-old Friedrich left Hamburg to join his two brothers in Guatemala, where they ran Nottebohm Hermanos. Having lived in Guatemala for almost thirty-five years as a German citizen, Friedrich happened to be visiting Gisela's father in Liechtenstein when the Second World War broke out. In October 1939 he hurriedly acquired citizenship from Liechtenstein and formally renounced his citizenship of Germany. In 1943 Guatemala refused to acknowledge that Nottebohm was not German, and seized all his property. On the request of the USA, Nottebohm was deported to the US, where he was held in an internment camp for two and a half years. After the war he was denied entry to Guatemala and returned to Liechtenstein. In 1951 Liechtenstein launched proceedings against Guatemala, arguing that it had broken international law against a citizen of Liechtenstein. The International Court of Justice needed to decide whether Guatemala had to recognise Nottebohm as a citizen of Liechtenstein. Liechtenstein lost the case. The court ruled that Nottebohm had no 'genuine link' with Liechtenstein. Thanks to the Nottebohm case, the concept of a 'genuine link' is needed in cases of diplomatic protection.
4 Jutta vividly remembered Friedrich's death in 1962, because of a remarkable piece of information she learned from her mother: 'My true father is dead' was how Gisela announced Friedrich's death. It was the first time Jutta was made aware of Gisela's suspicion that she was the product of an affair that Friedrich had had with his sister-in-law, Harriet, Gisela's mother.
5 See Norman Ohler, *Blitzed: Drugs in Nazi Germany* (London, 2016).
6 Thanks to her lawyer, the case did not reach the courts. Wally was instead ordered to pay a fine of 600 Reichsmark. StAL, EL 902/20 Bü 91743. Denazification Records, File of WG. Letter from her lawyer, Schmid, 5 December 1947.
7 *Stuttgarter Nachrichten*, 22 November 1947, 4, AG's obituary.
8 Peter Sichrovsky, *Born Guilty: Children of Nazi Families* (London, 1988), 3.
9 See Welzer, Moller and Tschuggnall (eds), '*Opa war kein Nazi*'.

Archives Consulted

Public and Private Archives, Collections and Libraries

Archiv bezpečnostních složek (Security Services Archive, Prague)
Archiv hlavního města Prahy (Prague City Archives)
Archives of the University of Hohenheim
Archives of the Zeppelin-Gymnasium (formerly the Reformrealgymnasium), Stuttgart
Archives Nationales de France (National Archive, Paris)
Bibliothek für Zeitgeschichte, Stuttgart (Library of Contemporary History)
Bundesarchiv, Berlin-Lichterfelde (German Federal Archive)
Bundesarchiv-Militararchiv (German Federal Military Archive, Freiburg)
The Central Registry Office of Prague, Vodičkova Street, Prague
Columbia University Law Library, New York
Cornell University Law Library, Ithaca
Daniel E. Koshland San Francisco History Center, San Francisco Library
Derzhavnyi arkhiv Kyivs'koi oblasti (The State Archives of the Kiev Oblast)
Deutsche Dienststelle (WASt), Berlin
Hauptstaatsarchiv Stuttgart (Main State Archive, Stuttgart)
Haus der Geschichte Baden-Württemberg, Stuttgart (House of Local History of Baden-Württemberg)
Hoover Institution Library and Archives, Stanford
Leo Baeck Institute Archive, Center for Jewish History, New York
Louisiana Research Collection, Howard-Tilton Memorial Library, Tulane University
Národní archiv v Praze (National Archive, Prague)
New Orleans Public Library, Louisiana Division / City Archives & Special Collections, New Orleans
The Notarial Archives Research Center, Civil District Court Building, New Orleans
Private Collection of Jochen and Irmela Griesinger
Private Collection of Peter Jehli
Private Collection of Jutta Mangold
Private Collection of Helga, Andrew and Christine Rothschild
Private Collection of Fritz and Barbara Schlegel
Staatsarchiv Ludwigsburg (State Archive, Ludwigsburg, Baden-Württemberg)
Stadtarchiv Stuttgart (City Archives of Stuttgart)
Stadtarchiv Tettnang (City Archives of Tettnang)

Stadtarchiv Tübingen (City Archives of Tübingen)
Státní okresní archiv Kroměříž (State District Archives of Kroměříž)
Státní oblastní archiv v Litoměřicicích (State Regional Archives Litoměřicicích)
Statni oblastni' archive v Plzni (Regional State Archives of Pilsen)
Williams Research Center, The Historic New Orleans Collection, New Orleans

Acknowledgements

This work would never have been attempted but for the kindness, support and understanding of the Griesinger family. Above all, I extend my deepest appreciation to Robert Griesinger's daughters, Jutta Mangold and Barbara Schlegel, who graciously opened their lives and hearts to a stranger intent on asking difficult questions about their family's past. My sincere and heartfelt thanks go to Jochen and Irmela Griesinger who placed at my disposal a copious store of papers, letters, photographs and diaries belonging to the Griesinger family. I am also very much indebted to Fritz Schlegel, Barbara's husband, for providing such a welcoming environment during our interviews. Finally, I owe a unique debt of gratitude to Eda Vendysova Bakalarova, Anna Marhold and Nathan Marhold, without whose unstinting generosity, *The SS Officer's Armchair* would be incomplete.

After doing research in seven countries, my respect for archivists and librarians has only increased. I would like to thank the unfailingly helpful and courteous staff of all the institutions I worked at, especially the Bundesarchiv, Berlin-Lichterfelde; the Staatsarchiv, Ludwigsburg; the Hauptstaatsarchiv, Stuttgart; the Stadtarchiv Stuttgart; the Bibliothek für Zeitgeschichte, Stuttgart; the Archiv bezpečnostních složek, Prague; the Notarial Archives Research Center, New Orleans; and the Hoover Institution Library, Stanford. Vlasta Měšťánková (the National Archives, Prague) and Mary Lou Eichhorn (The Williams Research Center, THNOC, New Orleans), stand out as requiring special note for pointing me towards important archival materials, as does Mary Munill, Stanford's interlibrary loan wizard, for so ably locating my almost impossible requests.

I first discovered the story of Robert Griesinger's Nazi-era documents while a Max Weber Postdoctoral Fellow at the European University Institute in Florence. Without Justin Valasek's kindness in agreeing to co-host so many dinner parties – and for Griesinger to dominate so many subsequent conversations at our flat on the Via dei Macci – this story would never have seen the light of day. Similarly, I should like to express gratitude to friends and colleagues first at the EUI and, later, after I left Florence, who have given generously of their time to help translate documents and decipher the scribbles produced by Griesinger and his family: Birgit Apitzsch, Christine Brocks, Max Drephal, Sabine Hanke, Lucia van Kaick, Stefan Lamp, Jannis Panagiotidis, Lea Pao, Philipp Rehm, Erika Rubesova, Luca Scholz, Jenny Simon, Andrea Wechsler, Seán Williams and Benjamin Ziemann. Special thanks to Maren Frömel who has helped to decipher more Nazi-era documents than she would care to remember.

During my travels in pursuit of Griesinger, I was fortunate to be able to call upon the generous help, hospitality and valuable advice of a number of people: Erin Albritton, Sigrid Brüggemann, Rob Cameron, Jaroslav Čvančara, Ivana Dejmková, Anna Magdalena Elsner, Dr Ulrich Fellmeth, Charles Gottlieb, Holger zur Hausen, Alena Kamenová, Daniela Karasová, Petra Krátká, Eduard Kubů, Stefanie Leisentritt, Jiří Linek, Peter Lundgren, Roland Maier, Jaroslava Milotová, Heribert Möhres, Melanie Moll, Melissa Monica, Dr Roland Müller, Josef Naßl, Greg Osborn, Jiří Padevět, Sharon Quiachon-Bechmann, Udo Rauch, Sally Reeves, Irina Renz, Jakob Roesler, Katerina Santurova, Eva Škvárová, Vincent Slatt, Barbora Stolleova, Judit Vamosi, Tereza Vlášková, Dr Anja Waller, Marina Wyler and Šárka Zouzalíková.

I am indebted to many scholars, colleagues and friends across the world whose helpful suggestions, kindness and goodwill mean far more than they can ever know: Laura Almagor, Arthur Asseraf, Jaromír Balcar, Antony Beevor, Jakub Beneš, Jane Caplan, Tom Carey, Giovanna Ceserani, Rebecca Clifford, Martin Conway, Chris Dillon,

Eugenio Donadoni, Rowan Dorin, Laura Lee Downs, Charlotte Fonrobert, Ben Frommer, Alexandra Garbarini, Robert Gildea, Emanuela Grama, Abigail Green, Wolf Gruner, Anna Hájková, Karen Harvey, Jacqueline Heaton, Alma Heckman, Alice Kaplan, Alexander Kruglov, Glenn Kurtz, Jan Láníček, Lisa Leff, Philippa Levine, Mary McLeod, Jürgen Matthäus, Andrea Mehrländer, Douglas G. Morris, Dirk Moses, Eliot Nidam Orvieto, Philipp Nielsen, Dieter Pohl, Felix Römer, Sandrine Sanos, Suzanne Schneider, Laura Schor, Stefanie Schüler-Springorum, Ben Shepherd, Anne Simonin, Martin Smok, David Stahel, Elli Stern, Elizabeth St George, Susan Rubin Suleiman, Fritz Tubach, Anna von der Goltz, Martha Weinman Lear, Natasha Wheatley, Tara Zahra and Volker Zimmermann. Special thanks are due to Hanna Diamond, for her guidance and commitment; to the unstinting generosity of Aron Rodrigue who afforded me the opportunity to spend a year at Stanford University, where most of this book was written; and to the patience of Talz Leman in whose swimming classes I was able to forget momentarily the Third Reich.

The greatest debts have been incurred closer to home. I am grateful to the department of history at the University of Sheffield for providing such an intellectually engaging and collegial academic home. I would like to express my thanks to a few colleagues (at the risk of appearing unjust to others), who have been a model community of support: Rebecca Freeman, Julie Gottlieb, Dina Gusejnova, Eirini Karamouzi, Sarah Miller-Davenport, Caoimhe Nic Dháibhéid and Mary Vincent. The School of History at Queen Mary University of London, my new academic home since September 2019, likewise deserves thanks for providing me with such a welcoming and stimulating environment during the final stages of this book.

For their thorough and helpful reading of portions of the manuscript and proposal, I owe many thanks to Hadley Freeman, Adam Freedman, Ann Jefferson and Anne Sebba. Marion Kaplan, Sue Vice and Gerhard Wolf patiently waded through the entire manuscript and offered insightful feedback. This is a better book because of their efforts, but they should not be held responsible for a word of it.

I am indebted to my agent, Peter Straus, for his invaluable advice and unstinting support, and to everyone at Rogers, Coleridge and White, especially Matt Turner. Thanks are also due to Lionel Leventhal, Michael Leventhal and Naomi Tongue for their help crafting the proposal. In Bea Hemming, I could not have asked for a more capable and gracious editor. I am indebted to all at Jonathan Cape and beyond for the care with which they have seen the book through the press: Marigold Atkey, Darren Bennett, Monique Corless, Mandy Greenfield, Daisy Watt. On the other side of the pond, I give thanks to my US agent Melanie Jackson and my editor Paul Whitlatch. Thanks are also due to David Lamb and Carrie Napolitano of Hachette for their generous editorial guidance.

My thanks for their help, often unconsciously rendered, go to my friends who have been wonderful throughout the writing of this book. Special thanks to Ludivine Broch, Carolina Corsello, Joey Hasson, Becca Marcus and Eddie Marshbaum for putting up with so many hours/months/years of conversation dedicated to Robert Griesinger, and for offering such unflagging support and wisdom. I cannot express enough gratitude to Asher Dresner who has, at every step of the way, provided me with wise advice and invaluable suggestions for improvement.

Most of all, I owe tremendous gratitude to my family. I would like to thank my brothers for their encouragement and continuous inspiration and my grandparents who offered unwavering guidance and never-ending affection. Profound thanks to my mother- and father-in law, Toni and Robert Marcus, for their constant support and motivation; they and my wife's sisters and their families welcomed me with more kindness and generosity into the Marcus clan than I could ever have hoped for.

My gratitude towards my parents is boundless. My dad merits colossal praise for his good humour, for encouraging me to pursue my interests, and for his belief in me. While he has likely long since forgotten the bedtime stories he told me as a child, the ways in which he told them have stayed with me and even found their way into the narrative of this book. I can't thank him enough for all his efforts. My mum has been the greatest source of inspiration throughout my life. It was she who instilled in me a love of reading and attention to detail. Without her countless sacrifices, unwavering love and incessant requests to play Scrabble and Boggle with her, I could not have become the person and historian I now am.

This book owes everything, as do I, to Elizabeth Marcus, who has tirelessly read multiple drafts of the manuscript, and has discussed every aspect of this project with me. I am grateful beyond words to her for challenging me to dig deeper, sharpen my focus, and rethink my own assumptions. Elizabeth's love, patience and laughter sustained me through some of this project's toughest stages. Thank you, EJ. As we enter a new decade, here's to many, many years of continued adventures.

Daniel Lee
London
New Year's Day 2020

Index